THE LIBERAL CATHOLIC MOVEMENT
IN ENGLAND

The Liberal Catholic Movement in England

The "Rambler" and its Contributors
1848-1864

by

JOSEF L. ALTHOLZ

Assistant Professor of History,
University of Minnesota

LONDON
BURNS & OATES

© Josef L. Altholz 1960

First published 1962

MADE AND PRINTED IN GREAT BRITAIN BY
THE DITCHLING PRESS LTD, HASSOCKS, SUSSEX, ENGLAND FOR
BURNS AND OATES LIMITED
25 ASHLEY PLACE, LONDON, S.W.1

TABLE OF CONTENTS

PREFACE

I AM writing the story of a great hope and a great failure.
The Liberal Catholic movement was a remarkable
attempt to find a *modus vivendi* between the Roman Catholic
Church and the secular principles of the nineteenth century.
The study of the English version of Liberal Catholicism may
shed some light on aspects both of Catholic and of English
history; it further possesses a fascination of its own, as the
story of a group of interesting personalities at work in a
period of intense intellectual excitement. The story of English
Liberal Catholicism has never been told in its entirety.
It has generally been treated as a minor aspect of a larger
history or of the biographies of such men as Newman,
Wiseman, Manning, Ward and, particularly, Lord Acton.
I have attempted to integrate in one narrative a story which
has been told piecemeal and portions of which have never
been told at all.

The Liberal Catholic movement was the product of the
interaction of a certain tendency of the Catholic mind with a
particular set of historical problems and circumstances.
It ought to be viewed simply as the object of disinterested
historical curiosity; but such disinterestedness is frequently
difficult to attain. Many of the intellectual problems with
which the Liberal Catholics dealt are problems which still
confront Catholics and others in this age. The tendency of
mind represented by Liberal Catholicism was not confined
to the nineteenth century: there are liberal Catholics, or
Catholic liberals, at the present time. Circumstances, however, have changed the practical significance of the term,
and no current movement can fairly claim historical continuity with the Liberal Catholic movement of the nineteenth
century, which, although some of its positions were subse-
quently adopted or allowed by the Church, effectively came
to an end by the early 1870s.

This work should be read as a purely historical study. I am

vii

not a member of the Catholic Church, and I do not intend to pass judgment on the merits of theological questions. I have deliberately abstained from giving my final judgment on the Liberal Catholic movement in England, for such a judgment must involve assumptions and values which are outside the province of the historian. "For to collect all that is to be known, to put the discourse in order and curiously to discuss every particular point, is the duty of the author of a history." (2 Maccabees 2: 31.)

I must acknowledge my indebtedness to His Eminence the Cardinal Archbishop of Westminster for permission to make use of the archives of the Archdiocese; to the Abbot of Downside for the use of the Acton materials at Downside Abbey; to Father C. Stephen Dessain of the Birmingham Oratory for the use of some of the Newman papers; to Abbé Alphonse Chapeau for assistance in connection with the Manning papers, in the possession of the Oblates of St. Charles at Bayswater; to Mr. and the Hon. Mrs. Douglas Woodruff for the use of the Acton papers in their possession and for other assistance; and to the authorities of the British Museum and of the Library of Cambridge University for the use of the Gladstone and Acton papers respectively.

I wish to give special mention to the assistance I have received from Abbé Victor Conzemius, the editor of the Acton-Döllinger correspondence, to be published shortly after the appearance of this book. In order not to delay my work, he very kindly sent me copies of the manuscripts which he was editing, in advance of his own publication. These documents may be checked against the complete texts in his edition. They have enabled me to make an extensive revision of my work, which originally appeared as a doctoral dissertation at Columbia University in 1960.

The kindness of Abbé Conzemius is an example of the friendly assistance I have received from many scholars in the course of my work. Among them I wish to thank Professors Garrett Mattingly, Herman Ausubel, R. K. Webb, Robert Cross and Jerome Buckley of Columbia University; D. H. Willson, Stanley Payne and others of my colleagues at the

University of Minnesota; Charles F. Mullett of the University of Missouri; and Herbert Butterfield, Master of Peterhouse, Cambridge. I am indebted also to the following: Father Bernard Fisher and Mr. Anthony Bracking for assistance with the archives of the Archdiocese of Westminster; Dom Aelred Watkin of Downside Abbey; Walter Houghton of the Wellesley Index to Victorian Periodicals; my fellow-students Richard Helmstadter, Robert Gutchen and Cornelius Darcy; H. L. Beales; Herr Rolf Geisler; and the staffs of the Libraries of Columbia, Fordham and Yale Universities and the University of Minnesota. To all these, to many others whom I have not space to mention, and to my parents I wish to express my deep appreciation.

JOSEF L. ALTHOLZ

Minneapolis
July, 1961

NOTE ON MANUSCRIPT MATERIAL

THE manuscript collections listed below have been extensively consulted in the preparation of this work. They will be referred to by the following abbreviations:

BM Add. MSS.   British Museum Additional Manuscripts [Gladstone Collection] (followed by volume and folio number).

CUL Add. MSS.   Cambridge University Library Additional Manuscripts [Acton Papers] (followed by catalogue number).

Downside MSS.   Papers in the Library of Downside Abbey, collected by Cardinal Gasquet, chiefly letters of Lord Acton to Richard Simpson and T. F. Wetherell.

Manning MSS.   Papers of Cardinal Manning, in the possession of the Oblates of St. Charles, Church of St. Mary of the Angels, Bayswater, London.

Newman MSS.   Papers of Cardinal Newman, at the Oratory, Birmingham.

Westminster Archives   Archives of the Archdiocese of Westminster, 1847-1865.

Woodruff MSS.   Correspondence of Lord Acton in the possession of Mr. Douglas Woodruff. Includes correspondence of Lord Acton with J. J. I. von Döllinger, being edited for publication by Abbé Victor Conzemius; my translation from the German.

THE CATHOLIC REVIVAL

THE Liberal Catholic movement of the nineteenth century was an attempt to bridge the gap between the doctrines of the Roman Catholic Church and the dominant secular principles of the age. It is difficult precisely to define Liberal Catholicism: it was neither liberal enough to satisfy the Liberals nor quite Catholic enough to please the Pope. Liberal Catholicism was not necessarily Liberal in politics: on the continent of Europe it tended towards moderate clericalism or conservative federalism. Nor was it invariably liberal in theology, and it must be clearly distinguished from such movements as Jansenism, Gallicanism or modernism. The liberalism of Liberal Catholicism consisted rather in its view of the relations between theology and politics: it was an intellectual liberalism, characterized by an emphasis upon the legitimacy and value of intellectual sources independent of the authority of the Church.

Such a tendency of mind is a perennial phenomenon among Catholics and has not been confined to any one period or country. But the formation of a Liberal Catholic movement—the association of various Catholics for the purpose of advancing a programme proceeding from this outlook—was the product of a particular time and set of circumstances. It was a response to the intellectual, social and political revolutions with which the nineteenth century was inaugurated; it arose in France, spread to Italy and Germany, and found an echo in England. Its English manifestation ran a course of its own, largely determined by the peculiar circumstances of English Catholicism.

The 1840s were years of intense creative excitement for the Catholics of England, marked by an intellectual revival, a wave of conversions, the re-creation of a diocesan hierarchy, the enjoyment of emancipation and the promise of a "second spring." During the years from 1845 to 1865, the basic elements of this Catholic revival—the re-awakening of the old Catholics, the conversions from the Oxford Movement, and the influx of Irish immigrants—were brought together to shape the future growth of Catholicism in England.

It is necessary, in order to understand the peculiar qualities of English Catholicism, to view it against the background of the invincible Protestantism of the English people. During two centuries of intolerance the Catholics had suffered persecution and exclusion from the life of the nation; it was only in the more tolerant eighteenth century that they could begin to find their place in English life. Their problem then became one of reviving that contact with English society and thought which had been virtually broken during the period of conflict and persecution, of moving from suspicion to toleration, from toleration to participation. The Catholic revival was therefore to be a two-sided process: the development of a greater sympathy towards Catholicism among the English Protestants, and a response by the Catholics to the challenges and opportunities of the new age.

When the period of emancipation began, towards the end of the eighteenth century, the Roman Catholics of England were a small unobtrusive group, less than one hundred thousand souls. The native Catholics consisted of the remnants of Catholic groups which had survived the Reformation in certain localities, and families of nobility and gentry scattered throughout the country; these, with a few poor Irish immigrants, formed a Church which "strove, as it were, to make herself invisible."[1] When the penal laws were repealed, it was due less to their efforts than to the good sense of the English Protestants and to the influence of the Catholics of Ireland, whose strength and unity offer a marked contrast to the feebleness and dissensions of their English brethren. Similarly, it was the action of the Irish Catholics which brought about Catholic Emancipation in 1829. The efforts of the English Catholics had broken down

---

[1] Paul Thureau-Dangin, *The English Catholic Revival in the Nineteenth Century,* trans. Wilfrid Wilberforce, 2 vols. (London, 1914), I, xxiii.

amid factional strife, which revealed the predominance among them of the "Cismontane" party, which was willing to accept a government veto on the appointment of bishops and to limit the prerogatives of the Pope in England. Such men belonged rather to the age of the Enlightenment than to the religious revival of the nineteenth century, and the future was not with them.

During the 1830s, however, signs of renewed activity began to appear. This development was in large part the work of Nicholas Wiseman, then rector of the English College in Rome. The news of the Oxford Movement led him to suspect that new opportunities might await the Catholic Church in England. He returned to deliver a course of lectures in 1835 and 1836, which resulted in a number of conversions and contributed to the development of a more friendly attitude towards Catholicism among many Englishmen. Before he returned to Rome, Wiseman founded the *Dublin Review*, which was to be the semi-official organ of English Catholicism in future decades. Other Catholic journals were soon founded; there was an increase in Church building and in the number of the clergy. The growth of the Church was indicated by the increase in the number of vicars-apostolic (who served in lieu of bishops) from four to eight in 1840. There was thus, even before the arrival of converts from the Oxford Movement, a modest but promising trend of Catholic revival in England.[2]

The Oxford converts offered to English Catholicism an opportunity to establish fruitful contact with that great body of Englishmen who had been brought up to regard the Roman Catholic Church as a completely alien institution. The men of the Oxford Movement had done their work in effective independence of Roman Catholicism, and when, in 1845, the first wave of conversions took place, few of the converts had ever met a Roman priest or attended a Roman service in England. "Catholics did not make us Catholics;

[2] For the history of this earlier Catholic revival, see Thureau-Dangin, *The English Catholic Revival*, and Bernard Ward, *The Sequel to Catholic Emancipation* (London, 1913).

Oxford made us Catholics," said Newman.[3] They had, in fact, converted themselves, and thrust themselves into an English Catholic body which was unprepared for their coming. A major problem for English Catholicism in the next two decades was to assimilate the increasing numbers of converts and to put them to work at the task of spreading Catholic doctrines in England.

The English Catholics, however, were unable to devote their full attention to this problem. While they generally welcomed the converts, there were some who viewed the new developments with distaste: "old Catholics," as they were called, who "were still under the influence of that timidity and inertia which centuries of persecution had engendered,"[4] who feared that they might be displaced by the more active and able converts, or who honestly thought that the converts would lead the Church into unfortunate courses. There had indeed been some opposition before 1845 to Wiseman's policy of encouraging the Oxford Movement. After the restoration of the hierarchy in 1850, these old-fashioned Catholics were to seem almost as much of a problem as the converts themselves. Another factor which tended to divert the energies of the English Catholics was the next major development in their history, the sudden influx of Irish immigrants after the potato famine of 1845. The resources of English Catholicism at this time were inadequate to provide the necessary services of religion to these crowds; churches, priests and schools were in short supply.

Thus in 1850, when the restoration of a diocesan hierarchy proclaimed to the world the fact of the Catholic revival in England, there was being posed the question whether this revival was adequate to meet the challenges faced by English Catholicism in the 1850s. Could the new hierarchy bring together such diverse elements as the old Catholics, the Irish immigrants and the converts, and make the Catholic body, increasing in numbers and activity, a significant part of English life?

---

[3] Louis Bouyer, *Newman: His Life and Spirituality*, trans. J. Lewis May (London and New York, 1958), p. 371.
[4] Thureau-Dangin, *The English Catholic Revival*, I, 306.

In the late 'forties there were few forebodings of failure among the English Catholics. It was a time of exaltation, when men spoke hopefully of "the conversion of England" and basked in the sunshine of the "second spring." The resurgent energy of English Catholicism was exerted over a wide range of circumstances and ideas, and manifested itself in many forms. In contrast with the almost apologetic obscurity of the older Catholics, the tendency was now rather to flaunt the Catholic religion in the face of Englishmen, to emphasize its distinctive aspects—its reliance upon Rome, its authoritarianism, its occasional obscurantism, its peculiar devotions. Father Faber led a party which introduced Italian devotions in what was considered an extreme form; later W. G. Ward and Manning were to emphasize, in an equally extreme manner, the ecclesiastical and authoritarian spirit of Rome. But this Ultramontanism, though it came eventually to be the dominant form of resurgent Catholicism, was not its only expression.

There was another, smaller, group, which was conscious, first, that Catholicism must be made to appear intellectually respectable in the eyes of Protestant England and must keep up with the new developments in science and thought which were engrossing the attention of society, and secondly, that all was not well among the Catholics themselves, that through poor education and wilful ignorance they were shockingly unprepared for the new age of science, industrialism and democracy. Newman was sympathetic with this group, but it was led by younger converts of less fame. Their distinguishing characteristic was a consciousness that they were living in a society whose tone and spirit had been formed by Protestantism, and which had to be Catholicized, if it were possible at all, from within. Their acceptance of intellectual sources independent of the Catholic Church was founded upon a trust that even the most independent inquiry must lead to a truth that was essentially Catholic. It was an adventure in faith, similar, in many ways, to the outlook of the Liberal Catholic movement on the Continent, of men such as Montalembert in France and Döllinger in Germany; but it had its own native roots. When this movement, in the course of its development, had assumed the character of a party within the English Catholic body, its members were given the name of Liberal Catholics.

Could this Liberal Catholic movement, intensely Catholic yet deeply penetrated by non-Catholic thought, survive and make its way in the new circumstances of English Catholicism? It was the fate of English Liberal Catholicism to reach its development during a period of grave crisis for the Catholic Church, when, in England, a new and nervous hierarchy was faced with problems it was unprepared to handle, and on the Continent, the tide of revolution and nationalism menaced the Catholic structure of society and even the Papal throne. It was in this atmosphere of tension that the Liberal Catholics, at first simply a group of individuals with a common tendency of thought, later a party with a definite programme, came forward and sought to find their place in the Catholic world. They found themselves, instead, the rejected children of the Catholic Revival.

Chapter I

JOHN MOORE CAPES AND THE *RAMBLER*, 1848-1854

ONE of the manifestations of the English Catholic revival was the development of a Catholic periodical press. Catholic journalism, indeed, dated back to the last years of the eighteenth century; but those earlier efforts had been short-lived. Few of the ventures of the 1830s and the 1840s escaped a similar fate, but there were two which were destined to survive: Nicholas Wiseman's *Dublin Review*, founded in 1836, and a weekly newspaper, *The Tablet*, founded in 1840 by Frederick Lucas, a convert from Quakerism.

The Oxford converts, with their superior education, intellectual abilities and religious zeal, afforded a great potential accession of strength to the Catholic press. For a number of reasons, however, they were slow to enter the field of journalism: they preferred to produce tracts, pamphlets and books of apologetic, controversy or devotion, which seemed to be demanded by the immediate circumstances. The importance of the periodical press was, in fact, little appreciated among English Catholics at that time. Nonetheless, some of the converts, as early as 1846, expressed an interest in a journalistic venture, which was actually commenced in 1848 with the founding of the *Rambler* by John Moore Capes.

Capes, a graduate of Oxford, had taken Anglican orders and received the living of St. John's, Bridgwater. Here he spent virtually all of his ample fortune building and endowing a new church. He was not at first an adherent of the Tractarian movement,[1] but found his own way to Rome.

---

[1] Edward George Kirwan Browne, *History of the Tractarian Movement* (Dublin, 1856), pp. 74 ff. Capes was reputed to have been a follower of W. G. ("Ideal") Ward, according to Richard William Church, *The Oxford Movement: Twelve Years, 1833-1845*, 3rd ed. (London, 1932), p. 394. This probably was a late

B   7

He was drawn to Roman Catholicism by a conviction of the absolute need for an infallible doctrinal authority, an infallibility which was claimed only by the Church of Rome. After a visit to Littlemore, where he found that Newman was moving in a similar direction, Capes was received into the Catholic Church at Oscott College on 27 July 1845, by Wiseman, who had become a bishop and was president of the college. Many of Capes' parishioners, his wife, and his brother Frederick, soon followed his example. The latter, a proctor in the ecclesiastical courts, had to give up a practice of over £1,000 a year. The financial sacrifice of the two brothers was hailed by Newman as "the greatest thing that has been done in money matters"[2] by converts.

As a married man, Capes was debarred from the priesthood. The struggling English Catholic body offered few openings for married "convert parsons"; Capes, more fortunate than most, found a position as professor of mathematics at Prior Park College, near Bath. Here, in 1846, he conceived the idea of founding a periodical in which he and other converts "should write for the present condition of the *English* mind, entering into all subjects of literary, philosophic and moral interest, treating them as a person would who believes Catholicism to be the only true religion."[3] He secured the warm approval of Bishop Ullathorne, then Vicar Apostolic of the Western District, and proposed the plan to Newman. Newman approved the project, but pointed out a number of practical difficulties.[4] Eventually all difficulties were overcome, and Capes, with the assistance of a few friends, among whom was James Spencer Northcote, another convert clergyman at Prior Park, brought out the first number of a new weekly, the *Rambler*,[5] on 1 January 1848.

development: Capes, while at Oxford, was rather stunned than convinced by Ward, if I am correct in identifying Ward with "Arlington" in Capes' autobiographical novel, *To Rome and Back* (London, 1873), pp. 96-108.

[2] Newman to Dalgairns, 10 Dec. 1845, cited by Wilfrid Ward, *The Life of John Henry Cardinal Newman*, 2 vols. (New York, 1912), I, 107. J. M. Capes lost both his living and the £10,000 he had spent on his new church.

[3] Capes to Newman, 15 July 1846, Newman MSS.

[4] For Newman's replies, see Abbot (later Cardinal) Gasquet, "Introduction" to *Lord Acton and his Circle* (London, 1906), pp. xii-xiv.

[5] The name, taken from Samuel Johnson, has no significance: it was chosen "simply for want of a better"; *Rambler*, I (1 Jan. 1848), 2.

The *Rambler* was essentially the organ of the lay converts, men of Oxford, who had so recently made the transition from the established Church to a communion which, in England, was small, humble, and weakened by centuries of persecution. Although they showed themselves, at the time of their conversion, extremely docile and disposed to see "all things under a *couleur de rose*,"[6] the converts were quickly disillusioned: it seemed to them that the "old Catholics" were intellectually backward, apathetic and timid, the clergy limited both in attainments and activity, and the laity isolated from the intellectual and public life of England. To a considerable extent, these criticisms were justified. The converts, however, in their zeal to remedy these defects, sometimes went to opposite extremes, and often provoked the alarm and resentment of the hereditary Catholics with their inclination toward greater freedom in thought and speech. Capes was one of the more moderate of the converts; yet he, too, was capable of quite sharp criticism of defects in the Catholic body, which necessarily led him into conflict with those who preferred a discreet silence to free discussion. He was particularly distressed at the intellectual deficiencies of the English Catholics: "I soon made up my mind that it was my function to devote myself to promoting that general culture of the English Catholic body in which, as I soon found, they were grievously deficient."[7] He hoped that his magazine would serve to raise the level of culture of the English Catholics and, by removing the reproach of intellectual backwardness, to enable them to exert their influence on other Englishmen.

Capes desired to improve the teaching and elevate the standards of the colleges which provided secondary and higher education for both the clergy and the upper-class laity. At the same time, he advocated the extension of Catholic schools among the poor, and urged greater financial support by the laity for education at all levels. This stress on lay action was one of the major characteristics of the

[6] Capes, *To Rome and Back*, p. 229.
[7] *Ibid.*, pp. 271-2.

Rambler,[8] which strove for a higher level and more intelligent
direction of activity by both laity and clergy. As part of this
activity, Capes sought to introduce those "Roman" devotions for which the converts were so enthusiastic, and which
the old Catholics, bred in the tradition of quiet piety
engendered by the centuries of persecution, tended to discourage. In this, however, the *Rambler* never went to the
lengths of the more extreme converts such as Father Faber,
the Superior of the London Oratory; it always preferred the
intellectual to the emotional side of religion.

The *Rambler* professed to abstain from both theology and
partisan politics. Capes strove, in its first years, to keep pure
theology out of its pages; but there is a large region of
thought, not in itself theological, which borders on theology
and is in frequent contact with it. The *Rambler* could not
avoid entering into this area of "mixed" questions, and was
soon led into theology itself. Capes was more successful in
avoiding politics; he was not greatly interested in the subject.
On those specific issues with which Catholics were particularly concerned, Capes took the side favoured by Wiseman,
with whom he always maintained friendly relations. In
foreign politics, the *Rambler*'s great interest was in the affairs
of Rome, where it maintained its "own correspondent"
during the critical year 1848; it took a safe position, praising
the reforms of Pius IX, and justifying his eventual break with
the Revolution.

One characteristic of the early years of the *Rambler*, which
it did not continue after Capes ceased to be editor, was a
marked tendency towards what may be called "social
Catholicism." "The great problem for the statesman of this
day is the reconciliation of rich and poor, or rather of riches
and poverty."[9] Capes feared that "social decay" arising from
neglect of the problems of the poor might lead to revolution:

---

[8] For all practical purposes, Capes and the *Rambler* are synonymous in this
period; Capes wrote the largest part of the journal and determined its policy.
I have employed the impersonal manner of speaking when referring to policies
or attitudes expressed by the *Rambler* which survived the period of Capes'
editorship, or which cannot be assigned to him personally. It should also be
noted that, although the *Rambler* was predominantly the work of converts, it
accepted contributions from old Catholics.

[9] "Rich and Poor," *Rambler*, I (22 April 1848), 345.

"If we will not care for the poor man from love, we must do it from dread."[10] Capes was inclined to believe, with some regret, that democracy was inevitable, and he sought to prepare the lower classes for it by bringing to them the benefits of education and religion. This was the motive for his zeal in urging the expansion of Catholic missions and schools among the poor. His social Catholicism, which was also based on a genuine love of the poor, had some curious manifestations; he opposed Sabbatarian legislation, much to the dismay of some Catholics, because it interfered with the innocent amusements of the poor. The *Rambler* serialized harrowing "tales" of "Scenes of Life in London" to dramatize its concern for the poor. This concern also brought it into sympathy with the Irish, who formed the bulk of the Catholic poor in the cities.

The most popular and successful section of the early *Rambler* was its artistic department. Capes was himself a competent musician, his brother Frederick was an art critic, and Northcote, a very able amateur archaeologist who travelled much in Italy, provided articles on the Roman catacombs and on foreign churches and shrines. The Capes brothers were inclined by temperament to favour the revival of Gothic art and architecture and of Gregorian chant. However, the social Catholicism of the *Rambler* overrode these preferences. It was more important, the *Rambler* asserted, to build many small, cheap churches among the poor than a few grandiose Gothic edifices; it was better to spend little on decoration and much on schools; and it was preferable to sacrifice the austere beauties of plain-chant in favour of popular hymns in English, such as Faber was writing. In the heyday of the Gothic revival, dominated by so vehement a leader as the architect Pugin, these notions could not pass without challenge. In fact, nothing provoked so much controversy during the early years of the *Rambler* as its architectural articles, nor was it ever subjected to fiercer denunciation than by the devotees of the Gothic style.

More important, however, in the light of the future

---

[10] This was his comment on the revolution in France: "The Fallen King," *Rambler*, I (2 March 1848), 178.

development of the magazine, was its constant interest in Catholic religious and political thought on the Continent. From the beginning, the *Rambler* showed an inclination towards those doctrines and thinkers known as "Liberal Catholic."[11] In the first number it began a series of articles on Lacordaire, translated from the *Correspondant.* Book reviews gave it an opportunity to examine the life of Lamennais and to praise the work of Döllinger. It felt a "deep and almost painful interest"[12] in America; suspecting that separation of Church and state was the inevitable tendency of the nineteenth century, it looked upon America as a praiseworthy example of a country in which the Church was allowed full freedom by a secular state. These views were not especially stressed by the early *Rambler,* but they indicated the direction of its thought.

With such views, expressed as they were with considerable vigour and ability, the *Rambler* was clearly destined for a life of controversy. It could not help attracting attention and interest, and the result was that it achieved an early success which raised it immediately into the front rank of Catholic periodicals. At the same time, Capes was sufficiently cautious in his expressions to retain the good will of most of the bishops, and especially of Wiseman; his conduct of the *Rambler* received "many cordial expressions of approbation."[13] By the seventh issue it had been found necessary to increase the size of the *Rambler* from sixteen to twenty-four pages. After two months Capes thought it desirable to give it the character of a weekly newspaper rather than a magazine, the better to deal with current events in that year of revolution.

This brought the *Rambler* into direct competition with *The Tablet,* until then the leading Catholic weekly newspaper. Just at this time *The Tablet* had fallen out of favour with the bishops. Under the vigorous editorship of Frederick Lucas, it had distinguished itself by its manly assertion of Catholic claims; but Lucas was addicted to harsh language, which quickly brought him into disfavour. He had taken up the

[11] The Continental Liberal Catholic movement will be discussed, in some detail, in Chapter III.

[12] *Rambler,* I (12 Feb. 1848), 120.

[13] "Permanent Enlargement of the Rambler," *Rambler,* I (5 Feb. 1848), 89.

Irish cause much too heartily for the taste of the English Catholics; he had attacked Lord Shrewsbury, a friend of Wiseman; he had opposed the project for diplomatic relations with Rome, against the wishes of most of the English bishops; and, at the beginning of 1848, *The Tablet* had given offence in Rome by publishing some letters which were deemed disrespectful to the Holy See. Wiseman, urged from Rome, publicly disavowed any connection with *The Tablet*, and was immediately denounced by it in reply.[14] The *Rambler*, with its more cautious policy, grew in episcopal favour as its rival declined; at one of Wiseman's *soirées* it was whispered that its becoming a newspaper was part of a plan, sponsored by Wiseman, to have it eventually supersede *The Tablet*.[15] Capes denied any such intention; he was, in fact, rather embarrassed by this episcopal sponsorship, and feared that people would think that Wiseman was forming a "convert party."[16]

The direct collision of the *Rambler* and *The Tablet* did not, however, last long. It seemed to be a law of the *Rambler*'s growth that it continually required to expand in scope and size. Capes felt that a weekly was not a suitable medium for the serious papers which he desired to publish. He also found that it was too great a burden to produce, almost single-handed, an issue every week. In September of 1848, therefore, the *Rambler* became a monthly magazine of eighty pages. This removed it from direct competition with *The Tablet*, which continued on its course of opposition to Wiseman until 1850, when Lucas, who had become a thorough Irish nationalist, removed it to Dublin.

The comparatively good repute of the *Rambler* did not exempt it from a considerable amount of criticism. "We are notoriously the most disputatious community in the kingdom," Capes observed, "quarreling with each other on every possible opportunity."[17] Noting the amount both "of severe

[14] For this controversy, see Bernard Ward, *The Sequel to Catholic Emancipation*, 2 vols. (London, 1915), II, pp. 174-5.
[15] Privately printed circular by Frederick Lucas, 1848; copy in Westminster Archives.
[16] Capes to Newman, 3 March 1848, Newman MSS.
[17] Preface to Vol. III of the *Rambler* (1848), p. iv.

animadversion and of zealous eulogy" that the *Rambler* had received, he felt it necessary to justify its "boldness in pressing upon its readers a variety of topics which the cautious conservative spirit of other days would have kept sacred from all public discussion," and to ask for "forbearance, and a candid consideration, both of the difficulties of the task we have undertaken, and of the absolute necessity which there exists for the infusion of a fresh vigour, and a deeper philosophy, into our present system of ideas."[18] It was frequently necessary to plead for the right of free debate. When objection was taken to the discussion of church decorations, a correspondent argued that "every person, be he who he may, ecclesiastic or layman, has an unquestionable right to publish and defend any opinion whatever that he pleases on those theological subjects which are not already ruled by the Church herself, and that the attempt to stifle such discussion is pregnant with mischief to the well-being of the Catholic Church."[19] This was a position held by the *Rambler* throughout its history. It also held that such debate need not be confined to the usual paths of Catholic apologetics; thus, when "Communism" was condemned by the Pope, the *Rambler* warned that "it must still be met with those arguments to which alone they who disown the rights of the Pope will consent to yield."[20] This sensitivity to thought outside the Church was another standing characteristic of the *Rambler*.

The first major controversy of the *Rambler* was on a question of architecture. It opened on 29 July 1848, with a letter by "X" on "Rood-Screens," opposing Pugin's practice of building rood-screens on "theologico-artistic" grounds, arguing that screens obstructed the congregation's view of the sacramental acts.[21] The editor, desiring to stir up some

---

[18] *Ibid.*, pp. iii, v, vi.

[19] Letter by "Z" on "The Right of Free Discussion," *Rambler*, I (19 Aug. 1848), 368.

[20] "Communism," *Rambler*, V (Feb. 1850), 113. In this article the *Rambler* advocated co-operatives and an increase in wages.

[21] *Rambler*, I, 292-7. All correspondence in the *Rambler* was anonymous, the correspondents arbitrarily choosing letters to identify themselves. Only one correspondent in this controversy identified himself by name: W. G. Ward, who later acknowledged that he was "H." Most articles were unsigned,

interest, invited discussion on the subject, and promptly found himself flooded with letters. The *Rambler*, in raising the question, had unwarily trod on a very sensitive area of feeling among Catholics.

The Gothic revival led by Pugin had found particular support among the old Catholics, who regarded it as the appropriate national style. The converts, who wished to follow Roman models as closely as possible, favoured "Italian" styles of decoration and devotion which had developed on the Continent after the end of the Middle Ages. Thus the architectural conflict merged with other conflicts between converts and old Catholics; at the same time, by becoming a battle between the "national" and the "Roman" tendencies in the Church, it took on quasi-theological over-tones. The *Rambler* took the "Roman" side, partly because Capes at that time shared the general attitude of the converts, but even more because he found that the Gothic style could not meet the actual needs of the English Catholics for numerous cheap churches, built among the poor, and suited to those devotions which they found most congenial. The controversy became embittered because of the tone and language of Pugin, who regarded Gothic as the only truly Catholic style, which it was almost a dogma of faith to support and heresy to oppose. Indeed, he was not above impugning the orthodoxy of his opponents. Pugin published a strong letter in *The Tablet* on 2 September 1848, warning against "a system of deadly enmity to the fundamentals of Church architecture and Christian art,"[22] and a pamphlet in 1850 denouncing "this miserable system of modern degener-acy" as a subversive attempt "to change the whole nature of the divine services of the Catholic Church" and as a display of "Methodism."[23] This brought forth a response from Capes, who was shocked and somewhat disillusioned by this style of controversy among Catholics, but who was quite capable of

including all those for which the editor considered himself responsible; some of the "communicated" articles were signed by initials.

[22] Cited in Bernard Ward, *Sequel to Catholic Emancipation*, II, 270.

[23] Augustus Welby Pugin, *An Earnest Appeal for the Revival of the Ancient Plain Song* (London, 1850), pp. 3-4. The controversy had spread from architecture to music, where the *Rambler* supported "modern" hymns for the people against medieval plain-chant.

replying in kind. Capes charged Pugin with speaking more
as an Anglican than as a Catholic, implying that the Church
had fallen in perfection since the Middle Ages, and fostering
"a belief that the Church has actually *done wrong* in adopting
the peculiar externals which characterise her in modern
times."[24] Pugin defended himself, and assailed the "archi-
tectual heresies" of the *Rambler*—"a body of mutineers" who
were "exciting this insane, I may almost say impious, movement against the restoration of old Catholic solemnity"[25]—
in a new pamphlet; and the small war between "Goths" and
"anti-Goths" continued. Only Pugin's death in 1852 put an
end to the controversy.

Meanwhile the *Rambler* had been engaged in another and
more serious controversy. The number for December 1848
contained an article on "Catholic and Protestant Collegiate
Education," criticizing the quality of the education given at
the Catholic colleges, charging that the Catholic laity were
worse educated than any corresponding class of Protestants,
and blaming this situation upon the mixing of lay students
with those destined for the Church, in which each class was
sacrificed to the interests of the other. Capes' criticisms were
based on his knowledge of Prior Park, which was notorious
for the mismanagement of its finances, and therefore some
of his statements were exaggerated; but "even then many of
the old Catholics regarded it as 'timely and in the main
correct'."[26] The article gave offence, however, to many
graduates of the colleges. Bishop Ullathorne, now vicar-
apostolic of the Central District residing in Birmingham, was
at that time engaged in a dispute with Newman and Faber
over the Oratorian "Lives of the Saints," which had offended
many old Catholics by their extreme Romanizing tendencies;
the *Rambler* had supported the Oratorians and had protested

---

[24] "Mr. Pugin and the 'Rambler'," *Rambler*, V (April 1850), 374. Newman
took much the same position as Capes in his remarks on architecture in the
Idea of a University (1854): "an obsolete discipline may be a present heresy."
John Henry Newman, *The Idea of a University defined and illustrated* (new impression, London, 1917), Discourse IV, p. 83.

[25] Pugin, *Some Remarks on the Articles which have recently appeared in the "Rambler"
relative to Ecclesiastical Architecture and Decoration* (London, 1851), pp. 8, 24-5.

[26] Dom Cuthbert Butler, *The Life and Times of Bishop Ullathorne*, 2 vols.
(London and New York, 1926), I, 128.

against the suppression of the "Lives of the Saints." Ullathorne was therefore ill-disposed towards the *Rambler*, and he saw in its criticism of collegiate education evidence of a "conspiracy against the old Catholics."[27] He attacked the *Rambler* article in a long letter in *The Tablet*, 9 December 1848, deploring the fact that "those who are but as children amongst us, forgetting their pupilage, have undertaken to rebuke, censure, and condemn the acts of those in authority in our Church."[28] In somewhat exaggerated language he objected to laymen speaking publicly on subjects, such as education, "which depend entirely on Church authority."[29] A more temperate criticism of the *Rambler* was made in its own pages in a letter from Frederick Oakeley, a convert, who had studied at St. Edmund's College, Old Hall.

The *Rambler* replied in an article in the next number, pleading for liberty of discussion on questions which are not of faith. "It has also pleased the Divine Head of the Church to confine the infallible guidance of the Church herself within certain definite boundaries, which leave an immense domain of subjects upon which the private Christian has no certain guide, and must make use of the ordinary means for ascertaining what is right and true."[30] It claimed that the inferiority of Catholic education in England was undeniable as a matter of fact, and was proved by the absence of any substantial Catholic English literature; it could only be good to bring out the truth and discuss it honestly.

The *Rambler*'s position was supported in a signed letter by W. G. Ward, one of the most prominent converts, who took the occasion to refute the notion of a "convert conspiracy": "It seems to have been the impression of many, that converts are criticizing old Catholic institutions from a sort of external position, as though not feeling ourselves bound up with those institutions . . . it is, on the contrary, precisely *because* we feel ourselves as fully part and parcel of the existing system as are the older Catholics themselves . . . that we are so constrained

[27] *Ibid.*, p. 160.
[28] *Ibid.*, p. 159.
[29] *Ibid.*
[30] "The Duties of Journalists—Catholic and Protestant Education," *Rambler*, III (Jan. 1849), 329.

to speak."[31] Capes also received the private support of
Newman, who described the article as "very clever and very
true," adding that "I cannot see on what principle you can
draw back from a *truth*, to which you have given publicity."[32]
Cautioning Capes to avoid the appearance of hostility to the
old Catholics, he admitted that Capes could not avoid giving
some offence no matter how much he moderated his language: "the *Rambler* is doing a great deal of good, and we
cannot do good without giving offence and incurring criticism."[33] Wiseman, too, privately sympathized with Capes
and disliked Ullathorne's attack on the *Rambler*.

Ullathorne continued to be unfriendly to Capes and the
Rambler. Capes thought that Ullathorne was one of those
who "simply disliked that independence of thought on
matters not of faith which he found in converts, as a result of
their liberal education; an independence most unpleasant to
prelates whose mind was absorbed in the idea that the one
function of bishops is to govern, and the one duty of priests
and laity to obey."[34] In 1851, in response to the Protestant
attack on the restoration of the Catholic hierarchy, Capes
proposed a scheme for lay lecturers who would speak in
defence of the Church, and himself delivered a series of
lectures, with the warm approval of Wiseman, who was now
Cardinal-Archbishop of Westminster. The lectures were
delivered in a church. Ullathorne disapproved of this; it
appeared to him that this was a form of "lay preaching."
When Capes spoke out vigorously in favour of the greatest
possible amount of lay action on behalf of the Church,
Ullathorne spoke of him as having uttered "rank heresy."[35]
Wiseman continued his support of Capes, even sending him
material with which to vindicate his position.[36] When Capes

[31] William George Ward, "The Necessities of Catholic Education," *Rambler*,
III (Feb. 1849), 446.

[32] Newman to Capes, 6 Dec. 1858, Newman MSS.

[33] Newman to Capes, 3 Jan. 1849, cited by Wilfrid Ward, *Life of Newman*, I,
245.

[34] Capes, *To Rome and Back*, p. 301. The reference is to an old Catholic
"prelate," not identified by name, whom I conjecturally identify as Ullathorne.

[35] Newman to Capes, 6 and 10 April 1851, Newman MSS.

[36] Wiseman to Capes, March 1851, Westminster Archives. Wiseman pointed
out that laymen were frequently allowed to preach from the pulpit in Rome
itself.

had to suspend his lectures on account of illness, Newman filled the breach himself by delivering his lectures on *The Present Position of Catholics in England*. Later, after Ullathorne had come to be on friendly terms with Newman, he ceased for a while to be hostile to the *Rambler* and even contributed a series of articles to it in 1856.

Capes was always on good terms with Newman, who encouraged his projects. Still the dominant figure among the converts, Newman was the symbol of the hopes of men such as Capes, although he shrank from assuming the leadership of a movement. Newman had the strongest conviction of the need for a revivification of Catholic thought and of the important role which the educated laity could play in this work. The extent, and also the limitations, of the liberalism of Newman's Catholicism were made evident in his Dublin lectures on *The Idea of a University*, delivered in 1852 to promote the Catholic University of which he was to be rector. The lectures sought to justify the pursuit of intellectual culture for its own sake, a pursuit which should be welcomed and unfettered by the authorities of the Church. Knowledge and reasons are the real allies of faith, for the common object of both science and theology is truth. The Church meets reason with the weapons of reason. Catholics have no special advantage in the pursuit of secular knowledge: "The Church has ever appealed and deferred to witnesses and authorities external to herself, in those matters in which she thought they had means of forming a judgment."[37] These were to be the basic tenets of the Liberal Catholic movement; but Newman balanced them with a sufficiency of *caveats*. If left to itself, liberal knowledge may work out results prejudicial to Catholicism, leading to an "intellectualism" which tends to produce a "mere philosophical theory of life and conduct, in the place of Revelation," and "gives birth to a rebellious stirring against miracle and mystery, against the severe and the terrible."[38] History, for example, takes a merely external view of revelation, and is liable to a perversion which substi-

[37] Newman, *The Idea of a University*, Discourse I, p. 6.
[38] *Ibid.*, Discourse IX, pp. 217, 218.

tutes the testimony of historical documents for that of revelation as the measure of religion.[39] The sciences, Newman felt,
may not pursue their course immune from theological criticism, and the Church may employ the weapons of authority
to discipline the unbridled intellect. If Newman's intellect
was liberal, his instincts were conservative.

Newman's assistance to Capes was rather limited. Want
of time, and a certain reluctance to offend Wiseman, who
had pressed him to write for the *Dublin Review*, prevented
Newman from contributing to the *Rambler*. However, he
brought Capes into contact with the members of his order,
the Oratorians of Birmingham and London, and some of
them wrote for the *Rambler*. In return for this support, the
Rambler gave publicity to the work of the Oratorians; Capes
also composed music for some of their functions. Eventually,
in 1850, he secured from Newman three poems in a series to
which Faber also contributed. In that year Capes also persuaded Newman to become "theological censor" of the
Rambler. These associations had created a widespread impression that the *Rambler* was in reality the organ of the Oratorians; in 1851, at Newman's urging, Capes had to deny this
publicly.[40] In 1852, due to his preoccupation with the Achilli
trial and the Dublin University, Newman resigned his
"censorship" of the *Rambler*.

His influence had always been exercised in favour of
caution, and the two years of his "censorship" coincided with
a period of temporary conservatism for the *Rambler*. The
Catholic diocesan hierarchy had been restored in 1850, and
the agitation against it had disillusioned many Catholics who
had hoped for friendlier relations with Protestants. For a
time the English Catholics tended to withdraw into the state
of isolation from which they had only recently emerged. The

[39] This was the basis of Newman's criticism of Döllinger in his *Letter to the
Duke of Norfolk* (1874). See Stephen J. Tonsor, "Lord Acton on Döllinger's
Historical Theology," *Journal of the History of Ideas*, XX (June-Sept. 1959),
352, and Thomas S. Bokenkotter, *Cardinal Newman as an Historian* (Louvain,
1959), p. 70.

[40] Newman to Capes, 6 and 11 May 1851, Newman MSS. *Rambler*, VII
(June 1851), 542. Newman had apparently been criticized by the Continental
Oratorians for conducting a secular journal. Capes, in denying this, took
occasion to contradict other rumours that the *Rambler* was the organ of Cardinal
Wiseman, or of the Jesuits.

Rambler, following this trend, published, in May 1851, an article which warned that the State was perpetually the enemy of the Church, and that its "toleration and favour are always transitory and fictitious. The Church and the world *cannot* coalesce and walk side by side for a single hour."[41] It denounced "liberalism" and those Catholics who abstained from actions which might irritate Protestants or who did not "live for Catholic objects."[42] Another article, in September, denounced the principle of religious liberty as "one of the most wicked delusions" and proclaimed that "Catholicism is the most intolerant of creeds."[43] This attitude, however, was alien to the spirit of the *Rambler*, and did not last long.

This temporary policy of isolation had its effect on the *Rambler*'s politics—its weakest department. The "papal aggression" agitation had broken the traditional connection of the Catholics with the Whigs. The *Rambler* advocated the formation of an independent Catholic opposition in Parliament to work for exclusively Catholic objects. However, the reality of the "Irish Independent Opposition" which was formed under the leadership of Lucas—a party which was devoted not merely to Catholicism but to tenant right—soon disillusioned the *Rambler*, and it relapsed into its earlier indifference to political parties.

Neither the occasional vacillations of its policy nor the controversies in which it was frequently engaged had prevented the *Rambler* from making good its footing as an established journal. This was no mean accomplishment, as Catholic periodicals were notorious for their instability. Capes frequently complained of the fickleness of the small Catholic reading public, "the most sensitive and touchy class of men in the world,"[44] who were inclined to cancel their subscriptions whenever an article gave some offence.

[41] "Our Position and Policy," *Rambler*, VII (May 1851), 378.
[42] *Ibid.*, 380.
[43] "Civil and Religious Liberty," *Rambler*, VIII (Sept. 1851), 177-8. The writer acknowledged that religious toleration might be justified as a political measure, though not as a doctrine. The style and spirit of this article suggest that it may have been written by Ward.
[44] "Cheap Books," *Rambler*, IV (Nov. 1849), 415.

The *Rambler* was considered "an unusually successful periodical, as Catholic matters go":[45] its circulation, rather less than one thousand copies, was regarded as satisfactory, and it did not lack for contributors, although it was essentially the work of "a single individual and a few friends."[46] Nonetheless, the financial returns barely sufficed to cover the expenses for printing and paper; contributors were infrequently paid; and Capes, despite some pecuniary aid from his friends, found himself in 1852 out of pocket by some £400. Convinced of the necessity of his work, he was not dismayed by this, and was determined to carry on. His difficulties did not deter him from testifying that "it is a wonderful thing to be a Catholic."[47]

In this spirit he celebrated the fourth anniversary of his conversion with an article on "Four Years' Experience of the Catholic Religion."[48] Arguing that submission to Rome did not enslave the intellect, he asserted that his own conversion could be justified by the same reasoning which is employed in any human science: "the balance of probabilities" was decidedly in favour of Rome, and he had embraced "the most probable of two alternatives."[49] This "probabilistic" argument was criticized by a Catholic theologian, in a private letter to Capes, on the ground that it was a point of doctrine that the certainty with which a Catholic believes in the Church was an absolute, not merely a moral, certainty, excluding the idea of probability. Capes, with his mathematical turn of mind, thought this doctrine a "logical monstrosity."[50] Christianity itself, he thought, was a matter of certainty only in the manner in which all other historical questions were certain, "depending, that is, upon documentary evidence, which could never rise to the certainty of abstract mathematical truth";[51] how then could Catholicism claim a greater degree of certainty? This doctrine of faith

[45] "The Struggles of Catholic Literature," *Rambler*, IX (April 1852), 262.
[46] "Hopes and Fears for 1850," *Rambler*, V (Jan. 1850), 10.
[47] *Ibid.*, 1.
[48] *Rambler*, IV (July, Aug., Sept. 1849), 161-171, 221-233, 283-295. A pirated edition was published in America (Philadelphia, 1849).
[49] *Ibid.* (July 1849), 164.
[50] Capes, *To Rome and Back*, p. 304.
[51] *Ibid.*, p. 303.

appeared to Capes to violate the immutable laws of reason.

This was the first shock to his faith in the Catholic Church. He could not find a solution to his difficulty; Newman, whom he consulted, apparently did not realize the nature of his problems and returned an unsatisfactory answer. Capes was nonetheless sure that an answer could be found or that his critic had overstated the teaching of the Church. "It was for a long time a puzzle rather than a recognised doubt. So thorough was my trust and my satisfaction, that the new thought was for years nothing but a haunting suspicion of the existence of some sort of intellectual problem, the solution of which must be readily accessible, if only I could find my way to it."[52] It was several years before he came to consider the question as one which required him to reconsider his faith in Catholicism. Its only immediate effect was to make him readier to admit the intellectual difficulties of Catholicism and to look with a critical eye on the shortcomings of ecclesiastical authorities. Only a few friends were ever told of his doubts; Newman, who was one of them, did not consider the difficulty very serious. As late as 1857 Newman was able to write: "Capes is too good a fellow for one to have any fears of *him*."[53] No hint of Capes' doubts ever appeared in the *Rambler*, and there is no reason to believe that they exercised any significant influence on his conduct of the magazine.

In 1852 Capes, on account of a chronic illness, found the burden of editing the *Rambler* too great, and persuaded his friend James Spencer Northcote to become editor. Capes remained proprietor of the magazine and continued to contribute articles. Northcote's editorship was not a success. In 1853 his wife became ill and then died; this incapacitated him for some time for his duties as editor. After his wife's death, he resolved to study for the priesthood, and was anxious to give up his secular occupations. Capes, meanwhile, had become dissatisfied with Northcote's conduct of the *Rambler*, complaining that "his cautiousness, and dry

[52] *Ibid.*, p. 302.
[53] Newman to Ambrose St. John, 7 May 1857, cited by Ward, *Life of Newman*, I, 437.

C

antiquarianism, made the sale fall off so much, that I felt obliged to resume the work as soon as I could."[54] Northcote resigned in October of 1854, and Capes resumed the editorship.

Capes' second editorship opened a new chapter in the history of the *Rambler*.[55] Hitherto, although it had supported, with some inconsistencies, those doctrines of bold inquiry and breadth of view which were later to be called "Liberal Catholic," it had done so simply by putting them into practice rather than by proclaiming them as a programme. In the middle 1850s, however, it began to take a more positive position.

[54] Letter of Capes to Mrs. Richard Simpson (date uncertain), Downside MSS. Northcote was ordained in 1857.

[55] On 1 Jan. 1854, as a promotional device to increase subscriptions, the *Rambler* commenced a "new series," beginning again with Vol. I. There is no special significance in this change. In 1859, another "new series" was commenced; and it has become customary to cite this (actually the third) series as the "new series." To avoid confusion, volumes of the "new" (second) series will be cited as "2nd ser."

CHAPTER II

RICHARD SIMPSON AND THE *RAMBLER*,
1854-1858

THE circumstances under which the *Rambler* had to be
conducted in the mid-1850s were different from those
of its founding in 1848. In the years of the "second
spring," when the energies of the Catholic body were
absorbed by the tasks of receiving converts and immigrants
and organizing the new hierarchy, there had been, despite
occasional differences, a consciousness of a common purpose
and a spirit of unity. This did not last. The Catholic revival
lost its original inspiration and direction and turned inwards
on itself.

In the middle and late 1850s, the English Catholic community was racked by internal dissensions. The reconciliation of old Catholics and converts did not take place; instead,
controversy continued and became more bitter. Cardinal
Wiseman, who favoured the converts, was meanwhile em-
broiled in difficulties with some of his bishops, including his
own coadjutor, Archbishop Errington. The converts themselves were divided. One party, of which Faber, Ward and
the future Cardinal Manning were the leading spirits, was
noted for its extravagance of devotion, its thoroughly
ecclesiastical spirit, and its emphasis on the role of church
authorities, especially the authority of Rome. Another party,
less numerous, for which Newman provided the inspiration
if not the leadership, sought to meet the intellectual needs
of the day, relying upon the work of the laity, combining
respect for Catholic authorities with freedom of inquiry and
consideration towards Protestants and unbelievers. This
divergence between the temperaments of Faber and Newman
was symbolized in the break between the Oratories of
London and Birmingham.

The *Rambler* sought to stand aloof from party struggles

25

among Catholics. Nonetheless, as the divergence became evident, it found itself more in sympathy with the spirit of Birmingham than with that of London. The tendency of the early *Rambler* towards bolder inquiry and criticism now became more pronounced. At the same time, Newman's personal influence, which had always been exercised in the direction of caution, was diminished because of his preoccupation with the Catholic University in Dublin.

The position of the *Rambler* in the field of Catholic journalism was also changing. A new weekly had come on the scene: the *Catholic Standard*, founded in 1849, which was published from 1855 under the title of the *Weekly Register*. In 1854 this journal had been acquired by Henry Wilberforce, a convert and friend of Newman. The *Weekly Register* took a Whig position in politics; it was hoped that it would counteract the Irish politics of Lucas' *Tablet*, which had come into conflict with the Irish bishops. But in 1855 Lucas died. *The Tablet* was acquired by John Wallis, who brought it back to England and reversed its politics, conducting it in the Tory interest. Wiseman, who was himself inclined to conservatism in politics, now showed *The Tablet* some favour, second, of course, to his own *Dublin Review*.

As a result of these developments, even without any deliberate intention on the part of its conductors, the *Rambler* was to be cast in the role of the organ of "the Catholic Left."[1] This tendency was accentuated by the presence of a new member on the staff of the *Rambler*, Richard Simpson. Capes, in April of 1854, had asked Simpson to become his assistant editor. Simpson declined this offer, but agreed to contribute substantially to each issue. Though he was not an editor, but merely a regular contributor,[2] Simpson's influence was soon felt in the conduct of the magazine.

Simpson, born in 1820, was a graduate of Newman's college, Oriel. He took orders, married, and was presented to the family living of Mitcham, Surrey. This he held for

---

[1] David Mathew, *Catholicism in England, 1535–1935* (London, 1936), p. 222.
[2] Memorandum by Simpson, n.d., Downside MSS. See also Abbot Gasquet, "Introduction" to *Lord Acton and his Circle* (London, 1906), p. xxi.

one year, resigning it on his conversion in 1845.[3] He had independent means, and travelled on the continent for some years after his conversion, acquiring an unusual command of languages. On his return to England he devoted himself to literary pursuits. His interests ranged over philosophy, literature, history and music. He was well regarded as a Shakespearian scholar, and was one of the earliest advocates of the theory that Shakespeare was a Catholic. In history he specialized in the Elizabethan period; his life of Edmund Campion was long the standard biography.

Simpson's intellectual ability is unquestioned. "In private life his genial disposition, sunny temper, and brilliant social gifts made him a general favourite. . . . No one could be more free from any tinge of the *odium theologicum*."[4] Those who knew him recognized the reality of his religious belief and his fervent though unobtrusive piety. Nonetheless, there have been those who have questioned the genuineness of his Catholicism, and his character has appeared an enigma to many observers. Part of the misunderstanding arises from the inability of some of his critics to comprehend how his liberalism could be reconciled with true submission to the Catholic Church.[5] His posthumous reputation has suffered from an exaggerated assertion that he assisted Gladstone in that statesman's attack on the Vatican Decrees.[6] Nonetheless, it must be acknowledged that much of the misunderstanding was the result of Simpson's own methods.

It was his literary creed that "the desire to know and tell the truth may be as religious a motive as the desire to give

[3] According to Wilfrid Ward, *The Life and Times of Cardinal Wiseman*, 2 vols. (London, 1897), II, 228, "Mr. Simpson, as an Anglican, had been at constant war with his Bishop." In *William George Ward and the Catholic Revival* (2nd ed., London, 1912), p. 143, he elaborates: "it was said by some of his friends that his disputes with his bishop had become such a necessary part of his daily life, that he could no more do without them than some men can dispense with a daily constitutional."

[4] "Richard Simpson," *Academy*, IX (22 April 1876), 381.

[5] Cf. Edwin Burton, "Richard Simpson," *Catholic Encyclopedia* (New Yo k 1913), XIV, 4: "Though he remained a practical Catholic his opinions were very liberal." In more unskilful hands this can be expanded to read: "although he remained in the Roman Catholic Church until his death . . . he was always liberal and even heretical in his views." *British Authors of the Nineteenth Century*, ed. S. J. Kunitz and H. Haycraft (New York, 1936), p. 561.

[6] This story may be found in most of the biographical notices. It is impossible to discuss it adequately here; a full discussion will be found in the Appendix, *q.v.*

edification."[7] This fierce integrity, which gave the appearance of pugnacity, led him to inquire and speculate fearlessly in history and philosophy, without concern for the effect of his writings on his more timid co-religionists. His intolerance of dishonesty and concealment was unmixed with malice or bitterness towards his opponents, with many of whom he was on the friendliest terms in personal intercourse. But it was overshadowed by "a certain Puckish spirit,"[8] a sharp wit, which he never hesitated to employ, regardless of the character or position of its target. Lord Acton, who became a close friend, described him as "a man of rare gifts and deep religion, but possessed with an incorrigible irreverence and sense of the comic."[9] Many things were attributed to him for which he was not responsible, and he was frequently misinterpreted; but he took no steps to avoid such misinterpretation. To Simpson, therefore, the faults of the *Rambler* were generally ascribed, even when they were the responsibility of others; and he never attempted to shift the burden from his shoulders. Indeed, he deliberately assumed the character of the impudent and reckless troublemaker, partly for the fun of it, but in large measure as a purposeful attempt to take on himself the odium which properly belonged to his party.

Simpson first came to public attention as a Catholic by defending the practice of invocation of saints in a debate with the Presbyterian Dr. Cumming. Characteristically, Simpson argued on his adversary's own ground, proving his case "from the Bible alone."[10] "All that I have attempted to show," Simpson said, "is that we are not the fools which the adversaries of the Catholic faith would make you believe; that we have some reason to give for the faith that is in us."[11] In 1851, Simpson was recommended by Newman to Capes as a possible participant in the latter's scheme for lecturers to

---

[7] Simpson to T. W. Marshall, n.d. (1862-4), Woodruff MSS.
[8] Douglas Woodruff, "Introduction" to Lord Acton, *Essays on Church and State* (London, 1952), p. 8.
[9] CUL Add. MSS. 4988.
[10] *Invocation of Saints proved from the Bible alone: Substance of an Address delivered by R. Simpson, Esq., B.A., at a discussion between him and Dr. Cumming, at Clapham, Tuesday, July 3d, 1849* (London, 1849).
[11] *Ibid.*, p. 29.

defend the Church against the "papal aggression" agitation.[12]

Simpson, who was Frederick Capes' neighbour at Clapham, began to contribute to the *Rambler* in 1850. The draft of his article on "Religion and Modern Philosophy" "startled" both Capes and Newman, but a revised version was accepted for publication.[13] Simpson argued that the Church need not fear the results of modern science. "In such cases it is not enough for a man to run away from doubts . . . a rational doubt must be met on rational grounds."[14] He dealt boldly with Biblical criticism and scientific objections to the Mosaic account of creation, pointing out that a Catholic is not bound to any particular theory concerning the mode or duration of the creation. "Hence in certain subjects a Catholic is quite free in his interpretation of Scripture, so that he need feel no anxiety though he find his scientific theories opposed to the commonly received and traditional interpretation, provided that he has satisfied himself by a rigid scrutiny that they are not subversive of any principle either of faith or morals."[15] Simpson adopted a figurative interpretation of the language of Genesis, treating the "days" of creation not as units of time but as operative principles of the divine purpose.[16] He compared the Mosaic account, thus interpreted, with the conclusions of modern science, as represented by Humboldt's *Cosmos*, and concluded that the Bible was remarkably accurate. This safe conclusion no doubt redeemed the daring speculation of this article, which is remarkable for its anticipation of the difficulties with which religious thought was to be beset in future years.

Simpson's instinct for "touchy" subjects was next shown in a discussion of the condemnation of Galileo, which had brought upon the Church the reproach of being opposed to science.[17] Again his boldness alarmed Newman, although the

[12] Newman to Capes, 21 Feb. 1851, in Gasquet, "Introduction," p. xxx.
[13] Capes to Newman, 18 July 1850, and Newman to Capes, 17 Aug. 1850, Newman MSS.
[14] "Religion and Modern Philosophy," *Rambler*, VI (Sept. 1850), 189. The article was continued in the next three issues.
[15] *Ibid.*, 194.
[16] He later justified this, and other such interpretations, by citing patristic authorities in a letter to the *Rambler*, VII (Feb. 1851), 177-9.
[17] This appears to have been an extension of his earlier articles. See letter of Bishop Grant of Southwark to Wiseman, 14 Jan. 1851, Westminster Archives:

article passed his censorship. Newman told Capes that Simpson "is the only one of your writers who puzzles me."[18] Simpson justified the decree in the case of Galileo, but pointed out that it did not bind the conscience of Catholics. Copernicanism had been condemned for a time, not as false in itself, but "simply as being accidentally contrary to the dignity and estimation of Scripture, and as being false in the sense of unproved."[19] The decree of the Index in 1616 was disciplinary, not doctrinal: Galileo was condemned for advancing the Copernican theory as positive truth when it was as yet an unproved hypothesis, and thereby creating doubts of the accuracy of Scripture without sufficient cause. "This office of the Church, as the vindicator of the outraged feelings of the public, is never to be confounded with her perfectly distinct office of teacher and infallible expounder of doctrines of faith and morals."[20] It was always permissible to advance the Copernican theory simply as a hypothesis; Galileo was too impatient to have it accepted as truth. Simpson argued that the Church was justified in requiring prudence and reserve in imparting knowledge to the public, in order to protect the faith of her weaker children. "If in pure matters of religion mere prematureness and un-seasonableness in the things propounded is enough to mark them with the note of heresy, the same thing may take place in a lower degree with regard to scientific theories."[21] But this restraint, Simpson asserted, was not ultimately un-favourable to the true advance of science. Thus he managed once more to come to a safe and even conservative conclusion after having dealt freely with an awkward topic.[22]

"Mr. Simpson of Clapham is writing on Humboldt's Cosmos etc. in the *Rambler*, and he desired a friend of his to ask me about the decree in the case of Galileo."

[18] Newman to Capes, 17 Dec. 1851, Newman MSS. Newman wanted Simpson to secure the "imprimatur" of his friends among the Redemptorists at Clapham.

[19] Simpson, "Galileo and his Condemnation," *Rambler*, IX (Jan. 1852), 18.

[20] *Ibid.*, 22. This argument was followed by Newman in *The Idea of a University* (London, 1917), Discourse IX, pp. 219-220.

[21] Simpson, "Galileo and his Condemnation," 23. This notion that heresy is the impatient and premature anticipation of truth is a favourite one of Newman's: see the *Apologia pro vita sua* (ed. Wilfrid Ward, London, 1931), pp. 350-1.

[22] It is possible that Simpson was the author of the article on "Savonarola" in the *Rambler* for November and December 1853, which is a similar treatment

Simpson's entry into the ranks of the regular contributors of the *Rambler* coincided with a greater boldness in the conduct of the periodical. An article on magic, in October of 1854, criticized the metaphysics of St. Thomas Aquinas. This provoked a letter by W. G. Ward in the next issue, vindicating the authority of Aquinas. In printing Ward's letter, Capes inserted an editorial note justifying the publication of a free criticism of scholastic philosophy.

> We think that no greater injury can be done to the cause of those who would promote the study of St. Thomas and the schoolmen, as theologians, than any attempt to identify their philosophical speculations with the truth of Catholicism, or to claim for their *modes* of reasoning on religious topics any thing more than an historical, as distinguished from a logical and necessary connection. . . . it is of great practical importance that the difference between the authority of the scholastic philosophy and that of the scholastic theology should be fully appreciated and distinctly brought out.[23]

In subsequent letters the writer of the offending article defended his statements, and asserted that "it would be almost impossible to teach St. Thomas now-a-days in the sense in which he was taught of old."[24]

In another article, the *Rambler* asserted that charity, not polemics, was the true principle of religious controversy, and that Catholics must attract the attention and agreement of Protestants by conciliatory means.

> The first step, therefore, to be taken by every man who would take part in the great controversy of our day, is the gaining of a thorough mastery of the actual condition of mind of the non-Catholics whom he would influence. . . . If we were asked to name the most urgent controversial need of our age, we should say that it was an application of the Baconian method of induction to the phenomena of religious error. Its interminable varieties . . . cannot be ascertained by

of a difficult subject. The article is remarkable for its frank acknowledgement of scandals in the history of the Church: "A Catholic cannot play tricks with Church history without injury to himself and others." *Rambler*, XII (Nov. 1853), 343.

[23] *Rambler*, 2nd ser., II (Nov. 1854), 450-1. This is typical of Capes, who never accepted scholastic metaphysics—a fact which was to be significant when he came to question certain of the doctrines of the Church.

[24] *Rambler*, 2nd ser., III (March 1855), 251.

any *a priori* reading, constructed on a purely theological
basis.[25]

The article decried the Catholic practice of questioning the
sincerity of one's opponents, and suggested that theological
science was inadequate to deal with the actual condition of
the Protestant mind.

These articles were indicative of a new and more aggressive
spirit in the *Rambler*; but it was not until a year later that the
periodical came to be regarded with suspicion by the
hierarchy. The occasion was provided by some writings of
Simpson. Converts like Simpson were aware, as born
Catholics were not, that much of the tendency towards
unbelief among Protestants was due to an ethical revulsion
from the Calvinistic doctrines of original sin and damnation
which had overshadowed their education;[26] they saw in this
an opportunity for Catholicism, with its milder theology, to
win new adherents. The definition of the Immaculate Conception in 1854 gave an occasion for a discussion of the nature
of that original sin from which Mary was held to be exempt
—a discussion which would at once remove Protestant
prejudices against the dogma and afford an opportunity for a
restatement of the Catholic doctrines on original sin and the
destiny of the unregenerate. Simpson wrote on this subject
in July of 1855, in the form of a letter to the editor, signed
"R.P.S."[27] This was followed by two other letters in May and
July of 1856 on the same topic.

Simpson held that original sin was a degradation from the
supernatural state of original justice to a state which was
simply natural, rather than being a positive defilement or

[25] "The True Principle of Religious Controversy," *Rambler*, 2nd ser., III
(April 1855), 256.
[26] For some illustrations of this, see a review of two books on Darwin by
Charles Coulston Gillispie in *Victorian Studies*, II (Dec. 1958), 167-9; see also
(for the case of Tennyson) Maisie Ward, *The Wilfrid Wards and the Transition*
(London, 1934), pp. 167-8.
[27] "The Immaculate Conception viewed in connection with the Doctrine of
Original Sin," *Rambler*, 2nd ser., IV (July 1855), 25-37. The form of a letter
was necessary in order to avoid editorial responsibility: a prefatory note (p. 25)
stated that the doctrines asserted were those of the author only. The *Rambler*
had earlier (May 1855) hailed the definition as a vindication of Newman's
theory of the development of dogma.

evil residing in the flesh. Thus the Immaculate Conception was simply a miracle of grace, by which Mary, alone among mortals, was restored to Adam's original state. For the rest of mankind, God had provided instead an economy of penance by which salvation was possible. This led Simpson to a discussion of the destiny of the unregenerate, whom Calvinists consigned indiscriminately to hellfire. Simpson argued that natural virtue among the unregenerate received its reward, even though the state of bliss was reserved for Christians; hell was not simply a state of punishment, but rather consisted of several states, including the limbo of Dante. In the course of this discussion Simpson found occasion to assert that the modern theory that man had evolved from the ape was not inconsistent with Catholic doctrine.

In attempting his theodicy, Simpson had used language which suggested that original sin was the result of a deliberate plan of God rather than a fault of man: "original sin comes not by propagation . . . but is caused by the decree of the all-merciful God, who places us on a level, because we should infallibly break our necks on the heights."[28] This was a clear theological error, though the fault lay more in Simpson's language than in his doctrines. Even where Simpson was on safe ground in theology he used language and introduced notions which seemed startling, if not actually dangerous, to Catholic readers. He cited reputable theologians to demonstrate that his opinions were at least admissible, but this did not prevent his letters from being denounced to the ecclesiastical authorities. Even the usually sympathetic Newman thought Simpson's letters "very unjustifiable."[29] In this he was reflecting the sentiments of his bishop, Ullathorne, who saw in Simpson's writings a manifestation of a "latitudinarian spirit."[30]

Cardinal Wiseman appointed a commission of three

[28] *Rambler*, 2nd ser., V (May 1856), 340.
[29] Newman to Capes, 19 Jan. 1857, quoted by Gasquet, "Introduction," p. xxiii. Newman's objection was to self-taught laymen writing theology, rather than to the theology itself.
[30] Cited in Dom Cuthbert Butler, *The Life and Times of Bishop Ullathorne*, 2 vols. (London and New York, 1926), I, 310. When Ullathorne publicly denounced the *Rambler* in 1862, Simpson's letters were severely criticized.

theologians in June 1856 to examine Simpson's doctrines. Simpson and Capes promptly declared their readiness to submit to whatever censures might result from this inquiry. A formal censure, however, was averted. Through a friend, Dr. Todd, Simpson proposed to Wiseman to insert a notice in the next *Rambler* to the effect that the writer of the letters, feeling that certain statements in them appear to require revision, desired to discontinue the discussion, and that His Eminence in consequence did not consider it necessary to continue the examination of his doctrines.[31] Wiseman agreed to terminate the proceedings but required two changes in the notice: an expression of regret, and a statement that the writer "withdraws from" rather than merely "desires to discontinue" the discussion.[32] This was done, the statement appearing in the *Rambler* for September 1856.[33]

As Wiseman acknowledged, Simpson's withdrawal statement "contains no retraction";[34] the "certain statements" requiring revision are not identified. Simpson was fully aware of this, and felt free to reassert many of his propositions in subsequent articles, although he never again dealt directly with the subject of original sin.[35] The result of this affair was that in later years Simpson came to be held responsible for all the objectionable features of the *Rambler*, even when he was not at fault.

The incident did not, however, lower Capes' opinion of Simpson. In the very month in which the withdrawal statement appeared, Simpson became assistant editor of the *Rambler*. Capes' poor health had made it necessary to secure an assistant; and, in fact, Simpson served as acting editor for the next four issues. It was during this period that the *Rambler* came into direct conflict with Cardinal Wiseman.

The *Rambler* for October 1856 contained a short notice of the American Catholic journal, *Brownson's Quarterly Review*,

[31] W. G. Todd to Wiseman, 17 July 1856, Westminster Archives.
[32] Wiseman to Todd, 22 July 1856 (copy), Downside MSS.
[33] Gasquet, "Introduction," pp. xxxi-xxxii.
[34] Wiseman to Todd, 22 July 1856, Downside MSS.
[35] When Ullathorne publicly criticized the letters in 1862, Simpson defended his position. He did not consider that he had been condemned. He added that all three letters had been read through by ecclesiastics before being published. See Richard Simpson, *Bishop Ullathorne and the Rambler* (London, 1862), p. 41.

which it praised as "the deepest, most solid, and most consistent periodical in our language."[36] This was returning the compliment which Brownson had paid the *Rambler* in July, when he had described it as

> after our own heart. It has a freedom and freshness about it, a boldness and independence, a force and earnestness, which we like, and from which we augur much good. . . . In a word, its editors seem to us to be more anxious to be living men than to be merely safe men, and more bent on quickening the thought and activity of the Catholic body than they are to obtain the negative merit of giving no offence, or of disturbing no one's tranquillity.[37]

Brownson made a few criticisms, however, on the *Rambler*'s style and language. To these Simpson thought it desirable to make a reply, in which he sought to explain why the *Rambler* was unable to meet the standards Brownson set for it:

> . . . England, and especially the little remnant of Catholic England, lives very much on tradition. . . . We have to write for those who consider that a periodical appearing three times a quarter has no business to enter into serious questions, which must be reserved for the more measured roll of the Quarterly. Our part, it seems, is to provide milk and water and sugar, insipid "amusement and instruction," from which all that might suggest and excite real thought has been carefully weeded. . . . any serious investigation of these sciences, made independently of the unauthoritative interpretations of Scripture that have hitherto been controlled and confined in the Catholic schools, would be discouraged as tending to infuse doubts into the minds of innocent Catholics, and to suggest speculation where faith now reigns. People, forsooth, to whom the pages of *The Times*, the *Athenaeum*, and the *Weekly Dispatch*, with all their masterly infidelity, lie open, will be exposed to the danger of losing their faith if a Catholic writer speculates a little on questions of moral, intellectual, social, or physical philosophy—if he directs his mind to any thing above writing nice stories in illustration of the pleasantness and peace of the Catholic religion . . . to any thing more honest than defending through thick and thin the governments of all tyrants that profess our religion, and proving . . . that the

[36] *Rambler*, 2nd ser., VI (Oct. 1856), 315.
[37] Cited, *ibid*.

interior of a Neapolitan prison is rather preferable to that of an English gaol. We only wish we saw our way clearly to be safe in speaking out in a manner still more completely after Dr. Brownson's heart.[38]

This article gave considerable offence: it seemed to be an unwarranted reflection on the intellectual shortcomings of the old Catholics, the "little remnant of Catholic England." What was worse, it appeared to be a direct hit at Cardinal Wiseman and his *Dublin Review*, part of it being a parody of a sentence from an article, attributed to Wiseman, in that journal.[39] There was a certain amount of petulance evident in the article, probably resulting from Simpson's recent encounter with Church authority over his letters on original sin.

This was followed in the next issue of the *Rambler* by an article on "The Rising Generation: Our Poor-Schools," by J. G. Wenham, a priest.[40] In other circumstances the article would not have given offence: it was a careful and sensible study of the weaknesses of Catholic poor-schools, with suggestions for their improvement. There were some clever paragraphs on two sorts of Catholics: the "croakers" who saw no good in what was being done, and the "*couleur-de-rose*" man who "lives in a poetical atmosphere of his own" in which all was "enchanting, hopeful, and glorious."[41] Both tendencies were gently satirized.

Cardinal Wiseman, who felt that the whole subject of education should be reserved to the bishops, was offended by the references to the "*couleur-de-rose*" tendency, which he interpreted, rather unjustly, as a personal criticism of himself. He connected Wenham's article with Simpson's, and wrote against both in the *Dublin Review* for December 1856. Wiseman complained that the conductors of the *Rambler* sought to set themselves apart from other Catholics, asserting the intellectual superiority of converts. "Its writers

---

[38] *Ibid.*, 316.

[39] Gasquet, "Introduction," p. xxxii.

[40] Gasquet (*ibid.*, p. xxvi) says this article was generally ascribed to Simpson. This is improbable, as it was prefaced by a note stating that it was written by a priest.

[41] *Rambler*, 2nd ser., VI (Nov. 1856), 321.

do not attempt to throw themselves into the true position of
Catholics. They stand aloof, and do not share the real
burthen of Catholic labour . . . they address us rather as a
speaker does from the hustings, from without and above the
crowd addressed."[42] He charged that "this intellectual
separation" from the main body of Catholics was "the creation of party, upon the very worst ground, that of a distinction of old, and new, Catholics."[43] He freely acknowledged
his own preference for the rosy view: "This Review was
founded upon a *couleur-de-rose* principle. It was started simply
in hopefulness, in buoyant bounding confidence that there
was a 'good time coming'."[44] Wiseman denied that Catholics
resisted the progress of scientific investigation, but said that
they "could not allow any doctrine of physiology to be
taught which led to a pre-Adamite theory, or one of plurality
of races, inconsistent with the doctrine of the fall, original
sin, and redemption."[45] Deploring the fact that dissensions
had arisen among Catholics, Wiseman ended with a plea for
unity.

Wiseman's distress at the "cynical remarks"[46] of the
Rambler was sincere, although there was in his article a trace
of the wounded pride of an author and editor. He was wrong
in interpreting the *Rambler*'s articles as an attack on the old
Catholics, but he had correctly sensed in Simpson's criticism
of intellectual timidity an attack on his own policy. Wiseman's primary concern, throughout his career, had been to
bring together the old and the new Catholics into one har-
monious community. He was therefore opposed to anything
savouring of a party spirit within the Catholic body. Wiseman was at this time beginning the great struggle of his
primacy against the "anti-Roman" and anti-convert old
Catholic clergy, led by his own coadjutor, Archbishop
Errington. It was therefore necessary for him to demonstrate
to the old Catholics that he was still one of them, that he had

---

[42] Wiseman, "The Present Catholic Dangers," *Dublin Review*, XLI (Dec.
1856), 450.
[43] *Ibid.*
[44] *Ibid.*, 465.
[45] *Ibid.*, 448. This may have been a reference to Simpson's articles.
[46] Wiseman to Henry Bagshawe, 20 June 1857, Westminster Archives.

not become the party leader of the converts. This was the reason for his sharp criticism of the *Rambler*.

The *Rambler* replied in an article in February 1857, protesting against "the unjust and uncharitable misrepresentations" of the *Dublin Review* as a "very indefensible piece of false criticism."[47] It denied that its articles were directed against the old Catholics. Admitting that the author of the article on Brownson might have been imprudent, it complained that the education article had been unfairly attacked. It pretended to be aggrieved by the criticism that the *Rambler*'s writers "do not share the burden of Catholic labour"; this, it cried, was an unwarranted personal attack. This last charge was denied by Wiseman in the next *Dublin Review*, in which he sought to put an end to the discussion.[48]

The *Rambler* was not appeased. In March appeared an article criticizing the tendency among Catholics to evade the difficulties presented by history and science. It called upon them to meet Protestant criticism by a greater honesty, rather than by the "shirking and cooking system"[49] of some Catholic apologists. "It is useless to proclaim that history and science are in harmony with our religion, unless we show that we think so by being ourselves foremost in telling the whole truth about the Church and her enemies."[50] It ridiculed the obsolete Mosaic geology of some Catholic writers; and, although it praised Wiseman's own lectures on "Science and Revealed Religion," his arguments were by implication included in this censure.

This new aggressive attitude of the *Rambler*—of which another sample was a letter in December 1856 criticizing the use of false etymologies by fathers and doctors of the Church[51] —began to alarm some of its friends, notably Brownson and Newman. The latter, who was "pained, and almost

---

[47] "The Rambler and the Dublin Review," *Rambler*, 2nd ser., VII (Feb. 1857), 140-1.

[48] *Dublin Review*, XLII (March 1857), 245-8.

[49] "Literary Cookery," *Rambler*, 2nd ser., VII (March 1857), 181.

[50] *Ibid.*, 168; Gasquet, "Introduction," pp. xxxiii-xxxiv.

[51] J. B. M.[orris], "Theologia Male Ferrata," *Rambler*, 2nd ser., VI (Dec. 1856), 40.

frightened,"[52] by the successive blows it was striking, communicated his fears to Capes. Meanwhile Manning, who was then beginning his rise in the hierarchy, advised Wiseman to handle the *Rambler* "after the manner of the Holy Office."[53] Capes did not regard the matter in so serious a light; but, having somewhat recovered his health, he resumed the editorship with the number for February 1857, and announced that fact to the public.[54] This implied no lack of confidence in Simpson, who continued as assistant editor.

In some matters, during this year 1857, the *Rambler* proceeded along approved paths. To make some amends for having offended the old Catholics, Simpson began a series of historical articles on the Catholic martyrs of the sixteenth and seventeenth centuries, which contained some of his most solid work. The *Rambler* supported Wiseman against the old Catholic opposition and proposed "Ultramontanism for England" in a leading article in July.[55] Capes was always anxious to maintain friendly relations with Wiseman, who had promised to write for the *Rambler*, and with whom he was personally on good terms.[56]

In large measure, the controversies of the *Rambler* had resulted from misunderstandings, and could have been avoided had the parties been able to look at matters from each other's standpoint. But no amount of sympathy could conceal the fact that there was a fundamental opposition between the principles on which the *Rambler*, even in the "safe" hands of Capes, was conducted, and those which Wiseman represented. Wiseman subordinated the laity to the clergy in all matters in which religion was concerned, including education and politics; the very idea of differences among Catholics on these matters was abhorrent to him. The

[52] Newman to Ambrose St. John, 7 May 1857, Ward, *Life of Newman*, I, 437. See also Newman to Capes, 19 Jan. 1857, quoted by Gasquet, "Introduction,' pp. xxiii-xxiv (with some omissions).
[53] Manning to Wiseman, 18 Feb. 1857, cited (but wrongly dated) by Edmund Sheridan Purcell, *Life of Cardinal Manning, Archbishop of Westminster*, 2 vols. (New York, 1896), II, 67.
[54] *Rambler*, VII (Feb. 1857), 162. The name of the editor was not mentioned, in conformity with the practice of anonymous writing.
[55] *Rambler*, 2nd ser., VIII (July 1857), 1-12.
[56] Capes to Wiseman, 1 Sept. 1857, Westminster Archives.

D

Rambler, on the other hand, exulted in the variety and freedom of Catholic thought on all things beyond matters of faith; it affirmed its right to speak on all matters not defined by the Church, and to proclaim the truth regardless of the inconvenience that might be caused or the reputations that might be damaged. Thus it came to be regarded by the hierarchy, ever fearful of anything that might disrupt the delicate balance of English Catholicism, as an *enfant terrible*.

The *Rambler* continued on its independent course. It asserted its right to "ridicule what is ridiculous," even when it happens to be found among the writings of Popes and saints: "once protect the absurdities of the theologian from ridicule by the sanctity of his character, and you make his sanctity responsible for his absurdities; that is, you make sanctity itself ridiculous."[57] Urging Catholic writers to pay more attention to the works of non-Catholic authors, it argued that "error bears witness to the truth. . . . we believe that the materials for perfecting the system of Catholic philosophy are being prepared, even by the labours of men without the communion of the Church."[58] It continued the controversy on education, despite Wiseman's express desire that the subject should be left to the bishops.[59] And it laid stress on the inordinate role of the clergy in the government of the Papal States, thereby contradicting the statements of Wiseman's spokesman in the House of Commons, Sir George Bowyer.[60]

This increasing boldness coincided with a remarkable improvement in the quality of the magazine in the years 1856 and 1857, for much of which Simpson was responsible.[61] These years also saw a further development of its policy, which brought it closer to a position that can be described as "liberal Catholic."

[57] *Rambler*, 2nd ser., VII (Feb. 1857), 159-161.

[58] *Rambler*, 2nd ser., VII (April 1857), 303.

[59] Scott Nasmyth Stokes, "The Controversy on the Poor-School Grant," *Rambler*, 2nd ser., VII (May 1857), 338-348. Signed "S.N.S."

[60] "Mr. Bowyer on the Papal States," *Rambler*, 2nd ser., VII (May 1857), 401-2.

[61] One sign of this was the disappearance of novels, or "tales," from its pages; these had been a feature of the early *Rambler*, and were not distinguished for any considerable literary merit. Since 1854 it had had a regular department of literary criticism.

The *Rambler*'s home politics remained unchanged: in the breakdown of the two-party system during the 1850s, it could find no reason to prefer one party above another. However, it now condemned all proposals to form a distinct Catholic party, urging that Catholics should work within the existing groups for their special ends. It was in foreign politics that a change was most apparent. Hitherto the *Rambler* had shared the general Catholic sentiment that Napoleon III ought to be supported because he had restored order and favoured the Church. Now, however, it condemned his government as "a hollow and vicious system, for which no present tranquillity can permanently compensate."[62] The occasion for this outburst was the Emperor's harassment of the Liberal Catholic leader Montalembert and his organ, the *Correspondant*.

The *Rambler* had always been sympathetic to Montalembert and other continental Liberal Catholics, without subscribing to their entire policy. Now it moved into closer alignment with them, giving a particularly favourable notice to the *Correspondant*, with whose "tone and principles" it felt "the liveliest sympathy": "Altogether the *Correspondant* is a journal which Catholics must regard with pride, as being conducted with talent, honour, liberality, and freedom, and in an excellent Catholic spirit."[63] The *Rambler* denied that Catholics were committed to the support of despotism and expressed the hope that Catholics would develop a love for political and social freedom.

It was, however, intellectual freedom which was the chief concern of the *Rambler*, particularly the freedom of the scientific historian. As early as 1854, it had taken favourable notice of the German historians, particularly Ranke, who, disregarding the interests of religious bodies, simply ascertained and candidly stated the facts.[64] Among Catholic historians, its model, whom it praised in extravagant terms, was Professor Döllinger of Munich. It expressed a preference, which it shared with Döllinger, for the methods of scientific

[62] "The French Emperor," *Rambler*, 2nd ser., VIII (Aug. 1857), 87.
[63] *Rambler*, 2nd ser., VIII (Dec. 1857), 456.
[64] "English and Foreign Historians: the Massacre of St. Bartholomew," *Rambler*, 2nd ser., I (Feb. 1854), 168-9.

history over those of theology, as more appropriate to the
modern age: "It is our firm belief that in these days the
Catholic cause will be best subserved by the study of facts.
. . . Theology is no longer the dominant science that it was
during the middle ages; and the authority of the syllogism of
Aristotle has received a counterpoise in the inductive method
laid down by Bacon."[65] The *Rambler* severely criticized those
Catholic historians who shirked manuscript research or
concealed embarrassing facts. On this account Simpson gave
an unfavourable review to Canon Flanagan's church history
of England, giving an example of his own fearless style of
criticism by asserting that the attempted deposition of
Elizabeth by St. Pius V had "sealed the loss of England to the
Church."[66]

It was a sign of this more detached attitude that the
Rambler was now inclined to question the reputed miracle of
La Salette, which it had earlier accepted. Suspending its
own judgment, it deplored the credulous "morbid passion
for modern miracles" as unsound both in history and in
theology: "Surely it is a serious error to confound the consideration of what is 'pious' with the consideration of what is
'true'."[67] This caused some sensation, and brought the
Rambler once again into conflict with Ullathorne, who had
proclaimed his own faith in the miracle. The *Rambler*
defended its position as strictly theological and common-
sense, urging the necessity of investigation before miracles
are accepted, and arguing that all the facts of Christianity
rest ultimately on some historical evidence.[68]

The bolder and more aggressive position which the
Rambler had assumed in these last years had considerably
altered its position in the Catholic body. It had commenced
as the organ of the converts generally; it now found itself

[65] *Rambler*, 2nd ser., VIII (July 1857), 76. This was in a review of Ozanam's
work on the fifth century.
[66] *Rambler*, 2nd ser., VIII (Nov. 1857), 353. A similar statement in Simpson's
life of Campion later aroused much controversy.
[67] "The Edinburgh Review on La Salette," *Rambler*, VIII (Sept. 1857), 197.
[68] "On Belief in Reputed Miracles," *Rambler*, 2nd ser., VIII (Oct. 1857),
290-301. This was a favourite philosophical position of Capes, who probably
wrote these articles. Simpson did not share in the criticism of the miracle of
La Salette, which he accepted with his surprisingly simple faith.

the organ only of a section of them, that smaller, more liberal section which held that Catholicism should keep pace with the progress of reason and science in an atmosphere of freedom. It stood now in direct collision with Wiseman and his *Dublin Review*. By the end of 1857, the *Rambler* had ceased to be the convert organ and had become the organ of a Liberal Catholic movement.

It was at this point that Capes ceased to be its editor. His health had not improved, and he had a blind and invalid wife. He had continued to lose money by the *Rambler* and had now come to the end of his financial resources. Finally, he had simply become weary of his editorial duties after a decade of apparently unfruitful endeavour. "I have long felt that I have had quite enough of it in the editorial way, and at last it was plain that if I did not altogether cease from everything which involved the anxieties of responsibility I should myself be speedily finished altogether."[69]

On 5 October 1857, Capes resigned the editorship, which was temporarily assumed by Simpson. Capes soon found it necessary to withdraw completely, selling the proprietorship of the magazine. It was divided into six fifty-pound shares; one each was taken by Simpson and Frederick Capes, and two by the young Sir John Acton, who became the first non-convert to take part in the conduct of the *Rambler*. The other two shares could find no takers, and were ultimately suppressed. Thus Capes' reward for ten years of journalistic effort was only two hundred pounds and the praise of Newman, who felt that "the Catholic body in this country owes you much gratitude, for the animus and object of your undertaking, the devotion you have shown to it for so long a

---

[69] Capes to Newman, 18 May 1858, Newman MSS. It is possible that Capes' decision to resign was also prompted by the recurrence of his religious doubts. However, I am inclined to believe that it was not until his retirement had provided him with leisure that he began to reconsider his religious position. There is no evidence that that reconsideration began earlier, and he himself states (*Reasons for returning to the Church of England*, [London, 1871]) that his doubts became acute thirteen years after his conversion, i.e., in 1858. Probably the nervous state to which he was apparently reduced by his various difficulties at this time contributed to shake his belief.

time, and the various important benefits it has done us."[70]

Simpson now became the regular editor of the *Rambler*, with Acton as his chief contributor and associate. The new arrangements took effect in February 1858.

[70] Newman to Capes, 17 May 1858, cited by Ward, *Life of Newman*, I, 439.

CHAPTER III

THE YOUNG ACTON:
HISTORY AND LIBERAL CATHOLICISM

SIR JOHN ACTON was unique among his Catholic contemporaries for the breadth and variety of his background and education. An Englishman by nationality, an aristocrat by inheritance, and a Catholic in religion, he had been made by circumstances of family and education into a thorough cosmopolitan, a competent scholar, and an accepted member of Protestant social and political circles.

The Actons were an old Shropshire family, with their seat at Aldenham, who had acquired a baronetcy in the seventeenth century and had been converted to Catholicism in the eighteenth. In 1791 the title and estate fell to John Acton, an adventurer, who succeeded in winning the affections of the Queen of Naples, the rank of Admiral in the Neapolitan navy, and eventually the position of Prime Minister of Naples. Of his two sons, the younger, who died in 1847, became a cardinal; the elder, Sir Richard, a diplomat, was the father of John Edward Emerich Dalberg Acton, who was born in Naples in 1834, and succeeded to the baronetcy on his father's premature death in 1837.

Acton's mother, Marie de Dalberg, was the heiress of the Dalbergs of Herrnsheim, barons of the Holy Roman Empire. Her uncle had been the last archbishop-elector of Mainz. Her father had entered the diplomatic service of France under Napoleon, becoming a minister of State and duke and peer of France. In 1840 the widowed Lady Acton took as her second husband Lord Leveson, later the second Earl Granville. Granville was a member of the Whig aristocracy, a rising politician, and a Protestant. In his stepfather's house in London, young Acton found himself in an environment with which few English Catholics were familiar: the Protestant and Whig aristocracy which had ruled England for a century

45

and a half. It was, however, his mother's devout Catholicism
which determined the course of his education.

Acton was sent in 1842 to a school near Paris operated by
Monsignor Dupanloup, later Bishop of Orléans. After a year,
however, he was removed to Oscott College for a more
conventional English Catholic education. Under Wiseman's
presidency, Oscott was the centre of English Catholicism at
the time; but it was nonetheless deficient as an educational
institution. Acton complained that he was restricted in his
reading and was dissatisfied with the rigid seminarian
discipline. Nonetheless he remained until 1848, completing
the course. He next spent two years at Edinburgh studying
privately under Dr. Logan, who had just been dismissed
from the Vice-Presidency of Oscott after a quarrel with
Bishop Ullathorne. Logan was a convert of a generation
earlier than the Oxford Movement; this rather unsatisfactory episode represents almost the only convert influence
on Acton's education.

Acton's family connections had given him a wider horizon
than most of the old Catholics and a breadth of view akin to
that of the converts. But he had not shared the experience of
the Oxford Movement; he was born to his Catholicism. The
Catholic faith was so natural to him, so much a part of the
atmosphere that he breathed, that he felt no need to display
it, and he seemed to be wanting in the enthusiasm which
characterized the converts.

It had been intended that Acton should complete his
studies at Cambridge; but the colleges to which he applied
refused him admission on account of his Catholicism. He was
therefore sent to Munich to study under the historian
Döllinger. There is a trace of Wiseman's influence here.
Wiseman, seeking to broaden the intellectual culture of the
old Catholics by an infusion of German scholarship, had
cultivated Döllinger's friendship in 1835 and had awakened
in him an interest in English Catholicism. Thenceforth
Döllinger was in the practice of keeping a number of young
English students in his house. Acton was to become the most
prominent of these pupils.

"The decisive fact of Acton's life was his apprenticeship

under Döllinger."[1] He formed Acton's religious, ethical, and political thought and developed in him a passion for the scientific study of history. It was also through Döllinger that Acton became connected with the Liberal Catholic movement which had become a significant factor in the Catholicism of the continent.

The Liberal Catholic movement developed from the Catholic revival which began with the opening of the nineteenth century. Chateaubriand, the prophet of romanticism, was also the herald of the revival of Catholicism. It derived a political theory from De Maistre's doctrine of the absolute supremacy of the Pope, and a philosophical basis from the traditionalism of Bonald. These tendencies were summed up and given a new turn in the life and work of Lamennais.

Lamennais was fired by the idea that "the Church was to be the principle of construction for the civilization of the future."[2] It was his doctrine that the individual reason was impotent, and that the test of truth was the universal consent of the general testimony, whose organ was the Church, speaking directly through the Pope. His *Essai sur l'Indifférence* (1817) brought him fame; he became the eloquent champion of the Church against infidelity and of Ultramontanism as opposed to Gallicanism. His extreme claims on behalf of the Pope brought Lamennais opposition from the French bishops, who retained something of the Gallicanism of past generations, and from the government of Charles X, which sought to use the Church as an instrument for its own purposes. Henceforth he rejected the monarchy as the enemy of the Church, and placed his trust in the people; in one bound he passed from legitimism to democracy.

Lamennais had come to think that the future belonged to the peoples, not the kings, and that "religion should not be involved in the fall of the old regime."[3] Rather, the Church

---

[1] Gertrude Himmelfarb, *Lord Acton: A Study in Conscience and Politics* (Chicago, 1952), p. 19.

[2] Wilfrid Ward, *William George Ward and the Catholic Revival* (2nd ed., London, 1912), p. 85.

[3] CUL Add. MS. 4905. This is one of Acton's notes for a projected biography.

should "baptize the Revolution" by reconciling the people
to religion through a common devotion to liberty. In this
development, he had been anticipated by Chateaubriand
and was paralleled by the Baron d'Eckstein, editor of *Le
Catholique*; but he drew his main support from a group of
able young men, of whom Montalembert and Lacordaire
were the most notable. Their organ was the *Avenir*, founded
in 1830. They drew inspiration from Ireland and America,
where the Church was independent of both the support and
the control of the State; they sensed that these countries,
ruled by Protestants, provided examples for Catholicism in
a future which was to be dominated by forces hitherto
hostile to the Catholic Church: democracy, Protestantism,
and nationalism. They welcomed the revolution of 1830 in
France, and found in the Belgian revolution, in which
Catholics worked side by side with Liberals, an expression of
their principles. Their cry was "God and Liberty." For the
Church, they demanded independence from the State; but
they insisted that the Church could not demand liberty for
herself without extending it to others. So they supported
liberty of conscience, of thought and of the press, and the
separation of Church and State.

The conductors of the *Avenir*[4] sought liberty in politics
precisely because they wished to establish the principle of
authority in the Church, free from the domination of the
States and the hostility of the peoples. When they met
continued opposition from the French bishops, they appealed
to Rome. Instead of the expected endorsement, they found
their doctrines rejected in 1832 by the encyclical *Mirari vos*,
in which Gregory XVI denounced the error of "indifferent-
ism," which proceeded from the doctrine of liberty of conscience, thought, and the press. Lamennais and his friends
promptly announced their submission. But Lamennais had
suffered a shattering blow: his philosophic system had

of Döllinger, which would have included a study of the Liberal Catholic
movement; see also Add. MSS. 4903-15, 4964, 4968-70, 5445.

[4] Montalembert and Lacordaire were not in entire agreement with Lamennais's democratic vision; there were several different currents in the *Avenir*
movement, which perhaps explain the different courses followed by its leaders
after its collapse. See Peter N. Stearns, "The Nature of the *Avenir* Movement,"
American Historical Review, LXV (July 1960), 837-847.

depended on the authority of the Pope, which had now been turned against him; the very exaggeration of his doctrines proved fatal to his faith. Two years later he left the communion of the Church.

Lamennais carried no one with him in his fall, and his disciples became the ablest defenders of Catholicism in France. The submission of Montalembert and Lacordaire did not mean, however, that they had abandoned all their former opinions or given up the hopes of refashioning Catholic life in conformity with the dominant principles of the age. It was possible, they held, to advocate as a matter of practice that which had been condemned as a matter of theory: the doctrines of liberalism might be tenable by Catholics if advanced merely as a practical and transitory adjustment to the necessities of the actual situation.[5] On this basis, the movement was reconstructed during the next decade.

Warned by the experience of 1832, the Liberal Catholics avoided philosophical speculation and confined themselves to activities less likely to arouse hostility. Lacordaire refounded the Dominican order in France and lectured at Notre Dame; Montalembert wrote on medieval history; and another leader, Ozanam, founded the Society of St. Vincent de Paul to engage in work among the poor. Then, in 1842, Montalembert organized a political party—not a liberal party, but a "Catholic" party. The issue was freedom of instruction for religious bodies, which was guaranteed by the constitution of 1830 but denied in practice. Montalembert was thus able to unite Catholics behind a cry for liberty. It was not a philosophy but a policy, more moderate than that of the *Avenir*: Montalembert no longer sought separation of Church and State, and was not favourable to democracy. But by forming "un parti catholique sur le terrain libéral"[6] he had achieved the aim of the *Avenir*, of a Catholicism in harmony with modern ideals, seeking liberty for the nation

---

[5] For a more thorough discussion of this distinction of "thesis" and "hypothesis," see C. Constantin, "Libéralisme Catholique," *Dictionnaire de Théologie Catholique*, 15 vols. (Paris, 1909-50), IX, 625-6.

[6] *Ibid.*, 571. Constantin makes a distinction between the "catholicisme libéral" of this period and the "libéralisme catholique" which is his name for the movement as a whole.

as well as for itself. The Revolution of 1848, and the conservative Republic which it brought forth, was a triumph for the Catholic party: bishops and priests were elected to the Chamber, and Lacordaire for a time even took his seat on the extreme Left. For a brief moment French Catholicism was in harmony with the spirit of the age, and it profited from this situation by the passage of the Falloux law, which granted the liberty of instruction.

1848 was the high-water mark of the Liberal Catholic movement; but for Liberal Catholicism, as for liberalism generally, it turned out to be the *annus mirabilis* that failed. The highest hopes were aroused by the fact that there was now on the papal throne a reputed liberal, Pius IX. When he amnestied political prisoners and granted a constitution, the Italian Liberal Catholics hailed him as their leader. Liberal Catholicism in Italy, led by Gioberti and Rosmini, differed from the French movement by its greater emphasis on nationalism; it sought an Italian federation under the presidency of the Pope. But Pius had no intention of placing himself at the head of an Italian nation, or of giving up his sovereignty over the States of the Church. After his liberal minister Rossi was murdered, he feared for his life amid the rising tide of revolution in Rome and fled to Gaeta. His authority in Rome was restored by French bayonets in 1849, and Pius returned in 1850, a disillusioned man. Henceforth he became the confirmed opponent of liberalism and nationalism, the leader of reaction in Europe. The opportunity for a Liberal Church had been lost.

In France, too, the hopes of the Liberal Catholics had faded. The Falloux law of 1850, which represented the triumph of the Catholic party, led to its split. An intransigent faction, led by Louis Veuillot, editor of the *Univers*, thought that the law did not go far enough. The issue divided the party into two sections, Liberal and Ultramontane—the latter a term which had originally designated the entire movement, with its emphasis on papal authority. Now that Pius IX had committed himself to a policy of opposition to the ideals of the modern world, the term "Ultramontane" came to designate that group which favoured his policy of

regarding the Church as being in a "state of siege," opposed
to the ruling tendencies of the age, isolated, self-regarding,
and militant, closely organized under the absolute authority
of the Pope. Opposed to them was the "Liberal" school of
Montalembert, which retained its hopes of a conciliation
between Catholicism and the modern world; its organ was
now the *Correspondant*. The cause of the Liberal Catholics
was ruined by their political policy. Montalembert, after
supporting Louis Napoleon, turned against him in 1852.
The majority of the French Catholics, however, rallied to
Napoleon as the saviour of society and protector of the
Church; Veuillot became a violent imperialist and carried
Catholic opinion with him. The party of Montalembert was
increasingly isolated.

The leadership of the Liberal Catholic movement now
passed to the Germans. The Catholic revival in Germany was
contemporaneous with the Romantic movement; it was
given an intellectual form through the works of Möhler and
Görres. A dispute between the Church and the Prussian
government in 1837 over the question of mixed marriages led
to the formation of a Catholic political party, which was
Ultramontane in the sense of being opposed to the domination of the State over the Church and devoted to the Holy
See. But the central issues in German Catholicism were not
political, as in France, or national, as in Italy, but intellectual.

"Germany was the only country in possession of theological
schools which, through their connection with the Universities
and their controversies with the different Church communities, remained in touch with the intellectual problems
and currents of the day."[7] Constant intercourse with their
Protestant neighbours had forced them to become familiar
with the arguments of the enemies of the Church, and to
realize the insufficiency of the conventional Catholic
apologetic. In this enforced competition of doctrines, only
the most thorough and objective statement of the truth could
be victorious. In order to meet the arguments of Protestants,

[7] Lady Blennerhasset, "The Late Lord Acton," *Edinburgh Review*, CXCVII
(April 1903), 501. Lady Blennerhasset, a pupil of Döllinger and friend of
Acton, is also the authoress of a survey of the Liberal Catholic movement in
"The Papacy and the Catholic Church," *Cambridge Modern History*, X, 131-168.

it was necessary for Catholics to match them in scientific impartiality; and so the German Liberal Catholics developed the doctrine that the Church must rely on the weapons of science, which would prove more efficacious than the obsolete arguments of scholasticism. Ultimately, the truths of religion and those of science must be compatible, and therefore it was in the interest of the Church to be disinterested, to pursue the truth for its own sake without regard for the consideration whether or not it would serve the Catholic cause in controversy. Civil and intellectual freedom was a necessary condition of this harmony of truths; therefore the principle of freedom had to be asserted, not merely for Catholics, but for other communities. "They sought to obtain for the ecclesiastical authority no immunity but that which it would enjoy from the promotion of political rights; and in philosophy, they provided no protection for religious doctrines but in the advancement of scientific truth."[8]

In the 1850s, there had developed a reaction against this scientific outlook, centred around the school of Mainz. The Mainz school was the representative in Germany of the new Ultramontanism, though it was more moderate than the party of Veuillot in France; it sought to bring the work of Catholic scholars under the control of the ecclesiastical authorities. There seemed to be a danger that the free inquiry of the Liberal Catholic scholars might lead them too far; two philosophers, Günther and Frohschammer, were condemned by the Index. Nonetheless, the liberal school, the school of Munich, continued on its course. After the deaths of Möhler and Görres, Döllinger was its most distinguished scholar.

Döllinger had taken orders in the days of Pius VII, the beginning of the Catholic revival, when the Church, having resisted the tyranny of Napoleon, seemed to have shaken off the defects of past centuries. This liberal vision of the Church coloured his early Ultramontanism. "By choice and by vocation a divine, having religion as the purpose of his life," he "judged that the loftier function, the more spiritual

---

[8] Acton, "Ultramontanism," *Essays on Church and State*, ed. Douglas Woodruff (London, 1952), p. 70.

service, was historical teaching. . . . Church history had long
been the weakest point and the cause of weakness among
Catholics, and it was the rising strength of the German
Protestants. Therefore it was the post of danger."[9] The
objectivity of his historical work thus concealed an apologetic
purpose.[10] Nonetheless, Döllinger became a convinced
advocate of the scientific attitude towards history. His
reputation was made by the four volumes of his *Church
History* (1833-1838); and with the appearance of his work on
the *Reformation* (1848), which challenged the authority of
Ranke, he became for a time the accepted spokesman of the
Catholic Church among historians.

Döllinger's historical studies formed his religious thought.
He was less interested in pure theology than in the practical
working of religion in the lives of men: he found the truths
of history more convincing than the truths of metaphysics.
He regarded Christianity as the product of history rather
than of philosophy and was therefore opposed to the methods
of the Scholastics. His inclination was to a theory of the
development of doctrine similar to that of Newman, whom
he admired.[11]

Döllinger was unusual among Catholic historians in that
he made Protestantism, as it had developed through the
centuries, an object of constant attention. As a German, he
took a particular interest in Lutheranism; but he followed
events in the Church of England and was in communication
with many leaders of the High Church party, notably
Pusey and Gladstone. It was the hope of his life that a reunion between the Churches might be achieved and that
history might serve in this work of conciliation by removing

[9] Acton, "Döllinger's Historical Work," *The History of Freedom and other Essays*,
ed. J. N. Figgis and R. V. Laurence (London, 1907), p. 379.

[10] "Conservatism was the keynote of Doellinger's life. The intent and
purpose . . . was to save as many institutions of the past from change and
extinction as possible. In an age of revolution he turned to history as the only
instrument he thought capable of performing this task." Stephen J. Tonsor,
"Ignaz von Doellinger: Lord Acton's Mentor," *Anglican Theological Review*,
XLI (July, 1959), 212.

[11] Newman reciprocated this admiration and arranged for the translation
of one of Döllinger's books by Father Darnell of the Oratory. Newman visited
Döllinger at Munich in 1847, and Acton arranged for them to meet in England
in 1851 and 1858.

unfounded prejudices. He sought understanding rather than
proselytes; his work was confined to the sphere of the
intellect, and to those of more ardent temperament he
appeared "hard, cold, and unimaginative."[12]

Döllinger had been in communication with the French
Liberal Catholics since the days of the *Avenir*, but he pursued
his course independently of them, finding them deficient in
scientific spirit. He had had a brief period of relative
political liberalism in 1848, when he was a delegate to the
Frankfurt Parliament. He voted for the exclusion of the
Jesuits and, preaching to the assembled German bishops at
Würzburg, told them that freedom was necessary to the
Church, and that Catholics must claim it for others as well
as themselves. But at heart Döllinger was a conservative:
even at Frankfurt he had taken his seat on the extreme Right.
As provost of the royal chapel at Munich, he was a devoted
servant of the Bavarian crown. His circle at Munich was
legitimist, conservative and clericalist; but in the genial
atmosphere of Bavaria these doctrines were not incompatible
with constitutionalism and toleration. In Church politics,
Döllinger was an Ultramontane of the old school, that is, one
who distrusted the interference of the State in the Church.
At the core of his politics was a hatred of absolute power in all
its forms, whether in Church or State; if this was liberal in
tendency, it was conservative in origin, and owed much to
Burke.

Döllinger's position as historian and Catholic was somewhat altered by the events of the 1850s. The rise of the school
of Mainz signified that his doctrine of the independence of
history was not to pass unchallenged by the new Ultramontanism. At the same time, the science of history was
itself undergoing a change. The critical school of history, in
whose spirit Döllinger worked, had been largely dependent
on old authorities newly interpreted. In 1854 Ranke came to
Munich to teach a science of history based on the use of

---

[12] Newman to Alfred Plummer, 21 Oct. 1873, cited in Frank Leslie Cross,
John Henry Newman (London, 1933), p. 175. The young Herbert Vaughan,
later Cardinal, visited him in 1855 and was "a little chilled" to find that
Döllinger did not say Mass every day: see J. G. Snead-Cox, *The Life of Cardinal
Vaughan*, 2 vols. (London, 1910), I, 64.

unpublished manuscripts, and in the next few years masses of archival material were opened to scholars. Döllinger had to train himself in the new methods and to revise his historical outlook in the light of his new studies. The discoveries of these years led him unconsciously to take a more independent attitude to the authorities of his Church. Acton, who had come to Munich to be Döllinger's pupil, became instead his fellow-apprentice in the new history and in Liberal Catholicism.

Acton spent six years with Döllinger in Munich, as disciple rather than as pupil; Capes described the relationship between them as that of father and son.[13] Acton was ready and willing to be formed by his teacher; he later acknowledged to Döllinger that "I am nothing but what you have made of me."[14] It was no longer possible for Acton, having succumbed to Döllinger's influence, to be content to return to the unintellectual life of the English Catholic aristocracy. He was irresistibly attracted to the life of scholarship and was converted to Döllinger's austere ideal of an independent, unbiased history. Acton was unusually well equipped for the work of the historian. By birth and education he was the child of all Europe, and he spoke several languages with equal fluency. He was an energetic reader of books, with great power of retention; and, although the productive power in him did not equal the receptive, this failing was not evident during his early years. The particular area of research to which he was attracted was the "wavy line"[15] between politics and religion.

Religion was for Acton, as for Döllinger, the motive of his life. Even more than Döllinger, he emphasized the ethical aspect of religion, the supremacy of the developed con-

[13] Capes to Newman, 29 Sept. 1858, Newman MSS. On 28 Jan. 1859, Capes wrote: "He is just to him what I should wish my own son to be to me."
[14] Acton to Döllinger, 10 Aug. 1866, cited in E. L. Woodward, "The Place of Lord Acton in the Liberal Movement of the Nineteenth Century," *Politica*, IV (1939), 249 (my translation). Acton signed his letters to Döllinger "Ihr Treuer Schüler" and referred to Germany as "meine zweite Heimath": Acton to Döllinger, 12 May [prob. 1855], Woodruff MSS.
[15] Acton to Mary Gladstone, 3 June 1881, *Letters of Lord Acton to Mary Gladstone*, ed. Herbert Paul (New York, 1904), pp. 208-9.

E

science.[16] This doctrine of conscience was the basis of his political thought: "A Christian must seek to extend as much as possible the field in which he is responsible only to his conscience."[17] The Christian, he thought, was committed to the politics of liberty, "that condition in which men are not prevented by men from obeying their duty to God. . . . It is reason controlled by reason, instead of will controlled by will; it is duty to God unhindered by man; it is the security of minorities; it is the reign of conscience."[18] Freedom was therefore a spiritual principle, and politics an expression of religion; but, once politics had been established on these principles, it could pursue its course as an independent science, and the Church was subject to the laws of political science as much as to those of physical science. The same moral code was valid in both the spiritual and the temporal orders. Catholics must judge governments, not by their subservience to the temporal interests of the Church, but by the test of whether they guarantee liberty and promote the authority of conscience.

The greatest enemy of the rule of conscience, and therefore of the Church, was absolutism—the State, whether autocratic or democratic, asserting itself as the object of all loyalty and obedience. No institution, Acton thought, has the right to claim the whole allegiance of man. A sound system of politics would seek to erect barriers against State absolutism: it would demand the security of minorities, the recognition of autonomous corporations within the society and the division of governmental powers. These were precisely the conditions necessary to the prosperity of the Catholic Church in Protestant countries such as Germany

[16] In later years, his ethical rigorism was to become intense and to lead to his alienation from Döllinger. But it would be wrong to read back these later views into the attitude of the young Acton. Acton's views were always developing, and the young Acton differed in many respects from the Acton of later years. I have therefore sought to exclude from my consideration any opinion, position, or writing of the later Acton unless, after examination, I am convinced that it represents the sentiments which Acton held as a young man. This is done for purely methodological reasons and does not prejudge the question whether Acton's thought represents a grand unity or is divided sharply into earlier and later stages. Cf. Lionel Kochan, *Acton on History* (London, 1954), p. 45.

[17] CUL Add. MS. 5751.

[18] CUL Add. MSS. 4969, 5644.

and England. These Catholic principles of government were embodied only in the constitution of Protestant England. Thus Acton was a Whig of the school of Burke, whom he recommended as "the law and the prophets."[19] He was anti-revolutionary and fearful of democracy; he opposed the plebiscitary dictatorship of Napoleon III and the democracy of the Northern States of America, both of which represented to him aspects of the centralized, absolute State. His Whiggism was conservative rather than liberal. Liberty was to be secured by the limitation of government in a pluralistic society.

Many of these views were to be modified in succeeding years, but Acton never lost his hatred of absolutism, whether in State or Church. Nonetheless, it is an oversimplification of his character to think of him simply as the author of the saying, "Power tends to corrupt, and absolute power corrupts absolutely," which has made him the hero of modern neo-conservatism. Acton possessed the faculty of seeing issues from many sides, of balancing conflicting viewpoints; he "believed that some truths need supplementing by others."[20] His vision of truth was always double-edged. Between his Whiggism and his Catholicism there was a certain tension. Acton's views were constantly developing, and within the grand unity of his philosophy there was room for much modification in practice and application.

Acton's education was not confined to the academic world. He travelled much, and was accepted in the best social circles of Europe. Part of nearly every year was spent in France, where he became acquainted with Montalembert and his friends, "the men with whom I most agree," especially the more scholarly members of the movement, the Prince de Broglie and "my old friend" Eckstein.[21] He

[19] Acton to Simpson, 4 Feb. 1859, *Lord Acton and his Circle*, ed. Abbot Gasquet (London, 1906), p. 60.

[20] G. E. Fasnacht, *Acton's Political Philosophy* (London, 1952), p. 228. For a competent study of the complexity and unity of Acton's character controlled by his deep religious sense, see Ulrich Noack, *Katholizität und Geistesfreiheit, nach den Schriften von John Dalberg-Acton, 1834-1902* (Frankfurt a.M., 1936). See also Kochan, *Acton on History*.

[21] Acton to Lady Granville (date uncertain), *Selected Correspondence of the First Lord Acton*, ed. J. N. Figgis and R. V. Laurence (London, 1917), p. 18. Eckstein was the closest of this group to Acton.

travelled to the United States in 1853 and to Russia in 1856, meeting the leaders of opinion in both countries. On his American journey Acton met Brownson, the ablest writer among American Catholics, and persuaded him to send his son to study under Döllinger; this episode "features Acton as a kind of primitive international clearing-house for Catholic intellectuals."[22]

The most important of these journeys was a visit with Döllinger to Rome in 1857, in search of manuscripts. "Döllinger used to commemorate his visit to Rome in 1857 as an epoch of emancipation."[23] He "came away depressed and disheartened" at the ignorance of Roman theologians and the misgovernment of the Papal States, although he was "neither shocked nor indignant at what he had observed."[24] Rather, having been somewhat taken aback by what he found, he pondered over it, and turned his studies to the modern history of the papacy. The discoveries he made during the next years, in which he learned that many of the claims of the papacy had been based on forgeries, were the beginning of the long process of reconsideration of his religious position which was to lead him away from Rome. But if Döllinger was disillusioned by his Roman experience, Acton was merely unillusioned. He had two interviews with the Pope, "and found him old and weak. . . . My impression is not of any ability and he seems less banally good-natured than his smiling pictures represent him to be."[25] Acton thought that Pius was weak as a theologian and ill-informed in politics; and he found him, as he found all Italians, ignorant of the state of other countries. But his view of the machinery of the papacy was critical rather than hostile; if it could not command his enthusiasm, it received his loyalty.

This loyalty was shown on his return to England in 1857. Granville, eager to launch his stepson in public life, offered

[22] Himmelfarb, *Lord Acton*, p. 32.
[23] Acton, "Döllinger's Historical Work," p. 410.
[24] CUL Add. MS. 4905.
[25] CUL Add. MS. 5751. This is Acton's notebook of his Roman journey, portions of which have been reprinted in Herbert Butterfield, "Journal of Lord Acton: Rome 1857," *Cambridge Historical Journal*, VIII (1946), 186-204.

to find him a nomination for an Irish seat in Parliament. Acton, though not ambitious, was willing; but he felt bound to warn Granville that he would be rendering "an uncertain service" to the Whig party by supporting him:

> I am of opinion that to a Catholic a certain sort of independence is indispensable. Reasons of religion must separate me occasionally from the Whigs. . . . I must therefore most positively declare that I cannot undertake always to vote with Lord Palmerston's Government or with any other. . . . The most serious matter that occurs to me on which I differ from the Government would be any interference in the affairs of the Pope.[26]

It is clear that at this stage of Acton's career "the Catholic motive in him was stronger than the Whig."[27] The political situation of the English Catholics was a peculiar one. Protestant prejudice made it virtually impossible for them to find English seats, or to rise to the higher offices. They were drawn to the Whigs by gratitude for their support of Catholic emancipation and by opposition to the Irish and Church policies of the Tories; but Russell's denunciation of the restoration of the hierarchy, and Palmerston's support of Italian nationalism, made them suspicious of Whig motives. Thus their political action was virtually confined to seeking redress of particular grievances, and they maintained "a certain sort of independence" of party affiliations. Nonetheless, Acton acknowledged that in general "there is no political party with which I could act so well"[28] as with the Whigs, whose principles were essentially his own. This satisfied Granville, who wrote: "I am glad to find that, though he is only a moderate Whig, he is also a very moderate Catholic."[29] Acton agreed to accept the nomination for Clare, and procured a letter of recommendation to his Catholic constituents from Cardinal Wiseman. But the

---

[26] Acton to Granville, 1857, *Selected Correspondence of Lord Acton*, pp. 28-9.

[27] Herbert Butterfield, *Lord Acton* ("Historical Association, General Series," London, 1948), p. 6.

[28] Acton to Granville, 1857, *Selected Correspondence of Lord Acton*, p. 28.

[29] Granville to Lord Canning, 10 March 1857, Lord Edmond Fitzmaurice, *The Life of Granville George Leveson Gower, Second Earl Granville*, 2 vols. (London, 1905), I, 227.

project fell through, and Acton remained out of public life for two more years.

"Acton proceeded to win intellectual and moral eminence at the expense of immediate practical influence."[30] He settled in England filled with the sense of a mission to educate his fellow-Catholics, by raising the standard of their scholarship and their politics and providing them with intellectual leadership adequate to the needs of the age. Fully acquainted with the narrow, unintellectual spirit of the old Catholics, Acton sought to gather together the intellectual resources that existed in the small Catholic body, so as to give it a respectable position in English life and thought. For this purpose he thought it desirable to found an institution of Catholic higher education for laymen in England.

The Catholic University of Dublin (on whose books Acton's and Döllinger's names had been entered by Newman) had failed to meet the needs of the English Catholics, and Newman resigned his position as rector in 1857. Acton considered publishing an open letter to Newman, urging him to found a Catholic university in England.[31] Instead of this, however, Acton gave his support to another plan, conceived by Newman and several converts, that of starting a Catholic public school under Newman's direction. Acton regarded this project as the first step to a university: the school, educating students up to the university level, would create a demand for a university to meet their further educational needs. "If this plan succeeds, the whole education of Catholics will have to be reformed."[32] Acton was very active in furthering this plan, which was to lead to the founding of the Edgbaston School a few years later.

Acton's more immediate activity was in literature. He took up several projects of historical writing and began the acquisition of his magnificent library. He first appeared in print in 1855 with some letters in the *Weekly Register*,

---

[30] John Neville Figgis, "Acton," *Dictionary of National Biography*, 2nd supplement (London, 1912), p. 8.
[31] A sketch of this project is in CUL Add. MS. 5751, dated 24 June 1857.
[32] Acton to Döllinger, 17 Feb. 1858, Woodruff MSS.

defending Döllinger's historical impartiality against a
zealous writer in the *Dublin Review* who had objected to
excessive candour among Catholic historians.[33] On Döllinger's
advice in 1857 he prepared a review of a biography of
Gustavus Adolphus and offered it to Cardinal Wiseman for
the *Dublin Review*; it was prepared too late to be published,
but another article was accepted at the end of the year.[34]
Wiseman was eager to publish the work of his former pupil,
but Acton did not find the cautious, unscientific policy of the
Dublin congenial. "Your Eminence is aware of the historical
method of the school in which I have studied. As it differs
from that which is often pursued in the *Dublin Review* I do
not know whether that might not be enough to exclude my
article."[35] Henry Wilberforce's *Weekly Register* was closer to
Acton's spirit, and he published his first articles in it.[36]
But a weekly was not a suitable medium for the scholarly
works which Acton proposed to write; and lecturing, which
he attempted occasionally in 1858, was equally unsuitable.[37]

What Acton wanted was an "organ"—a serious periodical,
in whose management he would have a share, which would
provide him with a dependable outlet for his writings as well
as an incentive to write.

> It will give me readiness and practise in writing and
> experience and familiarity in political questions which must
> under any circumstances be useful to me. The necessity of
> producing something regularly will keep me hard at work and
> in constant intellectual activity. . . . It will give me a position
> and an influence among Catholics which I hope to use well,
> and which must be of great advantage to me hereafter. I

[33] Victor Conzemius, "Aspects ecclésiologiques de l'évolution de Döllinger
et du vieux catholicisme," *Revue des sciences religieuses*, XXIV (1960), 255. See
[W. A. Finlayson], "Bad Popes," *Dublin Review*, XXXVIII (March 1855),
1-72, and "Luther," *ibid.*, XXXIX (Sept. 1855), 1-60.

[34] "Henri IV," *Dublin Review*, XLIV (March 1858), 1-31.

[35] Acton to Wiseman, 17 Feb. 1857, Westminster Archives.

[36] *Weekly Register*, 17 May 1856, p. 5, cols. 2-4; 29 Nov. 1856, p. 6, cols. 3-4;
6 Dec. 1856, pp. 8-9; 31 Jan. 1857, p. 5, cols. 4-5. (I am indebted for these
references to Abbé Victor Conzemius.) Acton to Döllinger, 27 Nov. and 4 Dec.
1856, Woodruff MSS., indicate that Acton was quite close to Wilberforce at
this time.

[37] Acton lectured on Russia in January and on education in Birmingham in
June. The latter speech was praised by Wiseman in a letter to Acton, 20 June
1858, Woodruff MSS.

reflected also that it was . . . a capital means of turning my German studies [to use in England].[38]

The *Rambler*, which had in recent years developed a set of principles similar to those of Acton, seemed destined to fill this role for him.[39] Capes' retirement provided him, at the right moment, with the opportunity to become one of the proprietors and conductors of the organ of Liberal Catholicism in England.

---

[38] Acton to Döllinger, 17 Feb. 1858, Woodruff MSS. This portion of the letter was written in English. Acton made his decision to join the staff of the *Rambler* before consulting Döllinger.

[39] The suggestion that Acton purchase shares in the *Rambler* was made by Simpson: Simpson to Acton, 9 March 1864, Woodruff MSS.

CHAPTER IV

ACTON, SIMPSON, AND THE *RAMBLER*, 1858

THE new management which assumed control of the *Rambler* at the beginning of 1858 was dedicated to the continuance of the policy of independence, liberalism, and breadth of view which the magazine had adopted in its first decade of existence. At the same time, the addition of the young Acton[1] to the *Rambler*'s staff meant a new infusion of energy; and Simpson's assumption of the editorship, no longer restrained by the comparative caution of Capes, signified that a more daring spirit, a greater boldness of inquiry and statement, would preside over its pages.

It was not, however, in an aggressive spirit that Acton and Simpson began their work. They proposed that the editor should be advised by a council composed of "everybody who is distinguished for position and talent and at the same time a friend of the *Rambler*,"[2] and included several persons, priests and laymen, who could not be described as Liberal Catholics. Acton was so little involved in the dissensions and factions of English Catholicism that he suggested for the council such men as Ward and Manning.[3] Simpson was even willing to accept a theological censor. Eventually, however, both council and censorship were abandoned. Acton feared that a council might become an instrument for controlling the editor in the interests of the bishops or of the publisher, James Burns, whom Acton distrusted. Acton and Simpson found that they formed a team which worked well together,

---

[1] Acton's correspondence with Simpson has been edited by Abbot (later Cardinal) Gasquet, *Lord Acton and his Circle* (London, 1906). Gasquet, an unsatisfactory editor, muted or suppressed many of Acton's stronger expressions. See [Dom] A[elred] Watkin and Herbert Butterfield, "Gasquet and the Acton-Simpson Correspondence," *Cambridge Historical Journal*, X (1950), 75-105.

[2] Acton to Simpson, 28 Feb. 1858, Gasquet, *Lord Acton and his Circle*, p. 10.

[3] Ward was asked to take charge of the theological department of the *Rambler*, but politely declined. Acton to Döllinger, 17 Feb. 1858, Woodruff MSS.

and they came to have a dread of outside interference.

For Simpson, his position as editor meant an increased opportunity to pursue his favourite lines of thought. He was responsible for the department of "general literature," including the special field of history. He also wrote on philosophy, produced an occasional light article, shared in the reviewing, and was in general responsible for ensuring that there was a sufficiency of material to fill the pages of the *Rambler*. Acton was fascinated by Simpson's industry and productiveness: no one else could produce hack work of such quality in such quantity. Acton was also attracted by Simpson's sincerity and integrity, and the two became close friends.

The remaining proprietor, Frederick Capes, took a comparatively small share in the conduct of the *Rambler*. His particular department was fine arts; he also acted as informal treasurer of the magazine, paying the printers' and stationers' bills. His connection with the *Rambler* was kept secret, "as his professional business might be damaged by some of the Bishops."[4] One new contributor joined the staff of the *Rambler*: Dr. Charles Meynell, a priest at Oscott, who supervised the department of philosophy for some time.

Acton contributed articles on history and reviews of foreign literature, but he was principally interested in the political department of the magazine. He had joined the *Rambler* "to have an organ of this kind, with full intention of getting into Parliament as soon as possible."[5] He did not, however, intend to pursue a conventional political career; he had no personal ambition, and his Catholicism limited the success he might obtain in English politics. Furthermore, he was extremely conscious at this time of his isolation from political parties. His ambition was rather to exert an influence on political thought, to be an educator of public opinion, especially Catholic opinion. "I would have a complete body of principles for the conduct of English Catholics in political affairs, and if I live and do well, I will gradually

---

[4] Simpson to Newman, 26 Feb. 1859, Newman MSS.
[5] Simpson to Newman, 5 May 1859, Newman MSS.

unfold them. The Catholics want political education."[6] In a letter to Simpson on 16 February, Acton set forth his ambitious programme for educating the English Catholics. They must be taught to prefer principle to expediency in political matters and to develop a sincere attachment to the principles of the English constitution as interpreted by Burke. Acton thought that "there is a philosophy of politics to be derived from Catholicism on the one hand and from the principles of our constitution on the other," for the two sets of principles "coincide and complete each other."[7]

One of Acton's first contributions to the *Rambler* was a review of a biography of Burke, "the wisest, the most sincere, and the most disinterested of all the advocates of the Catholic cause,"[8] England's soundest political thinker. For a while, however, Acton left political writing to others. Simpson wrote several articles on France, criticizing the despotism of Napoleon III and the "unnatural union between the priest and the soldier"[9] which sustained it. In home politics, Simpson urged English Catholics to "avoid all that looks like sectarianism."[10] Dr. Todd also wrote on the same theme, pointing out that it was allowable for Catholics to differ among themselves in political matters: "the Church, as such, takes no sides in politics; and her cause is best promoted by the maintenance of liberty of opinion in all these affairs."[11]

At the beginning of 1859 Acton gave a detailed exposition of his political doctrines in an article entitled "Political Thoughts on the Church." Acton argued that the Church cannot be indifferent to politics, for its mission is to transform the lives of men as well in the public as in the private sphere.

> The Christian notion of conscience imperatively demands a corresponding measure of personal liberty. The feeling of duty and responsibility to God is the only arbiter of a Christian's

---

[6] Acton to Simpson, 16 Feb. 1858, Gasquet, *Lord Acton and his Circle*, p. 4.
[7] *Ibid.*, p. 3.
[8] Acton, "The Life and Times of Edmund Burke," *Rambler*, 2nd ser., IX (April 1858), 268.
[9] Simpson, "France," *Rambler*, 2nd ser., X (Aug. 1858), 83.
[10] Simpson, "English Catholics and the English Government," *Rambler*, 2nd ser., IX (March 1858), 145.
[11] W. G. Todd, "The Mission of the Laity," *Rambler*, 2nd ser., IX (May 1858), 294.

actions. With this no human authority can be permitted to interfere. . . . The Church cannot tolerate any species of government in which this right is not recognised. She is the irreconcilable enemy of the despotism of the State, whatever its name or its forms may be.[12]

This liberty did not depend upon a particular form of government, but rather upon a spirit of constitutionalism and recognition of autonomous corporations within the society. In the nineteenth century this spirit could be found only in Protestant countries, especially Britain, which, though it had abandoned the Catholic faith, had preserved the Catholic principles in its constitution. It was therefore the duty of British Catholics to defend the constitution against both the dangerous principles of the Radicals and the lack of principles of the Tories.

This doctrine of constitutional liberty was disregarded by the Catholic nations on the Continent. Acton was unsparing in his criticism of those Catholic leaders, such as Louis Veuillot, who, relying on the State to support the claims of the Church, were willing to accommodate Catholicism to the demands of absolutism. "He that deems he can advocate the cause of religion without advocating at the same time the cause of freedom, is no better than a hypocrite and a traitor."[13] The party of Veuillot, Acton asserted, was doing the work of the enemies of the Church by alienating from it the best intellects of the day and by teaching Catholics to rely upon the aid of the State rather than on the words of Christ. Acton aligned the *Rambler* on the side of Montalembert, to whom he acknowledged the deepest feelings of sympathy and admiration. Montalembert reciprocated these sentiments: "He is anxious to be more *en rapport* with us, deeming our cause nearly identical with his own."[14] Acton brought Simpson into correspondence with Montalembert, and proposed a series of articles on the varieties of

---

[12] Acton, "Political Thoughts on the Church," *The History of Freedom and Other Essays*, ed. John Neville Figgis and Reginald Vere Laurence (London, 1907), p. 203; reprinted from the *Rambler*, 2nd ser., XI (Jan. 1859), 30-49.

[13] "The Count de Montalembert," *Rambler*, 2nd ser., X (Dec. 1858), 422. It was in this article that the term "Liberal Catholic" was first employed in the pages of the *Rambler* (p. 426).

[14] Acton to Simpson, 13 Feb. 1859, Gasquet, *Lord Acton and his Circle*, p. 61.

Catholic opinion on the Continent, of which he wrote two, on Lacordaire and Montalembert, and secured another, on Lamennais, from the Baron d'Eckstein.

If the *Rambler* was severe in criticizing those Catholics who fell short of the highest standards in politics, it was equally demanding of Catholic historians. "He who falsifies history falsifies the express teaching of the Supreme Judge. Nothing can be weaker than the ecclesiastical historian's concealment of ancient corruptions for fear of giving scandal."[15] Acton welcomed every opportunity to preach the doctrines of German historical science, the independence of history and the necessity of original research. Above all, he insisted that history should be studied for its own sake, without concern for the effect or the utility of the results. "I think our studies ought to be all but purposeless. They want to be pursued with chastity, like mathematics."[16]

There were times when it proved difficult to sustain this chaste attitude to history. In March 1858, the *Rambler* received for review Cardinal Wiseman's *Recollections of the Last Four Popes*. Acton found the book lacking in taste and talent: "There is absolutely nothing new to be learned from it."[17] Acton could not bring himself to write the favourable review which was expected of a Catholic magazine. He left the task to Simpson, who solved the problem by an evasion: "It is a work not so much of the critical faculties as of the affections and sentiments. . . . Such a scope as this takes the Cardinal's book out of the sphere of history."[18] Simpson was thus able to give it a favourable treatment.

Only in this instance was the *Rambler*'s criticism muted. In a review of a book of documents edited by Theiner, the Vatican librarian, Acton exposed the hindrances to which Theiner had been subjected by the authorities at Rome in his attempts to publish material from the Vatican archives,

[15] *Rambler*, 2nd ser., IX (June 1858), 424. This was written by Simpson.
[16] Acton to Simpson, 22 Jan. 1859, Gasquet, *Lord Acton and his Circle*, p. 57. Gasquet prints this letter as part of the letter of 19 Jan.
[17] Acton to Döllinger, 1858, quoted by E. L. Woodward, "The Place of Lord Acton in the Liberal Movement of the Nineteenth Century," *Politica*, IV (1939), 253.
[18] Simpson, "Sunny Memories of Rome," *Rambler*, 2nd ser., IX (April 1858), 274.

and criticized the practice of concealing historical evidence:
"in history, where ignorance is equivalent to error, secrecy is
fraud."[19] Acton held that historical science presented no
danger to the Catholic faith, which would best be served by
impartial examination and statement of all the facts. Science,
operating according to its own laws, must lead to truths
which could not be inconsistent with those of religion. "His
principle is that whatever is *true* in speculation ought to be
said at any time; and we ought to take on *faith* that it *must*
do good."[20]

Acton and Simpson were not unaware that the discoveries
of science might, in unfriendly hands, be made to appear
destructive to religious faith. They recognized that the
greatest danger to religion in the nineteenth century was the
spirit of "infidelity and indifference"[21] which dominated the
intellectual movements of the day, and which was, in part,
a response to modern scientific discoveries and theories. The
great weakness of Catholic thought, they felt, was that it had
failed to address itself to an age of unbelief. The *Rambler* had
always been sensitive to the trends of non-Catholic thought;
and it now addressed itself to the danger of scientific infidelity.

Acton and Simpson contended that the apparent hostility
of science to religion was due to a superficial and unscientific
interpretation of scientific knowledge by non-religious
philosophers. In 1858 they directed their criticism particularly against the positivism of Comte and his followers.
In this connection they projected a series of reviews of
Buckle's *History of Civilization in England*. Two of these reviews
were printed, one, by Simpson, criticizing Buckle from the
philosophical standpoint, and the other, by Acton, criticizing
him as an historian.[22]

---

[19] Acton, "Father Theiner's Publications," *Rambler*, 2nd ser., X (Oct. 1858),
267. The Pope himself was exempted from these criticisms.

[20] Ward to Newman, "Mid-Lent Sunday" 1859, quoted by Wilfrid Ward,
William George Ward and the Catholic Revival (London, 1912), p. 451.

[21] Simpson, "The Influence of Catholics in England," *Rambler*, 2nd ser., X
(July 1858), 26.

[22] Simpson, "Mr. Buckle's Thesis and Method," *Rambler*, 2nd ser., X (July
1858), 27-42; and Acton, "Mr. Buckle's Philosophy of History," *ibid.* (Aug.
1858), 88-104. Both articles have been republished, under Acton's name, in his

If non-Catholics had often misinterpreted science, Catholics were often ignorant of it; and this defect, more than any other, prevented Catholic writers from having any influence on the educated Protestant public. Acton and Simpson thought that this defect was evident in Catholic theology, which was unacquainted with the critical spirit of historical and biblical scholarship: "I should be no theologian unless I studied painfully, and in the sources, the genesis and growth of the doctrines of the Church. . . . It is the absence of scientific method and of original learning in nearly all even of our best writers that makes it impossible for me to be really interested in their writings."[23] Acton did not shrink from the reconstruction of theology which was required: "theology is not a stationary science, so that a man who says nothing that has not been said before does not march with his age."[24] The scholastic theology was regarded patronizingly as "a system of ideology which, in spite of some old-fashioned errors, is entitled to the veneration of every Catholic mind";[25] but it must be brought up to date.

In their recognition of the backwardness of Catholic thought, Acton and Simpson were joined by W. G. Ward, who was fond of saying that "at the present time the Catholic world to the Protestant world is in much the same relation as barbarians to civilized men."[26] But the reconstruction of theology proposed by Acton, in which the theologian was transformed into the historian, was far more radical than the revival of Thomism which Ward had in mind. It meant a fluid rather than a static theology, a perpetual adaptation to increasing secular knowledge. It should be remembered, however, that when Acton and Simpson proposed a change in theology they did not mean that the defined dogmas of the Church should be subject to change; in this they differed from the "Modernists" of a later generation. Acton and

---

Historical Essays and Studies, ed. J. N. Figgis and R. V. Laurence (London, 1908), pp. 305-343.

[23] Acton to Simpson, 22 Jan. 1859, Gasquet, *Lord Acton and his Circle*, p. 56.
[24] Acton to Simpson, 11 June 1858, *ibid.*, p. 25.
[25] "Ideology of St. Thomas," *Rambler*, 2nd ser., IX (Jan. 1858), 50.
[26] Ward to Simpson, 15 Feb. 1858, Gasquet, *Lord Acton and his Circle*, p. 37n.

Simpson regarded dogma as the "central core"[27] of faith, immutable and incapable of being affected by scientific criticism. It was not the principles of faith, but rather the theological forms of expression and explanation of those principles, which they proposed to adjust in order to meet modern needs. This attitude brought them into sympathy with the Paulist Father Hecker in America[28] and with Newman in England.

Newman was the symbol of the *Rambler's* hopes. He represented a Catholicism in which religious sentiments were balanced by intellectual cultivation and sympathetic insight into the minds of those outside the Church. His *Essay on the Development of Doctrine* (1845) had been the beginning of historical theology in England: it "did more than any other book of his time to make his countrymen think historically."[29] Newman acknowledged the need for a new formulation of theology designed to meet the requirements of the age and recognized the role which an intelligent, well-instructed laity could perform in the work of making Catholicism intellectually respectable and attractive to Protestants. Thus he was inclined to be sympathetic to the *Rambler,* whose proprietors reciprocated his sympathy. Simpson wrote to Acton: "I would as soon be boiled as betray Newman. He is the man of whose approbation I should feel more proud than of any other person, and under whom I hope some day to work."[30] Acton respected Newman as the finest intellect and best writer among the English Catholics, but he had less personal affection for him and was less able to regard him as a leader. Acton recognized that Newman, for all the daring of his

[27] Simpson, "Reason and Faith," *Rambler,* n.s., V (July 1861), 182. Modernists regard dogma as itself subject to change in conformity with scientific criticism. Simpson sometimes used language which seemed to imply the same thing, but he had too high a regard for dogma to be a Modernist. Although the Liberal Catholics advanced "many suggestive ideas which might have been taken up and developed by the modernists . . . there is no evidence of any direct relation between the two movements." Alec R. Vidler, *The Modernist Movement in the Roman Church* (Cambridge, 1934), p. 50.

[28] The *Rambler* recommended Hecker's *Aspirations of Nature* as "perhaps the most important work for the present day that we have yet had to review" (2nd ser., IX [Jan. 1858], 49). For Hecker, see Robert D. Cross, *The Emergence of Liberal Catholicism in America* (Cambridge, Mass., 1958).

[29] CUL Add. MS. 4987.   [30] Quoted by Acton, CUL Add. MS. 4987.

speculations and the liberalism of his sympathies, was cautious and conservative in temperament, submissive to authority, conscious of difficulties, inclined to compromise. Newman saw too much to be a man of action or the leader of a party. Conscious of the importance and value of the work which was being done by the *Rambler*, he was yet fearful of its tendencies; his main concern was to keep it from collision with the ecclesiastical authorities. Thus he could never fully engage himself in the work of the Liberal Catholics, and he remained their symbol rather than their leader.

In 1858 Newman, recovering from his failure at Dublin, was projecting new schemes to raise the intellectual level of British Catholicism.[31] One of these was the foundation of a Catholic public school for lay boys, which was opened at Edgbaston in 1859; Acton was one of the sponsors. Another project was a magazine which he had founded just before leaving Dublin, the *Atlantis*, a semi-annual journal conducted by the faculty of Dublin University under the editorship of Professor Sullivan. The *Atlantis*, although it included every subject taught in the University, was primarily intended to keep Catholic readers abreast of the latest trends of science. Acton, who found that a monthly such as the *Rambler* was not an altogether suitable medium for the long scholarly articles which he wished to write, offered to contribute to the *Atlantis*. He saw in it an opportunity to extend the influence of the *Rambler* and hoped by this means to draw Newman from his virtual retirement at Birmingham into a greater association with the work of the Liberal Catholics. Acton proposed to make the *Atlantis* into a quarterly, with the material for the additional two issues to be supplied by himself and his friends, under Newman's superintendence; the scope of the magazine would be enlarged to give greater emphasis to history, politics, and philosophy. Newman, on the other hand, was anxious to limit the scope of the *Atlantis* to scientific topics, avoiding the dangerous ground of theology. Caution was uppermost in his mind, and he

[31] Newman's experiences in Ireland and particularly his contact with the Young Irelanders had moved him to a more liberal political position and a greater interest in the role of the laity. See Alvan S. Ryan, "The Development of Newman's Political Thought," *Review of Politics*, VII (April 1945), 219.

F

stressed the difficulties of the project. Acton, confident of his own wealth and energy, was sanguine that all difficulties could be overcome; but Newman remained hesitant, and no conclusion had been reached by the end of 1858.[32]

In this year Acton and his friends came close to capturing the most important of the English Catholic periodicals, the *Dublin Review*. In the early days of the Catholic Revival, the *Dublin* had played a distinguished role as the leading organ of Catholic thought; but it had lately fallen into disrepute and was regarded as dull and dreary. Its early prestige was largely due to the articles of Wiseman, its proprietor, but he had virtually ceased to contribute. He retained his control over the review, which was edited by Henry Bagshaw, a barrister; under their cautious management all difficult topics were avoided, and the quality of the articles deteriorated. It was difficult to secure able contributors because the publisher, Thomas Richardson, allotted only a small sum to pay for articles. Bagshawe, in despair, resigned his editorship at the beginning of July 1858.[33] It appeared that the *Dublin* would have to be given up, as no new editor could be found.

At this juncture Thomas W. Allies, one of the contributors to the *Dublin*, proposed to Acton that he should take it over. Here was an opportunity for the *Rambler* to extend its influence. Under Capes, the possibility of amalgamating the two magazines had been considered; but Acton proposed to continue them both, under a common management. Newman, whose advice was solicited, told Acton that "I should very much like to see it in your hands,"[34] although he stressed the difficulties of the plan. Burns, the publisher of the *Rambler*, agreed to take the *Dublin* out of Richardson's hands and offered to give it adequate financial assistance. Acton now formally offered to take the editorship of the *Dublin*,

---

[32] The correspondence between Acton and Newman on this subject is included in the Woodruff and Newman MSS. Portions of the letters of Acton to Newman, 10 and 20 Dec. 1858, have been reprinted in Douglas Woodruff, "Introduction" to Lord Acton, *Essays on Church and State* (London, 1952), pp. 17-18.

[33] Henry R. Bagshawe, Circular "To the Catholic Public," 25 June 1858; copy in Newman MSS.

[34] Newman to Acton, 14 July 1858, Woodruff MSS.

and Wiseman and Bagshawe seemed inclined to accept his proposal.

Wiseman, however, now began to have second thoughts on the matter. Acton had stipulated that he must have absolute control over the review, free from episcopal censorship, and he was determined to make Simpson his sub-editor.[35] This was unacceptable to Wiseman, who had long been suspicious of Simpson and was unwilling to abandon all control over the leading Catholic organ. He felt that Acton and Simpson were speculating on the difficulties of the *Dublin* and calculating on taking its place in the Catholic body.[36] In August Wiseman broke off the negotiations and persuaded Bagshawe to resume the office of editor.

Acton had begun the year in high favour with Wiseman; but by August the Cardinal had come to be suspicious of Acton's influence. Wiseman thought it the duty of a Catholic journal "to steer clear of matter which could give rise to quarrels and divisions, especially among Catholics."[37] Certain articles in the *Rambler* had aroused his resentment, and he had begun to hear reports about its conductors which raised doubts as to their orthodoxy.

One of these reports was based on the activities of J. M. Capes, the former editor of the *Rambler*. In the months after his resignation from the editorship, Capes experienced a recurrence of the religious doubts which had assailed him in 1849. He found himself unable to accept the doctrine that the Catholic faith must be held as absolutely certain, not as merely probable. The demand for the absolute submission of the intellect seemed to him "equivalent to a demand for the surrender of my reasoning faculties."[38] Capes began to question other Catholic doctrines: transubstantiation, which seemed to him a metaphysical impossibility, and penance, which he considered an inducement to morbidity. He was

---

[35] Acton to Newman, 9, 25, and 29 July 1858, Newman MSS. Acton wanted Newman to act as theological adviser, to keep a rein on Simpson; he also hoped that Newman would contribute to the new *Dublin*.

[36] Wiseman to Bagshawe, n.d. (July or Aug. 1858), Westminster Archives.

[37] Bagshawe, Circular "To the Catholic Public."

[38] John Moore Capes, *To Rome and Back* (London, 1873), p. 320.

convinced that the Church was ruled by an anti-historical school of Ultramontanes, whose object was to enslave the intellect. Thus he came to reconsider the grounds of his conversion to Catholicism, the belief in the necessity of an absolute doctrinal infallibility. Capes now believed that there was, after all, no final source of certainty, no infallible authority, to which Christians might have recourse; he found himself unable to accept "a literal orthodoxy as an explanation of the great mystery of life."[39] At this point he quietly ceased to communicate in the Roman Catholic Church and took up a position apart from all religious bodies.[40]

Capes, who had never allowed others to become aware of his doubts, kept his new position secret and retained his associations with his Catholic friends. He even took over the editorship of the July 1858 number of the *Rambler* in order to allow Acton and Simpson to go to the Continent. Soon afterwards he made known his position to them. Simpson wanted to "cut him off,"[41] but Acton was anxious to avoid giving Capes any annoyance which might confirm him in his present state of mind. Acton hoped that Capes might yet be brought back to the Church, and extended himself to that end, recommending books for him to read and arranging for him to meet Döllinger on the latter's visit to England in September.

Meanwhile Capes had privately printed a statement of his difficulties, which he sent to a few friends. Among these was Newman, who was shocked by the news; even now he found it difficult to grasp the point of Capes' difficulties. After an agitated correspondence, Newman formulated an answer to Capes' greatest problem, the certainty of faith. The argument from probability leads us, Newman said, only to the

[39] Capes to Newman, 11 May 1863, Newman MSS.
[40] Capes, *To Rome and Back*, pp. 353ff. See also his *Reasons for Returning to the Church of England* (London, 1871). In 1870, after the definition of Papal Infallibility, Capes rejoined the Anglican Church. Before his death, however, he returned to the Church of Rome.
[41] Acton to Simpson, 2 July 1858, Downside MSS. Part of this letter is published by Gasquet, *Lord Acton and his Circle*, p. 29; but Gasquet excised Capes' name. Acton criticized Capes for his dislike for prayer and asceticism and for an "intellectual contempt for fellow-Catholics."

point where we recognize an obligation to believe; at this point, it is a matter of duty, by an act of will, to direct the mind to believe with absolute faith: "we are so constituted as to be bound by our reason to believe what we cannot prove."[42] It is possible that this discussion was the genesis of Newman's *Grammar of Assent*, published in 1870.[43] But Capes, whose logical mind demanded more rigorous proof, found Newman's arguments unsatisfactory. Nor was he convinced by Dollinger, Acton and Simpson, when he met them at Aldenham in September. Capes continued his drift away from Rome.

The meeting at Aldenham was to have unfortunate results for the conductors of the *Rambler*. Although Capes insisted on secrecy, news of the meeting leaked out.[44] The meeting had been held for the purpose of inducing Capes to remain in the Church; but rumours perverted the facts and made it appear that the gathering was for some seditious purpose. These rumours reached the ears of the most influential Englishman in Rome, Monsignor George Talbot. Talbot, a convert, had been appointed one of the Pope's chamberlains, and exercised a great influence on English Catholic affairs; he was Wiseman's agent in Rome. Talbot reported to Wiseman at the end of October that he had heard a disedifying account of the meeting at Aldenham: "the spirit was most detestable that was manifested in it. The only subject of conversation was abusing your Eminence, the Bishops, all Ecclesiastical Superiors, and ridiculing old Catholics."[45] This was the first of the secret denunciations of the *Rambler* that were to be sent to Wiseman.

[42] Newman to Capes, 1 Oct. 1858, quoted by Wilfrid Ward, *Life of John Henry Cardinal Newman*, 2 vols. (London, 1912), I, 443. Portions of Newman's other letters are quoted by Ward, *ibid.*, 440-3; Capes' letters are in the Newman MSS.

[43] See Ward, *Life of Newman*, II, 245-6. Ward cites a memorandum by Newman on "Fluctuations of Human Opinion," dated 1860, giving the viewpoint of a sceptic; the arguments are essentially those of Capes. The *Grammar of Assent* was Newman's final answer to the problems therein posed. For Simpson's critique of the *Grammar of Assent*, see his review in the *North British Review*, LII (July 1870), 220-233.

[44] Simpson to Acton, 20 Feb. 1859, Woodruff MSS.

[45] Talbot to Wiseman, 30 Oct. 1858, Manning MSS. Talbot also wrote to Canon James Patterson, one of Wiseman's confidants, in the same sense (but in more extreme language), 9 Nov. 1858, Westminster Archives.

Meanwhile Wiseman had come to have his own suspicions about the new management of the *Rambler*. When Simpson reviewed Wiseman's *Last Four Popes* in April, he gave special attention to a passage in which Wiseman had sought to refute the story that the historian Lingard had been made a cardinal *in petto* by Leo XII in 1826; Simpson described Wiseman's arguments as "solid and conclusive."[46] This attempt to please Wiseman displeased Lingard's biographer, Canon Tierney, who was one of the old Catholic clergy and an opponent of Wiseman's programme of "Romanizing" the Church in England. Tierney took umbrage at Wiseman's remarks on Lingard, regarding them as an attempt to defame one of the greatest of the old Catholics. Tierney wrote a long and violent letter to the *Rambler*, published in June, denouncing Wiseman's "misrepresentations,"[47] and attempting to prove that Lingard had in fact been made a cardinal. Simpson prefaced this letter with an editorial note to the effect that "we willingly insert the following correction of a mistake into which we fell in an article in our April Number."[48] This was simply an attempt on Simpson's part to pacify Tierney; but his words "we willingly insert" gave the impression that the *Rambler* was siding with Tierney in his attack on Wiseman.

Wiseman, who believed that the cardinal created in 1826 was not Lingard but Lamennais, printed a letter addressed to the canons of Westminster, setting forth his arguments at length. He had at first considered replying in the *Rambler*, but finally chose to reply in a letter which was "printed, not published,"[49] and sent only to a limited number of influential Catholics, in order to prevent a public controversy. At

---

[46] *Rambler*, 2nd ser., IX (April 1858), 280. A cardinal *in petto* is one who is created but not proclaimed as cardinal, the appointment remaining "in the Pope's breast."

[47] Mark Aloysius Tierney, "Was Dr. Lingard Actually a Cardinal?," *Rambler*, 2nd ser., IX (June 1858), 425. Tierney, canon of Southwark and chaplain to the Duke of Norfolk, had clashed with Wiseman several years earlier on the same issue.

[48] *Rambler*, 2nd ser., IX (June 1858), 425.

[49] Nicholas Wiseman, *Letter to the Canons of the Cathedral Chapter of Westminster* (London, 1858). The pamphlet bears the following postscript (p. 26): "Whoever receives this letter is sincerely requested not to allow it to be published, entire or in part."

Wiseman's request, it was not reviewed by the *Rambler*; but Tierney replied in a pamphlet which he sent to the recipients of Wiseman's letter.[50]

It is impossible to ascertain whether Tierney was right in asserting that Lingard had been made a cardinal, since the cardinalate remained "in the breast" of Leo XII and died with him. The only thing certain is that Lingard himself believed the story. The *Rambler*, when it finally gave its own judgment on the matter a year later, concluded that both Lingard and Lamennais had probably been made cardinals.[51]

Simpson and Acton, whose sole purpose throughout the affair had been to avoid offending either side, endeavoured to smooth things over. They both wrote to Wiseman, emphasizing that the *Rambler* did not endorse Tierney's attack on him:

> The *Rambler* has been independent from the first, and it will remain so. But the proprietors do not consider that independence means personal opposition to you. They know that you are the head and representative in England of the religion which they defend and profess, and that a systematic opposition to you, so far from being real independence, would be only slavery to passion and to an uncatholic idea.[52]

Wiseman accepted their disclaimers of opposition; but it was too late to allay the irritation which the incident had caused.

The *Rambler* soon gave more positive offence. In an article on Bossuet, in June, Acton asserted that Bossuet had held Jansenistic opinions on the subject of grace: "he considered himself, rightly or wrongly, a thorough Augustinian."[53]

---

[50] Tierney, *A Reply to Cardinal Wiseman's Letter to His Chapter* ("not published").

[51] "Dr. Lingard's Alleged Cardinalate," *Rambler*, n.s., II (Nov. 1859), 75-83; signed by "Z." For a more thorough discussion of the question, see Joseph Gillow, "John Lingard," *Bibliographical Dictionary of the English Catholics*, 5 vols. (London, n.d.), IV, 254-278, and Edmund Bonney, "John Lingard," *Catholic Encyclopedia* (New York, 1913), XI, 270-2.

[52] Simpson to Wiseman, 20 Nov. 1858, Downside MSS. Other portions of this letter have been printed by Gasquet, *Lord Acton and his Circle*, pp. 38n-39n. Acton's letter to Wiseman is summarized in Acton to Simpson, 13 Nov. 1858, Watkin and Butterfield, "Gasquet and the Acton-Simpson Correspondence," pp. 88-90.

[53] "Bossuet," *Rambler*, IX (June 1858), 388. The article had been begun in the previous issue, pp. 320-337. It is reprinted (somewhat abridged) in *Essays on Church and State*, pp. 230-245.

This implicit equation of the Jansenist heresy with the doctrines of St. Augustine provoked no reaction until it was repeated by Acton in August, in a review of Chéruel's life of Catherine de Medici. Protesting against the tendency of Catholic historians to be partial and uncritical in discussing eminent Catholics, Acton argued for perfect impartiality and openness: "nor because St. Augustine was the greatest doctor of the West, need we conceal the fact that he was also the father of Jansenism."[54] This time there was a sharp reaction, and many protesting letters were sent to the editor.

Simpson attempted to placate the critics with a notice in the September issue: "we protest that we never intended to identify any errors which the Church has proscribed with the teaching of 'the greatest doctor of the West' when properly understood; and that we most sincerely hold and profess whatever the Holy See has propounded, and condemn what it has condemned, on the questions of grace, free-will, and justification."[55] But Acton was not inclined to be conciliatory:

> I do most deliberately hold that errors condemned by the Church are to be found in the works of the Doctor Gratiae. I think it is worth following up, in order that men may learn that we do not choose even our illustrations without delibera- tion, and are ready to justify everything we write. There could be no better opportunity than this, as it will at the same time help to break down that narrow and invincible ignorance with which our theologians judge the writings of other people.[56]

Acton chose this as the field of battle on which he would defend the integrity of Catholic history. Having no doubts about the historical propriety of the phrase he had used, Acton wrote to Döllinger and secured from him a letter which justified, on historical and theological grounds, the description of Augustine as the "father of Jansenism."

[54] *Rambler*, X (Aug. 1858), 135. It is possible that the phrase was deliberately inserted by Acton in order to arouse a reaction: in preparing the short notices for the previous issue, he had said that he would "take care to say a few startling things." Acton to Simpson, 6 June 1858, Gasquet, *Lord Acton and his Circle*, p. 22.

[55] *Rambler*, X (Sept. 1858), 216.

[56] Acton to Simpson, Sept. 1858, Gasquet, *Lord Acton and his Circle*, pp. 34-5. Gasquet altered the phrase "I do *most* deliberately" to read "I do *not* deliber- ately"; he also garbled the concluding words. See Watkin and Butterfield, "Gasquet and the Acton-Simpson Correspondence," p. 88n.

Döllinger pointed out that Augustine was not accused of fathering Jansenism in the same manner as Luther had fathered Lutheranism; the phrase meant only that "in his dispute with Pelagians and semi-Pelagians Augustine did not merely state and defend the universal doctrine of the Church, but in some points went beyond it." These peculiar doctrines, of which the Jansenists took possession, were at no time the teaching of the Church—a fact which would be denied by no theologian who had studied the subject "accurately and in the source themselves." Therefore "Jansenius and his school were not altogether in the wrong when they proudly called themselves the disciples of St. Augustine."[57] Jansen had derived his doctrine from a thorough study of the saint's writings. Augustine's later theories of predestination and the resistlessness of grace had, in fact, been criticized by many leading Catholic theologians since the sixteenth century, as Döllinger proved by copious citations. In suspecting that Augustine's writings provided a basis for Jansenist heresies, Acton had been in "very good, I may say, in most select company. I know none better in the Church."[58]

Döllinger's letter, published in the December *Rambler*, was a challenge to the old-fashioned theologians who taught in the English Catholic schools. Its provocativeness was enhanced by the editorial note prefixed to it by Simpson, who protested against the "unfounded accusations" made against the *Rambler*, intended to "cramp our independence by sowing suspicions of our orthodoxy. It is our right . . . to prove that the denunciations made against us spring rather from the timidity of ignorance, the dogmatism of party views, or a ceremonious reverence to great names, than from such a knowledge of the subject in dispute as could give those who accuse us any right to sit in judgment on our opinions."[59] Döllinger's letter was unsigned, Simpson describing its author merely as "a divine of European reputation both as a

---

[57] J. J. I. von Döllinger, "The Paternity of Jansenism," *Rambler*, 2nd ser., X (Dec. 1858), 362-3.

[58] *Ibid.*, 373.

[59] *Rambler*, 2nd ser., X (Dec. 1858), 360. Simpson's review of Mansel's Bampton lectures, in the same issue, was turned into an attack on this tendency of some Catholics to denounce their fellow-Catholics as unorthodox: *ibid.*, 415.

theologian and as a historian."[60] However, Döllinger's authorship was generally known, as Acton had made no secret of it.

Acton had thought that the letter would "astonish rather than offend";[61] but it did, in fact, give great offence among the English Catholics. Several protesting letters were sent to Acton and Simpson. The *Weekly Register* for 11 December published two letters criticizing the *Rambler*, one by a professor of theology at Ushaw College, Dr. Gillow, who later published a pamphlet on the subject.[62] More serious was the reaction of Father Faber of the London Oratory, who denounced Acton to Cardinal Wiseman.[63]

Wiseman was now placed in a difficult position. He was still fond of Acton, and he had long been bound to Döllinger by sentiments of friendship and admiration; but the letter on the paternity of Jansenism had distressed him and scandalized his subjects. Wiseman determined to delate Döllinger's letter to the Congregation of the Index in Rome. "I am sorry," he wrote to Simpson, "that the letter in defence of St. Augustine's 'paternity of Jansenism' is exciting considerable uneasiness, likely to lead to the principles and opinions contained in it being referred to authority superior to mine."[64] It appeared likely that the *Rambler* would be condemned.

On 30 December, Acton called on Newman at the Birmingham Oratory to inform him of this development. Newman, who did not share in the general disapproval of the position taken by Acton and Döllinger, was shocked and

---

[60] *Ibid.*, 360.

[61] Acton to Simpson, 13 Nov. 1858, quoted by Watkin and Butterfield, "Gasquet and the Acton-Simpson Correspondence," p. 89. Acton had written to Wiseman to prepare him for a "stunning reply" in the December number.

[62] Joseph Gillow, "John Gillow," *Bibliographical Dictionary of the English Catholics*, II, 479.

[63] See Acton to Father Darnell, 3 Feb. 1859 (Newman MSS.), referring to a time when Faber "had not yet denounced me as you wot." Cited by David Mathew, *Acton: The Formative Years* (London, 1946), p. 121, n. 1. This explains the reference to "Brompton" (the London Oratory) in Acton to Simpson, 1 Jan. 1859, Gasquet, *Lord Acton and his Circle*, p. 47.

[64] Wiseman to Simpson, 22 Dec. 1858, Downside MSS. That the delation was actually made is attested by letters from Dr. Weathers (of Oscott) to Simpson, 14 Jan. 1859 (Downside MSS.), and Newman to Acton, 25 Jan. 1859 (Woodruff MSS.). Nothing, however, seems to have resulted from the delation.

indignant on learning of the denunciation of Döllinger's article: "He was quite miserable when I told him the news and moaned for a long time, rocking himself backwards and forwards over the fire, like an old woman with a toothache."[65] Newman cast aside his usual reserve, much to Acton's surprise, and talked freely about the tendency of men in power to tyrannize and the ignorance and presumption of English Catholic theologians. The result of the meeting was that Newman finally agreed to Acton's proposal to make the *Atlantis* a quarterly, thus providing a second organ for the Liberal Catholics.

Acton believed that he had succeeded in drawing Newman from his virtual retirement into active collaboration with himself and Simpson, and he rejoiced over this accession of strength more than he lamented the threatened condemnation by Rome. Newman, as it turned out, was not prepared to go quite so far. His agreement to expand the *Atlantis* was intended to draw some of the sting from the *Rambler*. He stipulated that the *Rambler* should cease to treat theology in its pages and announce that fact to the public; the *Rambler* would confine itself to history and politics, leaving weightier matters such as theology to the *Atlantis*. Acton agreed to this, without any confidence that it would restore the *Rambler*'s good repute: "People of the kind we have to conciliate are quite as sensitive and as intolerant in such subjects as history and politics as in theology. . . . There is a dread not only of particular conclusions, but of the free and sincere inquiry which may lead to them."[66]

It was this dread of free inquiry which had caused the denunciation of the *Rambler*, and which Acton was resolved to combat. Acton had come to have a distaste for periodical literature, which he found "inconsistent with the sort of studies I have pursued and with my slow and pacific habits of thought";[67] he wished to be able to retire to Aldenham and engage in serious historical work. But the unintellectual

---

[65] Acton to Simpson, 1 Jan. 1859, Gasquet, *Lord Acton and his Circle*, p. 47. Acton, as this letter shows, had little personal reverence for Newman, whom he referred to as "old Noggs."

[66] Acton to Newman, 4 Jan. 1859, Newman MSS.

[67] Acton to Simpson, 1 Feb. 1859, Downside MSS.

habits of the English Catholics made it necessary for a Catholic scholar to spend "almost as much time justifying his intellectual pursuits as pursuing them."[68] The denunciation of the *Rambler* aroused in Acton a determination to fight for the freedom of the Catholic scholar, regardless of the consequences; "and it is upon this ground that I shall say when we are condemned *Eppur si muove*."[69]

[68] Cross, *The Emergence of Liberal Catholicism in America*, p. 148.
[69] "But it does move"—the protest of Galileo when forced to recant. Acton to Simpson, 22 Jan. 1859, Downside MSS. This clause, which follows the passage about the "chastity" of mathematics (cited, p. 67), was omitted by Gasquet.

CHAPTER V

THE *RAMBLER*, THE BISHOPS, AND NEWMAN, 1859

B Y THE beginning of 1859 it had become clear that the proprietors and friends of the *Rambler* constituted a distinct party within the English Catholic body. The initial unity of the Catholic revival had broken down, and Cardinal Wiseman, who had been so anxious to prevent the formation of parties, had himself become a party leader. He was at this time at the height of his conflict with some of the old Catholics, led by Archbishop Errington; for this reason he was especially displeased to see the formation of a second opposition group led by Acton and Simpson. In this conflict with them, Wiseman could rely on the support of a majority of the English Catholics. "The popular view," Acton observed with some exaggeration, "is that a crowd of converts have conspired together, half to become apostates, the rest to remain [in the Church] in the hope that, as ostensible Catholics, they might do more harm through the *Rambler*."[1] A more temperate statement of the grounds of opposition to the *Rambler* was given by *The Tablet*:

> What we suspect to have been the actual ground of misgiving about the *Rambler* is not so much any isolated views which were identified with it (displeasing as these may have been), as its general tone and temper. It was felt, in one word, that there was an absence, or deficiency, of "religiousness" about it. Things were habitually discussed in it in a cold, hard, and worldly spirit. The grand mistake made in its administration seems to us to have been that of forgetting that Catholicism is an atmosphere, and not a mere creed; that it is a medium which colours almost everything which comes before us, except pure mathematics. The intellectual state of

[1] Cited in J. Friedrich, *Ignaz von Döllinger*, 3 vols. (München, 1901), III, 210. This was in connection with the meeting of Acton, Döllinger, Simpson and Capes at Aldenham in September.

a man who considers all ground open to free discussion which is not closed up by the rigid terms of the Faith, is somewhat analogous to the moral state of those invulnerable but most unsatisfactory Christians who go to confession once a year.[2]

In opposition to the principles of the *Rambler*, there was formed a party which emphasized the authority of the Church as the solution to intellectual difficulties and the guide for practical action. This Ultramontane party, largely composed of converts, was led by W. G. Ward and Father Faber. Manning, the future Cardinal, was in full accord with them, but at this time he was occupied with the controversy with Errington and the old Catholics. When Wiseman sought to counteract the dangerous independence of the *Rambler*, he came to rely on these Ultramontanes.

After he had rebuffed Acton's attempt to take over the *Dublin Review*, Wiseman sought the aid of Ward and his friends in rehabilitating the moribund journal. Faber was active in urging on these negotiations; but the poor state of the review, and Wiseman's insistence on retaining control, deterred even the Ultramontanes. It was not until the beginning of 1859 that they agreed to take over the *Dublin*. What principally motivated them, besides their "detestation of the *Rambler*" and their "wish to serve the Cardinal in his war against it," was a desire to secure Wiseman's support in the struggle between the converts and the old Catholics—"to try that the Cardinal should feel that the converts would *help* him, and so tend towards keeping up that *estrangement from Errington* which seems the best thing under our deplorable circumstances."[3]

The *Rambler* shared Ward's dislike of Errington and the conservative old Catholics, who overemphasized the national element in the Church in England; Acton regarded their "Gallicanism" as the product of "an imperfect state of learning impossible now-a-days in men who are up to the

---

[2] *The Tablet*, 21 May 1859; cited in Dom Cuthbert Butler, *The Life and Times of Bishop Ullathorne*, 2 vols. (New York, 1926), I, 313.

[3] W. G. Ward to Newman, 8 March 1859, quoted by Wilfrid Ward, *Life of John Henry Cardinal Newman*, 2 vols. (London, 1912), I, 489-90. See also E. Healy Thompson to Newman, 15 Feb. 1859, Newman MSS.

mark."[4] But Ward's Ultramontanism, Acton maintained, was equally unsatisfactory: it relied too much on ecclesiastical authority, and forgot that there are other truths than those of religion. On the issue of freedom versus authority there was a gulf between the *Rambler* and its Ultramontane opponents which could not be bridged. Newman attempted to occupy a middle position; deeply as he sympathized with the principles of the *Rambler*, he was bound to Ward and his associates by ties of friendship from the days of the Oxford Movement, and was always submissive to episcopal authority. He avoided committing himself, urged caution on Acton and Simpson, and declined invitations to contribute to the new *Dublin* and to Henry Wilberforce's *Weekly Register*.

Acton used the occasion of the re-organization of the *Dublin* to publish an article in the *Rambler* setting forth his views on what a Catholic review ought to be. This article, "The Catholic Press," published in February 1859, was actually a manifesto of the Liberal Catholic movement in the form of a critique of the *Dublin Review*. It must be admitted, Acton said, that the English Catholics had produced no serious or durable literature of their own: "we have not half a dozen books which will bear critical examination, or which we are not ashamed of before Protestants and foreigners; and we contribute nothing to the literature of the Church."[5] This, Acton argued, was largely the fault of the old *Dublin Review*, which had accustomed Catholics to intellectual indolence. In its early days, it had performed a useful service in meeting the challenge posed by the Oxford Movement; but new opponents had arisen, and the *Dublin* had failed to respond to them. Instead, it had restricted its sphere to "safe" topics, forcing other Catholic journals to occupy the vacant positions. The *Dublin* had fallen behind the march of intellect and "encouraged the insane delusion that scientific infidelity is not, like heresy, an antagonist that it

---

[4] Acton to Simpson, 4 July 1858, cited in [Dom] A[elred] Watkin and Herbert Butterfield, "Gasquet and the Acton-Simpson Correspondence," *Cambridge Historical Journal*, X (1950), 81. Acton himself was an old Catholic, but was intellectually more at ease among the converts.

[5] Acton, "The Catholic Press," *Essays on Church and State*, ed. Douglas Woodruff (London, 1952), p. 262; reprinted from *Rambler*, 2nd ser., XI (Feb. 1859), 73-90.

behoves Catholics to encounter."[6] It had left Catholics
unprepared to meet the new intellectual challenge presented
by the advances of science.

It was the duty of a Catholic review, Acton said, not
merely to uphold the Catholic cause and to command the
respect of Protestants, but also to educate the Catholic public.
It should keep Catholics informed of the progress of Catholic
learning and of the state of Catholicism in other countries.
It should serve as a guide and an example in literature.
It should be a guide for Catholics in political matters,
teaching them to consider principles rather than interests, to
uphold representative institutions and to resist the increasing
power of the state. Above all, it should teach Catholics to
understand science and to accept it as the necessary ally of
the Church, "claiming for the Church the principle of
scientific investigation which seemed to threaten her."[7]
It would combat scientific infidelity; but it would also wage
war on those within the Church who feared the advance of
science.

Here Acton found occasion to strike back at his opponents
who had denounced the *Rambler* for its policy of free inquiry
and discussion:

> Solicitude for religion is merely a pretext for opposition to
> the free course of scientific research, which threatens, not the
> authority of the Church, but the precarious influence of indi-
> viduals. The growth of knowledge cannot in the long run be
> detrimental to religion; but it renders impossible the usurpation
> of authority by teachers who defend their own false opinions
> under pretence of defending the faith. . . . They want to shelter
> their own ignorance by preserving that of others. But religion
> is not served by denying facts, or by denouncing those who
> proclaim them.[8]

The "one thing needful" was to accept science as the ally of
the Church, to save Catholicism from the "twin dangers of
unbelief and superstition. . . . Every branch of learning
pursued for the sake of its own conclusions will result in the
vindication of religion, and in the discomfiture of those who

[6] *Ibid.*, p. 266.
[7] *Ibid.*, p. 271.
[8] *Ibid.*, p. 272.

believe in their antagonism."[9] This was especially true in history, where impartial learning had achieved great results in vindicating the Church. "The impartiality of scientific research is our surest ally if we adopt it, and if we reject it is sure to cover us with confusion. . . . We must have confidence in the power of argument and reason to give victory to truth."[10]

Acton welcomed the new *Dublin*, hoping that it would prove a worthy representative of Catholic culture, adopting and teaching sound principles. In concluding the article, he made on behalf of the *Rambler* the statement, which Newman had desired, disclaiming any intention of dealing with theology; but he phrased it, not as an apology for previous indiscretions, but rather as a reaffirmation of the *Rambler*'s principles:

> We wish it to be distinctly understood that the *Rambler* is not a theological Review, and that we do not design to treat questions of theology, or to transgress that line which separates secular from religious knowledge. The principle of independent inquiry, within the bounds, and for the promotion, of the Catholic faith, it is our pride and our duty to maintain.[11]

The boldness and eloquence of this article concealed a certain sense of discouragement. Acton had been disillusioned about the character of the Catholic reading public and dismayed by its narrowness and ignorance. He was conscious that he had acquired a "questionable" reputation among Catholics by his journalistic activities. This consciousness reconciled Acton to the prospect of a "temporary disappearance"[12] from the English scene, which had become advisable for financial reasons: he had determined, as a measure of economy, to live on the continent for a while. Acton left his interest in the *Rambler* in the hands of Simpson, whom he regarded as "the only English Catholic possessing

[9] *Ibid.*, p. 273.
[10] *Ibid.*, p. 275.
[11] *Ibid.*, p. 277.
[12] Acton to Newman, 25 Jan. 1859, Newman MSS. Acton was quite wealthy; but there were many charges on the Aldenham estate, and it was too expensive to keep up the establishment unless the house were lived in all the time. His financial difficulty was (at least temporarily) relieved after his mother's death in 1860.

G

the positive qualifications for conducting such a review as the *Rambler* strives to be."[13]

Only a few days after Acton penned this tribute to his co-worker, Simpson's qualifications as an editor were brought into question by the English bishops. The issue in this case was education, a subject on which the *Rambler* had clashed with the episcopate in 1848-9 and again in 1856-7. Catholic education was one of those "mixed" questions which, because of their partially religious character, the bishops regarded as subject to their jurisdiction. The bishops had appointed a Catholic Poor School Committee through which they communicated with the Government on educational matters. Those Catholic schools which accepted Government grants were subject to Government inspection; but it had been arranged that the inspectors were to be Catholics, approved by the bishops, and restricted to the purely secular aspects of education, religious teaching being expressly excepted from their inspection.

In 1858 a Royal Commission was appointed to inquire into the condition of education in England. No Catholics were members of the Commission, which was to investigate Catholic schools as well as others. The Catholic Poor School Committee had failed to notice the appointment of the Commission until it was too late to change its composition or its instructions. When at last the bishops awoke to its existence, they misunderstood its character: they saw it as a breach of faith on the part of the Government, an attempt to force Protestant inspectors on Catholic schools and to subject religious teaching to inspection. Efforts were made to have the Commission reorganized with the addition of a Catholic member, or to secure the appointment of Catholic assistant commissioners. When these efforts failed, the bishops resolved to instruct the clergy to decline to co-operate with the Commission and to refuse its inspectors admission to Catholic schools.[14]

---

[13] Acton to Simpson, 4 Feb. 1859, Abbot Gasquet, *Lord Acton and his Circle* (London, 1906), p. 60.
[14] Circular to the clergy by Wiseman, 9 Nov. 1858; copy in Westminster

The decision of the bishops caused dismay among the educated laity, who felt that the hierarchy had placed itself in an impossible position. This dismay was expressed in an article in the *Rambler* for January 1859 by Scott Nasmyth Stokes, one of the Catholic inspectors of schools and "undoubtedly the principal authority on the subject in the Catholic body."[15] Simpson was aware that the bishops would resent a discussion of the subject, but printed the article on the advice of Acton, who was not "particular about accepting Stokes' seditious dissertation on education, as it cannot give more offence than the December Number."[16] Stokes urged Catholics to co-operate with the Commission, in order not to risk the loss of government grants. He said that Catholics had been misinformed on the subject, and that false issues had been raised. He professed due submission to ecclesiastical authorities, but gave offence by a reference to those "whose infirm and baby minds are gratified by mischief."[17]

Many of the converts sympathized with Stokes' article; but the bishops considered that he had attempted "to answer difficulties which he has not mastered."[18] *The Tablet* denounced Stokes' article, asserting that the question had been decided by the ecclesiastical authorities, and that Catholics were simply bound to carry out their plans. In the face of this criticism, Acton asked Stokes to write another article: "right or wrong, it is important that things so serious should be 'ventilated'."[19] Stokes' second article was published in the February *Rambler*.

Stokes asserted that no decision by the bishops had been made public: "we decline to infer the sentiments of Bishops from hints in newspapers; respect for the hierarchy leads us

Archives. The clergy were advised to avoid the danger of uneasiness and excitement among their flocks by not reading the circular in church to the congregation.

[15] Butler, *Life of Ullathorne*, I, 310.

[16] Acton to Simpson, 12 Dec. 1858, Downside MSS. Acton thought the article "excellent."

[17] Scott Nasmyth Stokes, "The Royal Commission on Education," *Rambler*, 2nd ser., XI (Jan. 1859), 17.

[18] Newman to Acton, 16 Jan. 1859 [dated 1858], Woodruff MSS. Newman himself regarded the article as "startling."

[19] Acton to Simpson, 19 Jan. 1859, Downside MSS. See also the letter of 11 Jan.

rather to regard as wisely tentative and provisional whatever views may have been entertained upon a question which avowedly involves no religious principle, and which we know from undoubted testimony to have been neither thoroughly discussed nor properly understood."[20] This was no question of faith or morals, but one of politics, on which religious men might be mistaken. Stokes urged the bishops to reconsider their policies, and recapitulated his arguments in favour of co-operating with the Commission. He hoped the question would not be decided without ample discussion: "In doubtful questions, unanimity is best secured by discussion. . . . Concealed discontents injure more than avowed difference of opinion."[21] A note appended to this article (probably by Simpson) cited a similar discussion in America as an illustration of the consequences of losing state aid for Catholic schools. "It is to preserve us from this consummation . . . that we again respectfully and earnestly implore our authorities to weigh the arguments we have advanced, and to reconsider the determination which the newspapers assume they have come to."[22]

Stokes had maintained that he was not challenging the bishops' decision, but rather that no final decision had been made, and that he was merely offering them advice before they committed themselves. This argument failed to impress the bishops, who objected to his articles on the ground that as a layman he had no right publicly to offer advice on the subject of education, which was reserved to the episcopate not only as to decision but as to discussion. This was a position which few of the laity were inclined to accept: even the Ultramontane Ward recognized the importance of "the right of a Catholic layman's independent thought,"[23] and sympathized with Stokes' articles. But the bishops were primarily concerned with the need for unanimity of Catholic action,

[20] Stokes, "The Royal Commission and the 'Tablet'," *Rambler*, 2nd ser., XI (Feb. 1859), 105.

[21] *Ibid.*, 111.

[22] *Ibid.*, 113. It was in connection with this note that Acton referred to Simpson's "pugnacity," in Acton to Simpson, 13 Jan. 1859, Gasquet, *Lord Acton and his Circle*, p. 53.

[23] Ward to Simpson, Feb. 1859, quoted by Gasquet, "Introduction" to *Lord Acton and his Circle*, pp. xlviii-xlix.

particularly in dealing with the Government. They decided
that it was necessary to assert their authority by striking at
the *Rambler*.

On 12 February 1859, a meeting was held in London of
Cardinal Wiseman, his coadjutor Archbishop Errington,
Bishop Ullathorne of Birmingham and Bishop Grant of
Southwark. They agreed that something must be done about
the *Rambler*, that it must be taken out of the hands of its
present management: "nothing short of Mr. Simpson's
retiring from the editorship will satisfy, as he plainly cannot
judge what is, and what is not, sound in language."[24] It was
agreed that Ullathorne should write to Newman, who was
known to be in the confidence of Simpson and Acton, and
that Newman should be asked to intervene to secure Simpson's withdrawal. It was made clear that, if Simpson did not
resign, the *Rambler* would be censured in the Bishops' forthcoming Pastoral Letters.

The bishops' reliance upon Newman caused him some
embarrassment. He had long thought that the *Rambler*'s
opposition to the bishops had placed it in a "false position":
"if the *Rambler* perseveres in its present course, it will find it
cannot hold on—but must come to an end."[25] On the other
hand, he thought that its censure would be a disastrous blow
to the growth of an intelligent and educated laity, and he felt
much personal sympathy for Simpson: "I have a great
opinion of his powers, and a great respect for his character,
and a great personal liking for him."[26] He had sought to
avert a collision between the *Rambler* and the hierarchy, and
now he found himself the only possible intermediary between
them.

Newman wrote at once to Simpson, informing him that
the bishops were determined to act promptly and severely,
and urging him to come to Birmingham as speedily as
possible. Simpson went to Birmingham on 18 February, and

[24] Ullathorne to Newman, 16 Feb. 1859, quoted by Wilfrid Ward, *Life and
Times of Cardinal Wiseman*, 2 vols. (London, 1897), II, 245.
[25] Newman to Acton, 31 Dec. 1858, quoted by Ward, *Life of Newman*, I, 484.
[26] Newman to Acton, 13 Jan. 1859, *ibid.*, 485-6.

put himself entirely in Newman's hands. He agreed to resign the editorship of the *Rambler*: "With a protest against the Bishops' want of consideration in giving me no notice of their intentions . . . and of their want of openness in not making any definite accusations against me or my writings, I yield to their threats, but only provisionally, and on the condition of my being [able] to find another editor, and of the proprietors being able to carry on the magazine in the same or in a different form."[27] He stipulated, in order to preserve the rights of his fellow-proprietors, that if his resignation should lead to the suspension of the magazine, he would be free to make public an account of the entire transaction; and he demanded that, if the March number of the *Rambler*, which was already in print, should be suppressed, the Bishops should reimburse his expenses on it. Newman, on behalf of the bishops, agreed to these conditions. Newman also agreed, on his own behalf, to take over the editorship himself, carrying on the *Rambler* as a bi-monthly to the end of the year, when a permanent editor could be found. Simpson engaged, for himself and his fellow-proprietors, to give their support and assistance to Newman. To Simpson, despite his bitterness about the manner in which he had been treated, it seemed that he had emerged triumphant over the bishops, having secured, through Newman's editorship, the continuance of the *Rambler* with its old staff and its old principles. "I rejoice greatly, because though I am conquered personally, they have got anything but their revenge."[28]

Newman wrote about Simpson's resignation to Ullathorne, who appeared satisfied with it; but Wiseman was less disposed to accept the concessions Newman had made on his behalf. He would agree not to mention the *Rambler* by name in his forthcoming Pastoral, but he would not promise to refrain from mentioning the education controversy; and he refused to reimburse Simpson for his expenses on the

---

[27] Simpson to Newman, 19 Feb. 1859, Newman MSS. Simpson was under considerable mental strain at the time. His brother, a priest, had just been stricken with a severe illness, and Bishop Grant had sent him to be cared for by Simpson.

[28] Simpson to Acton, 20 Feb. 1859, Woodruff MSS.

suppressed March issue. Furthermore, Wiseman said, "the whole compact will be nugatory if Mr. Simpson merely retires from the post of Editor for the purpose of disarming the Bishops, and yet he contributes in the same spirit as hitherto, or Mr. Stokes or others are allowed to write in the same strain. . . . Mr. Simpson's retirement will be worth nothing without some guarantee against the repetition of the same faults."[29] When Newman was informed of this letter, he said to Ullathorne, "Then, my Lord, the whole negociation is at an end."[30] But on the next day Ullathorne showed Newman another letter from Wiseman, in which the Cardinal stated the real ground of his objection, the fear that Simpson might be replaced by Acton, which would leave the management of the *Rambler* substantially unchanged. This immediately altered Newman's decision to withdraw. "The Cardinal's letter," he said, "I felt almost to force me to be Editor";[31] for otherwise he would be open to the imputation that he had evaded the real difficulty and had failed to effect a change in the management of the *Rambler*.

Newman had begun to have second thoughts about taking over the *Rambler* almost as soon as he had engaged to do so. His closest friend, Father Ambrose St. John, cautioned him against involving himself in a "somewhat perilous undertaking";[32] and Burns, the *Rambler*'s publisher, while urging Newman to take it over in order to prevent its collapse, warned him against working too closely with Simpson. Simpson offered Newman the entire property of the *Rambler*, with complete freedom to do what he liked with it; but Simpson's very eagerness to have him take it over aroused Newman's suspicions. The result was that Newman spent an entire month seeking excuses to avoid taking the *Rambler* before he finally committed himself.

One difficulty which occurred to Newman was the relationship that would exist between the new *Rambler* and

[29] Wiseman to Ullathorne, 22 Feb. 1859 (copy), Newman MSS.

[30] Memorandum by Newman, 25 Feb. 1859, Newman MSS. See also Newman to Simpson, 25 Feb. 1859, Newman MSS.

[31] Note by Newman, n.d., in the "Simpson" volume of the Newman MSS. See also Newman to Wiseman, 21 March 1859, Newman MSS.

[32] St. John to Newman, 28 Feb. 1859, Newman MSS.

the other Catholic periodicals. It was impossible for Newman to continue his work for the *Atlantis* while editing the *Rambler*, and he rejected Simpson's proposal to merge the two journals. The result was that Newman ceased to contribute to the *Atlantis*, which struggled along for a few years without his aid, and then died. The *Dublin Review* presented a more pressing problem. The bi-monthly *Rambler* in Newman's hands would be too strong a competitor for the *Dublin*, and the converts, who still revered the former leader of the Oxford Movement, would probably decline to write for a rival journal. Faber had already advised Ward that, if Newman took the *Rambler*, "the *Dublin* is a gone coon."[33] Simpson frankly urged Newman to accept the editorship of the *Rambler* in order to "destroy the *Dublin*."[34] This suggestion irritated Newman; it seemed that Simpson "had acquired an unusual aptitude for brushing Newman the wrong way."[35] Newman had no intention of entering into rivalry with the *Dublin*, and he was beginning to fear that Simpson was using him as an instrument of party warfare.

Actually, Wiseman's project of rehabilitating the *Dublin* by giving it over to the Ultramontane converts had already collapsed. The news that Newman would edit the *Rambler* provided Ward and his friends with "a good excuse for retiring."[36] They were more in sympathy with the *Rambler* than with the bishops on the education question, and Wiseman's severity towards the *Rambler* made them less eager to support him. Indeed, things seemed to Ward to be "tending to a kind of union of converts against ecclesiastical authorities."[37] Edward Healy Thompson, who was to have been the sub-editor of the *Dublin*, withdrew from the scheme after learning how the *Rambler* had been treated by the bishops: "My sympathies are certainly with the smitten, and not with the smiters. . . . I am sure that with my notions of what the

[33] Quoted in Simpson to Newman, 2 March 1859, Newman MSS.

[34] Simpson to Newman, 2 March 1859, Newman MSS. In the letter of 7 March, Simpson admitted that he could not help "feeling a satisfaction that this struggle, which has been all along one of rival editors, should end not in changing the *Rambler* alone, but in multiplying the difficulties of its rival also."

[35] CUL Add. MS. 4988.

[36] Ward to Newman, 8 March 1859, quoted by Ward, *Life of Newman*, I, 489.

[37] Ward to Simpson, 1 March 1859, cited in Gasquet, "Introduction," p. li.

Review ought to be . . . I should have received a whack of
the pastoral staff before six months had gone."[38] Ward
notified Wiseman that he and his friends had withdrawn
from the *Dublin*, which was left to continue its "precarious
and scrambling existence"[39] under the inefficient editorship
of Bagshawe.

Meanwhile the bishops had published their Lenten
Pastorals, which did not mention the *Rambler* by name but
alluded indirectly to the education controversy. Wiseman
spoke of "the enemy" choosing education "for the field in
which to sow the tares of division among Catholics," and
regretted that there were those who sought to lead Catholics
astray "from the simple path of right and dutiful feeling,
on a matter so obviously belonging to the ecclesiastical
authority."[40] Ullathorne referred to "one or two, here and
there, using the public press as a weapon against the conduct
of the episcopacy."[41] Father Formby, in an article in the
Weekly Register, termed this an allusion to the *Rambler*, and
attacked its conduct in the education controversy.

Simpson regarded these statements as a breach of the
bishops' engagement not to mention the *Rambler*, and
threatened, if Newman did not accept the editorship, to put
out a final issue of the magazine making public the entire
story of its suppression. Although he had earlier described his
surrender of the *Rambler* to Newman as absolute and uncon-
ditional, he now reminded Newman that "there was one
condition of the surrender of the *Rambler* which neither of us
named in writing, but both of us understood, namely that
whatever else it gave up, it should preserve its independence."[42] Simpson subjected Newman to every possible
pressure to persuade him to accept the *Rambler*. He sent him a
letter from Acton, urging him not to withdraw, and adding

[38] Thompson to Simpson, 3 March 1859, Downside MSS. Thompson had not
entered into the party warfare against the *Rambler*. Simpson was so impressed by
Thompson's friendly spirit that he suggested him to Newman as a possible sub-
editor of the *Rambler*.
[39] Dr. Charles Russell to Wiseman, 7 April 1859, Westminster Archives.
[40] Cited in *Rambler*, n.s., I (May 1859), 117.
[41] *Ibid.*, 118.
[42] Simpson to Newman, 10 March 1859, Newman MSS. See also the letter
of 15 March.

that Döllinger considered that the *Rambler*'s disappearance would be "an irreparable loss."[43]

Newman was growing restive under this pressure. Ward was urging him, if he took the *Rambler*, to change its name, so as to dissociate himself from the "detestable principles" of its former management. Newman rejected the idea of changing its name, as this would be an insult to its former conductors; his objection had not been to its principles, but to its tone.[44] Then he received a letter from Wiseman, which stated that the *Rambler* in Newman's hands would render the existence of the *Dublin* "not only critical, but, I fear, impossible"; it would leave "no chance for a second periodical."[45] Wiseman stated that he was prepared to accept the downfall of his beloved *Dublin* and had no objections to Newman's taking the *Rambler*; but Newman misinterpreted the letter, and thought that the Cardinal wanted him to withdraw from the *Rambler*. When, therefore, a letter by Simpson irritated Newman by reiterating the condition that he must preserve the independence of the *Rambler*, Newman replied petulantly, refusing to pledge himself to any principles, and proposing to terminate the negotiations.[46]

Simpson, in alarm, immediately went to Birmingham to discuss the matter with Newman in person. Newman evidently made his position clear to Simpson, who agreed to give the *Rambler* to him without conditions, in the confidence that he would preserve its essential principles. Newman only awaited the approval of Wiseman, to whom he had written explaining his intentions; when Wiseman did not reply, Newman understood that there was no objection to his taking the *Rambler*. On 21 March, he formally accepted the editorship. Acton, Simpson, and Frederick Capes were to

[43] Acton to Simpson, 8 March 1859, Downside MSS. Cited in Simpson to Newman, 14 March 1859, Newman MSS. Acton had assured Simpson of his full support for any arrangement which he might conclude with Newman.

[44] Newman to Ward, 10 March 1859, quoted by Ward, *Life of Newman*, I, 490-1. See also a memorandum by Newman, 24 May 1882, cited in Louis Bouyer, *Newman: His Life and Spirituality*, trans. J. Lewis May (New York, 1958), p. 329.

[45] Wiseman to Newman, 14 March 1859, quoted by Ward, *Life of Wiseman*, II, 247.

[46] Newman to Simpson, 16 March 1859, replying to Simpson to Newman, 15 March, Newman MSS.

remain proprietors and contributors, leasing the magazine to Newman, who was to have full control.

From the day when Ullathorne had shown him Wiseman's letter insisting that Acton as well as Simpson should be excluded from the editorship, Newman had felt that he would have to take it over himself, in order to satisfy the bishops. The alternative would have been to put an end to the *Rambler*, but this he would not do, because he wished to preserve a periodical which had done, and might still do, much good. Yet he was hesitant, fearful of becoming involved in controversies, and unwilling to take on another burden; he had to consider the interests of his Oratory at Birmingham, and of the Edgbaston School which was about to open. For a month, he sought to evade the unpleasant task; and even in accepting it he did so only "for the present."[47]

Nonetheless, his decision satisfied all parties. Wiseman professed himself "perfectly satisfied about the future principles of the *Rambler*"[48] in Newman's hands. Simpson delightedly expressed "the gratitude which I feel to you for having rescued me at so great a personal sacrifice from a position to which I was not equal."[49] And Acton, writing from Munich, was "persuaded that this revolution in our affairs will end by consolidating our party and strengthening our opinion and influence."[50] Newman represented many things to many people.

[47] Newman to Simpson, 21 March 1859, Newman MSS.
[48] Wiseman to Newman, 22 March 1859, Newman MSS. Wiseman added that he would, after all, be able to keep the *Dublin Review* in existence.
[49] Simpson to Newman, 22 March 1859, Newman MSS.
[50] Acton to Simpson, 1 April 1859, Downside MSS.

Chapter VI

FATHER NEWMAN CONSULTS THE LAITY

NEWMAN's editorship of the *Rambler* represented the last opportunity to bridge the chasm which separated the Liberal Catholics from their Ultramontane opponents. Newman hoped to restore the *Rambler* to the good graces of the hierarchy by changing what was offensive in its style and tone; at the same time he sought, in the spirit of its former conductors, to meet the intellectual challenges of the day and to develop an educated Catholic laity.

In order to reduce the burden of the editorship, the *Rambler* was changed from a monthly to a bi-monthly. This allowed it to emulate the style of a quarterly review while avoiding direct competition with the *Dublin*. This change, and the new format adopted by the magazine, justified the beginning of a "new series." On this occasion Newman sent a prospectus to the subscribers, announcing its new form and intentions. He stated that the *Rambler* would abstain from direct discussion of theology and, in dealing with mixed questions into which theology indirectly entered, would seek to reconcile freedom of inquiry with faith and reverence. In order to allow a wide range of discussion, the *Rambler* would be divided into three main sections: "editorial" articles, for which the editor was directly responsible, "communicable" articles, and correspondence, for which he assumed "only such general responsibility"[1] as was involved in publishing them. By this device it was hoped that free discussion could be carried on without involving the *Rambler* in the opinions of its contributors. To emphasize this distinction, "communicated" articles were to be signed (usually with fictitious initials) and to employ the personal "I" rather than the editorial "we." In addition to these main sections, the "Literary Notices" were to be increased, and a new section

[1] *Rambler*, n.s., III (Sept. 1860), 388n.

of "Contemporary Events," dealing with news of the day, was to be added; these sections were "editorial" in character.

Newman made every effort to preserve the continuity of the *Rambler*. He made no public announcement of his assumption of the editorship; instead he adopted the journalistic conventions of editorial anonymity and the corporate identity of the magazine. This was against the advice of Ward and of John Wallis, the editor of *The Tablet*, who urged Newman to change the name of the *Rambler* and to transform it into a new and distinct periodical.[2] Newman rejected this advice:

> Not a word was said of any change of matter, drift, objects, tone, etc. of the *Rambler*, though my purpose was in fact to change what had in so many ways displeased me. But I had no wish to damage the fair fame of men who I believed were at bottom sincere Catholics, and I thought it unfair, ungenerous, impertinent, and cowardly to make on their behalf acts of confession and contrition, and to make a display of change of editorship.[3]

Simpson acknowledged Newman's "great generosity" and "kindness towards the old proprietors."[4] Although he had no official position on the staff of the *Rambler*, Simpson performed many of the functions of a sub-editor, correcting proofs, making arrangements with the printers, and writing short reviews. The former conductors of the *Rambler* were welcomed as contributors. Newman's first issue contained an article by Simpson on "Religious Associations in the Sixteenth Century." The article is notable for its assertion that the persecuted Elizabethan Catholics organized themselves as "a secret society."[5] Newman, disregarding the modern Church's opposition to secret societies, admitted the article in the "editorial" section. Its conclusion, a plea for

---

[2] John Wallis to Newman, 23 May 1859, cited in Wilfrid Ward, *Life of John Henry Cardinal Newman*, 2 vols. (London, 1912), I, 633.

[3] Memorandum by Newman, 24 May 1882, *ibid.*, 494.

[4] Simpson to Newman, 15 April 1859, Newman MSS. For Simpson's assistance to Newman, see Simpson to Newman, 5 and 19 May 1859, Newman MSS.

[5] Simpson, "Religious Associations in the Sixteenth Century," *Rambler*, n.s., I (May 1859), 23. This article was severely criticized a half-century later by J. H. Pollen, S.J., "An Error in Simpson's 'Campion'," *The Month*, CV (June 1905), 592-599.

the impartial treatment of Catholic history, may have represented his own views.[6]

A spirit of liberality governed Newman's conduct of the *Rambler*. Although he approved the policies of Napoleon III, Newman accepted an article sharply criticizing the French Emperor.[7] Newman even invited Döllinger to reply in the *Rambler* to Dr. Gillow's pamphlet against his article on the "Paternity of Jansenism." Döllinger, however, cautiously declined to write, feeling that it would be unwise to do so in the present state of Catholic opinion and that it would prejudice the position and influence of the *Rambler*.[8] Controversies flourished in the "Correspondence" section, where great freedom was allowed. Although the *Rambler* professed to abstain from theology, a correspondent was allowed to raise the question: "How far is it allowable, or desirable, for laymen to study theology?"[9] Another correspondent inquired whether Döllinger had implied that the traditional theology of the schools was opposed to real historical and patristic learning, and was answered by Simpson, who criticized the school theologians for knowing the Fathers only from compendia rather than from the sources themselves.[10] A mild controversy developed over the question whether temporal prosperity was a "note" or sign of the Church, with reference to the state of Catholic countries. It was natural, then, for *The Tablet* to foresee a danger that licence would be given, in the "correspondence" section of the *Rambler*, for the expression of dangerous views, or that it might become "the

[6] Thomas S. Bokenkotter, *Cardinal Newman as an Historian* (Louvain, 1959), 61. Fr. Bokenkotter describes Simpson's article as "a solid contribution to historical scholarship."

[7] "Sigma" [Thomas F. Wetherell], "Thoughts on the Causes of the Present War," *Rambler*, n.s., I (July 1859), 186-198. Newman replied in a letter (signed "J.O.") in the next issue, "Napoleonism not Impious," *ibid.* (Sept. 1859), 378-9, to which Wetherell reponded in November.

[8] Ward, *Life of Newman*, I, 493-4. Apparently the delation of Döllinger's article had produced no effect in Rome. William Burke, Wiseman's nephew, told Simpson that there was no case for the Index. See Simpson to Acton, 20 Feb. 1859, Woodruff MSS.

[9] "H.L.," "Questions and Answers," *Rambler*, n.s., I (May 1859), 109. Answered by "H" (probably Simpson), "Lay Students in Theology," *ibid.* (July 1859), 238-41, to the effect that it was permissible within limits; Simpson had consulted the Belgian Fr. de Buck on this point.

[10] "R.S.," "Traditions of Historical Points in the Schools," *Rambler*, n.s., I (July 1859), 242-4.

safety valve for intellectual crotchets."[11] It seemed, indeed, that Newman was giving himself over to the Liberal Catholics.

The real test of Newman's editorship was to be his handling of the education controversy which had led to Simpson's retirement. The bishops had since made public their decision against co-operating with the Royal Commission, and it was now necessary for the *Rambler* to make some statement on the subject, in order to explain its previous conduct and put an end to the controversy. Newman began his statement with a full submission to the decision of the bishops, and cited copious extracts from their Pastoral Letters. He argued that their remarks did not contain any particular allusion to the *Rambler*. He further claimed that Stokes' articles had not, in fact, opposed the decision as such, since no formal decision had been made public when Stokes wrote:

> Episcopal decisions are matters too serious to admit of being made except in form. We did not know the Bishops had spoken formally, and we do not know what is meant by an informal decision. . . . We did not know that they had actually put the question out of their hands by any irreversible act or judgment; we are very sorry for our mistake, but we are not sure, from what is reported, that they have done so even now.[12]

He then went on to make a plea for greater consideration of lay opinion:

> Acknowledging, then, most fully the prerogatives of the episcopate, we do unfeignedly believe . . . that their Lordships really desire to know the opinion of the laity on subjects in which the laity are especially concerned. If even in the preparation of a dogmatic definition the faithful are consulted, as lately in the instance of the Immaculate Conception, it is at least as natural to anticipate such an act of kind feeling and sympathy in great practical questions . . . surely we are not disrespectful in thinking, and in having thought, that the

[11] *The Tablet*, 21 May 1859; cited in Dom Cuthbert Butler, *The Life and Times of Bishop Ullathorne*, 2 vols. (New York, 1906), I, 313.

[12] "Judgment of the English Bishops on the Royal Commission," *Rambler*, n.s., I (May 1859), 122. The article was printed as part of the "Contemporary Events."

Bishops would like to know the sentiments of an influential portion of the laity before they took any step which perhaps they could not recall.[13]

Newman had intended to satisfy the bishops without repudiating the writers in the *Rambler*, but the effect of this article was to give the impression that he had fully identified his new *Rambler* with the old. Simpson thanked him "for the generosity with which you take the past sins of the *Rambler* on your own shoulders."[14] Wiseman, on the other hand, complained that the new *Rambler* was "just as bad as the old."[15] Newman himself later admitted that "I took up and defended (in my own way) its cause on the Education Question."[16] In attempting to exculpate Stokes, Newman had done more than merely explain away his offence; he had implied that the bishops' decision had been made improperly and without due form. This was no less offensive than Stokes' criticism had been.

The most severe criticism of Newman's article, however, was made on theological grounds. Dr. Gillow, professor of theology at Ushaw College, objected to the passage in which Newman stated that "even in the preparation of a dogmatic definition the faithful are consulted." A correspondence ensued between Gillow and Newman, which the latter felt obliged to show to his bishop, Ullathorne. At the same time, Newman asked Ullathorne to appoint a theological censor for future issues of the *Rambler*.

On 22 May, Ullathorne came to the Oratory to discuss the matter with Newman. Ullathorne declined to appoint a censor for the *Rambler*, first, because it was not published in his diocese, and secondly, because its style made censorship virtually impossible: "the theological difficulties cropped up in half sentences." He agreed with many of the criticisms that had been made of the new *Rambler*, and he regretted that the old spirit had not gone out of it. "The Catholics of England were a peaceable people; the Church was peace.

---

[13] *Ibid.*

[14] Simpson to Newman, 1 May 1859, Newman MSS.

[15] According to Henry Wilberforce. See Acton to Simpson, 1 June 1859, Downside MSS.

[16] Newman to Acton, 20 June 1860, cited in Ward, *Life of Newman*, I, 636.

Catholics never had a doubt; it pained them to know that
things could be considered doubtful which they had ever
implicitly believed. The *Rambler* was irritating."[17] Newman
urged the importance of giving due consideration to the
educated laity, but Ullathorne would not allow the weight
of his argument. Newman then mentioned how great an
annoyance it had been to accept the *Rambler*, and how
relieved he would have been not to have done so; whereupon
Ullathorne abruptly suggested that he give it up. Newman
objected that this would mean giving it back to its old
proprietors; but Ullathorne, disregarding the objection,
said that there would be no difficulty if he gave them fair
notice and edited one more issue. Newman, ever responsive
to the wishes of his bishop, promised to resign the *Rambler*
after the July number. "I never have resisted, nor can resist,
the voice of a lawful Superior speaking in his own province.
I should have been in an utterly false position if I had
continued, without a revision, . . . a work, of the very object
and principle of which my diocesan disapproved."[18]

Newman's editorship had been a source of embarrassment
to the bishops: their triumph of having secured Simpson's
resignation had been virtually nullified when it became
apparent that Newman, with his greater prestige, was con-
tinuing many of the old *Rambler*'s policies. Newman, some
years later, observed that what he required for the *Rambler*
was "elbow room—but this was impossible."[19] Ullathorne
was on the friendliest terms with Newman; but this bluff,
unintellectual old-Catholic bishop found it difficult to
comprehend the range of Newman's ideas and could not
accept his views on the rights of the laity. The bishops, having
brought Newman into the *Rambler*, soon became anxious that
he should leave it.

Ullathorne's attitude was a great blow to Newman. His
life as a Catholic, at least since 1852, had been a succession of
frustrations and failures, and now another failure was added

[17] Newman to E. H. Thompson, May 1859, cited in Ward, *Life of Newman*, I,
496.
[18] *Ibid.*
[19] Newman to Miss E. Bowles, 19 May 1863, quoted by Ward, *Life of Newman*,
I, 587.

H

to the list. To the intellectual converts—whether liberal or
Ultramontane—Newman's resignation was a great mortifi-
cation, a sign that their wider views could command no
sympathy from the ecclesiastical authorities. Thompson
wrote to Newman that what was needed was a convert
bishop, and Henry Wilberforce felt that "our bishops do not
understand England and the English."[20]

Newman's resignation meant that the *Rambler* would be
returned to its old proprietors after the July issue. It was
resolved that Simpson should not resume his editorship, since
his reputation as an editor had been compromised by the
conflict with the bishops, and the renewed association of his
name with the *Rambler* would prejudice its chances of acceptance by the Catholic public. Simpson cheerfully accepted
the necessity of his self-effacement and suggested that Acton
should be the new editor, with the *Rambler* becoming more
distinctly political in its character. Acton was, in fact, the
inevitable choice to succeed Newman.

Acton had given his confidence to Simpson throughout the
negotiations with Newman; he had welcomed Newman's
acceptance of the editorship, and contributed to his first
issue. While travelling on the Continent, Acton had met
Montalembert and arranged for Simpson, deprived of an
organ in the *Rambler*, to contribute to the *Correspondant*.[21]
Later Acton had proposed that he and Simpson should buy
shares in the *Weekly Register*, which Henry Wilberforce,
frightened by the bishops' treatment of the *Rambler*, seemed
disposed to sell. This proposal did not materialize, but
Simpson contributed to the *Weekly Register* later in the year,
making it for a while a second organ of Liberal Catholicism.[22]

In April Acton was hurriedly called back to England by

[20] Cited in Ward, *Life of Newman*, I, 501. Thompson wished to consult Ward
on the situation, but Newman forbade this, calling Ward a "prodigious blab."
[21] Acton to Simpson, 20 and 21 April and 30 Sept. 1859, in Abbot Gasquet,
Lord Acton and his Circle (London, 1906), pp. 68, 70 and 87. The following articles
in the *Correspondant* (n.s., Vols. XVII and XVIII) appear to be by Simpson:
"Lettre sur le rôle des catholiques dans les dernières élections en Angleterre,"
May 1859, 167-171; "Lettre de Londres," June 1859, 374-377; "Lettre de
Londres," Sept. 1859, 174-180. The second letter provoked a critic to reply:
"Lettre de Londres," July 1859, 544-548.
[22] Acton to Simpson, 21 May, 1 June and 10 Aug. 1859, Downside MSS.

Lord Granville, on the occasion of the dissolution of Parliament. The general election offered Acton an opportunity to enter political life, and Granville was eager to sponsor him. Acton was not enthusiastic, but he felt obliged to stand for election, "*pour acquit de conscience*,"[23] and also to avoid being named sheriff of his county. He sought nomination at Cashel, Waterford City and Dublin, without success. Acton attributed his failure to the influence of Wiseman,[24] who favoured Lord Derby's government, partly because it had shown some sympathy with Catholic grievances, and partly because the Tories were less hostile than the Liberals to the Pope's Temporal Power. Eventually Acton received the nomination for Carlow, a borough with a somewhat disreputable parliamentary history, where the Catholic Liberals had been unable to secure a candidate.

Acton, who was ill at the time, did not visit Carlow until after the election, but was nominated *in absentia*. He stood as a Catholic first, and then as a Liberal; his principal supporter was a local priest; his opponent was a Protestant, a Tory, and a landlord. Acton's only contribution to the campaign, aside from some finances, was a letter to the priest, Father Maher, leaving the question of his party affiliation rather vague, but stating that he would oppose the existing Tory government: "I had rather reckon on Liberal principles than on the fears of the Tories."[25] He favoured Reform, the Ballot, Tenant Right, and non-intervention in Continental politics; but his greatest stress was on his Catholicism, and he made use of the letter of recommendation which Wiseman had given him in 1857. In an election marked by the exertions of Father Maher, a considerable amount of mob violence, and at least the suspicion of bribery, Acton unexpectedly defeated his opponent, and found himself, rather to his dismay, a member of Parliament.

Newman feared that Acton's new parliamentary responsi-

---

[23] Acton to Simpson, 5 April 1859, Gasquet, *Lord Acton and his Circle*, p. 67.
[24] Acton to Simpson, 19 April 1859, Downside MSS.
[25] Acton to Father Maher, 8 May 1859, cited in James J. Auchmuty, "Acton's Election as an Irish Member of Parliament," *English Historical Review*, LXI (Sept. 1946), 401—an excellent study of this curious election. Auchmuty was not aware of the reason of Acton's absence, his illness, for which see Acton to Simpson, 2 May 1859, Downside MSS.

bilities would not allow him to accept the editorship of the *Rambler*; but Acton thought that the two positions could be combined. Simpson suggested that the *Rambler* be made the organ of the small band of Catholic Liberal members of Parliament. Acton, though approving a greater emphasis on political affairs, did not wish to make the *Rambler* the organ of any parliamentary group. He was still uncertain of his political affiliation, although he voted with the Liberals in the division which overthrew the Derby government. His friends were in power, but he desired and received no office. This left him free to edit the *Rambler* as a magazine independent of party. Newman was relieved that Acton was willing to accept the editorship; Acton was not eager but was resigned to it as inevitable: "I hardly see how the *Rambler* can survive unless I undertake the editing of it."[26]

While Acton was arranging to take over the *Rambler* in the summer, Newman was preparing the July issue which was to be his last. It was necessary for him to defend his statement in the May issue that "even in the preparation of a dogmatic definition the faithful [i.e. the laity] are consulted." Gillow had objected to this statement as unsound in theology, because the word "consult" has, in Latin, a theological meaning incompatible with the use to which Newman put it in English. But Newman wished to do more than merely to justify his use of the word. He sought to take advantage of the occasion to make a plea for the recognition of the place of the laity in Catholic thought, a cause which had always been dear to him, for "in all times the laity have been the measure of Catholicism."[27]

Newman's article "On Consulting the Faithful in Matters of Doctrine"[28] began with an attempt to explain away the

---

[26] Acton to Newman, Corpus Christi 1859, Newman MSS.

[27] Quoted by Gasquet, "Introduction" to *Lord Acton and his Circle*, p. xxii.

[28] Newman, "On Consulting the Faithful in Matters of Doctrine," *Rambler*, n.s., I (July 1859), 198-230. The article was "communicated" rather than "editorial," the author signing himself "O" and referring to Newman in the third person. Newman did not reprint it in his collected works, although a portion was inserted as an appendix to the third edition of his *Arians of the Fourth Century* (London, 1871), pp. 454-72. The only complete republication of the article in English is in *Cross Currents*, II (Summer 1954), 69-97.

offensive word "consult," which, he said, might legitimately be used in popular English writing, even if such usage appeared unscientific in theology. While the opinion or judgment of the laity is not "consulted" in defining dogma, the fact of their belief is sought for, as a testimony of the apostolic tradition. The belief of the faithful, the *consensus fidelium*, is considered by the Church before it proceeds to a definition. "The body of the faithful is one of the witnesses to the fact of the tradition of revealed doctrine . . . their *consensus* through Christendom is the voice of the Infallible Church."[29] Newman cited several theological authorities for his doctrine of the *consensus fidelium*, particularly the Jesuit Perrone, who had been influential in securing the definition of the Immaculate Conception in 1854, when the Pope had made inquiries about the belief of the laity on the subject.

Newman might have ended the article at this point, having explained his remarks in the May issue; but he chose to go further and give an historical example of the principle of the *consensus fidelium*. In the fourth century, during the struggles with the Arians and semi-Arians, a majority of the bishops had been willing to compromise on questions of dogma, but the body of the laity and lower clergy had been firm in defence of orthodoxy. Newman argued that in those days "the divine tradition committed to the infallible Church was proclaimed and maintained far more by the faithful than by the Episcopate. . . . the body of the episcopate was unfaithful to its commission, while the body of the laity was faithful to its baptism." At various times Popes, bishops and councils had obscured or compromised revealed dogma, while the people had supported Athanasius and other defenders of orthodoxy—"a palmary example of a state of the Church during which, in order to know the tradition of the Apostles, we must have recourse to the faithful."[30] It was the *ecclesia discens*, the body of the faithful, rather than the *ecclesia docens*, the episcopate or "teaching Church," that saved the faith in this crisis: "there was a temporary suspense of the functions

---

[29] Newman, "Consulting the Faithful," p. 205.
[30] *Ibid.*, p. 213.

of the 'Ecclesia docens'. The body of Bishops failed in their confession of the faith."[31]

At the present time, Newman said, the bishops could be relied on to preserve the faith; but still it would be well to consider the sentiments of the laity. "I think certainly that the *Ecclesia docens* is more happy when she has such enthusiastic partisans about her ... than when she cuts off the faithful from the study of her divine doctrines ... and requires from them a *fides implicita* in her word, which in the educated classes will terminate in indifference, and in the poorer in superstition."[32]

Newman's article was more than a defence of his earlier remarks[33] or a continuation of the controversy over the role of the laity. It was an exposition of his doctrine of the development of dogma, the theory that the dogmatic formulation of the contents of revelation developed gradually in the course of the Church's history. This historical outlook did not involve any contradiction of the scholastic philosophy but it appeared strange and vaguely unorthodox to men trained only in the formal logic of the schools.[34] In demonstrating the role which the laity had played in the development of dogma in the fourth century, Newman had disregarded the traditional way of viewing Catholic doctrine. His historical statements could not be controverted, but his language gave much offence, especially his phrase "there was a temporary suspense of the functions of the *Ecclesia docens*." It appeared to many readers that Newman had asserted that the divine authority or *magisterium* of the Church had failed in the fourth century, that the teaching Church had been fallible, and that the episcopate in its corporate capacity had been guilty of heresy. Such assertions would have been heretical, but Newman had not in fact

[31] *Ibid.*, p. 214.
[32] *Ibid.*, p. 230.
[33] Newman later said that in the article "I retract the word 'consult'." Newman to Acton, 31 July 1859, Woodruff MSS.
[34] Acton (CUL Add. MSS. 4988) later made much of this apparent antagonism, as the explanation of the distrust with which Newman was regarded by many Catholics. See also Acton to Lady Blennerhasset, 14 April 1894 and 13 Sept. 1900, *Selections from the Correspondence of the First Lord Acton*, ed. J. N. Figgis and R. V. Laurence (London, 1917), pp. 77, 82.

made them. Nonetheless, his historical statements were interpreted in this theological sense, divorced from their original context. Monsignor Talbot, in Rome, thought that Newman's *consensus fidelium* meant the consensus of the laity in opposition to the clergy; this was "detestable" as it tended "to encourage the laity to dogmatize."[35] The theologians of Ushaw College, particularly Dr. Gillow, also criticized the article.

Newman was aware of some of these criticisms, though he underestimated their significance. "I know that the article . . . had annoyed the Ushaw people, but nothing more. . . . I have no misgiving about my real meaning as being sound dogmatically."[36] The reaction to the article did, however, confirm Newman in his decision to resign the editorship of the *Rambler*, which was quietly transferred to Acton in July.

The worst was yet to come. Bishop Brown of Newport, offended by the phrase "there was a temporary suspense of the functions of the *Ecclesia docens*," delated the article to the authorities at Rome on grounds of heresy.[37] Cardinal Barnabò, who as Prefect of Propaganda had oversight over English Catholic affairs, asked Ullathorne to bring the matter to Newman's attention and to secure from him an explanation of his article. Cardinal Wiseman, shocked by the denunciation, promised to do everything he could to help Newman clear himself. Wiseman attributed the denunciation to an old Catholic attempt to discredit the converts.

> There has been an unceasing undermining action going on against converts—the Oratory and Oblates [Manning's congregation] particularly, through letters to Barnabò. The *Rambler* opinions have been thrown into the scale. The late articles have given great pain, and Dr. Ullathorne is charged

[35] Talbot to Msgr. Patterson, 12 Nov. 1859, Westminster Archives.
[36] Newman to Ward, 20 Oct. 1859, cited in Wilfrid Ward, *William George Ward and the Catholic Revival* (London, 1912), p. 461. He also learned that his articles on "Ancient Saints" had somehow given offence. Newman to Acton, 5 July 1859, cited in Ward, *Life of Newman*, I, 634; also CUL Add. MS. 4988.
[37] The delation was made somewhat informally in letters to Mgr. Bedini of Propaganda and to Msgr. Talbot. Brown, who was generally suspicious of the converts, regarded Newman's words as positively heretical; some of the difficulty was caused by Brown's Latin translation which was not faithful to the sense of Newman's English. See Vincent F. Blehl, S.J., "Newman's Delation: Some Hitherto Unpublished Letters," *Dublin Review* (Winter, 1960-1), 296-305.

with a mission of peace to Dr. N[ewman]. It is wished he would write an Art[icle] explaining them rightly. I have spoken as well and soothingly as possible.[38]

Newman, when informed of the denunciation by Ullathorne, wrote to Wiseman on 19 January 1860, expressing his willingness to comply with Barnabò's wishes. Newman stated his readiness to explain his article, to accept and profess the dogmatic propositions which he had allegedly impugned, to explain his position in strict accordance with these propositions and to show that his words were consistent with them. He asked only that he be first informed as to the precise passages in his article which had given offence and the propositions which they had supposedly impugned.[39]

Newman's case was now in Wiseman's hands. He showed Newman's letter to Manning and Talbot, but absentmindedly laid it aside among his papers and never presented it to Propaganda. The only explanation for his failure is that he was seriously ill at the time, and on his recovery his mind was occupied with his quarrel with Errington, then in its final stages. Manning and Talbot also failed to inform Propaganda of Newman's letter. Newman thus lost the opportunity to justify himself, while Barnabò was left with the impression that he had refused to do so. Nothing further was done about the affair, and some months later Manning told Newman informally that it had been settled.[40]

But the matter had not been settled; it was merely allowed to drift. Barnabò believed that Newman had disobediently refused to explain his article. Despite Ullathorne's attempts to clarify the situation,[41] the affair had been so mishandled by Wiseman that, for seven years, Newman remained "under a cloud" at Rome, and the suspicion with which Rome regarded him was eventually communicated to the English Catholics. These seven years were the unhappiest period of

[38] Wiseman to Manning, St. Agnes' Day [21 Jan.] 1860, in "More Letters of Wiseman and Manning," *Dublin Review*, CLXXII (Jan. 1923), 121; originals in Manning MSS.

[39] Newman to Wiseman, 19 Jan. 1860, cited in Ward, *Life of Newman*, II, 171n. See also a letter of Ullathorne to Newman, 9 May 1867, *ibid.*, 171-2.

[40] Newman to Ambrose St. John, 7 May 1867, *ibid.*, 170.

[41] See Butler, *Life of Ullathorne*, I, 319-20. As late as 1861 Barnabò believed that Newman was still the editor of the *Rambler*.

Newman's life. Although he believed that the affair of his article had been hushed up, he was aware that it had left a bad impression and might be revived at any time. From 1861 to 1864, he published nothing, being unwilling to expose himself to further attacks. "How can I fight with such a chain on my arm?"[42]

Such were the effects of his brief editorship of the *Rambler* on Newman's career and reputation. For his failure he was himself partly to blame: he had gone farther than was necessary in explaining Stokes' articles and in defending his own remarks on consulting the laity. Yet it is questionable whether any amount of caution in language would have saved him from criticism, once it had become clear that in many matters of principle his own position was not far from that of Acton and Simpson. Newman, although never fully committed to the Liberal Catholic movement, had "entered the front lines of the battle with his *Essay on Consulting the Faithful* and when it backfired retreated to the rear as one of the first casualties."[43]

In obtaining Newman's withdrawal from the *Rambler*, the bishops had removed from the Liberal Catholics an influence which had always been exercised in the direction of caution and moderation. Manning foresaw the possible consequences:

> Now, there is another matter which gives me real anxiety, and that is the state of many of our ablest and most active laymen. There is a tone in matters of education, government, politics, and theology, which is free up to the boundary of legitimate freedom, if not beyond it, and they are men who deserve a good and fair treatment. Moreover, they cannot be put down or checked like boys. I am seriously afraid that we shall have a kind of De Lamennais School among some who, like him, were intellectual champions of the Church, and nothing will produce this so surely as snubbing. They could be easily directed by any one whom they thought fair or friendly, especially if, in the way Dr. N[ewman] has done, he grapples with their intellectual difficulties.[44]

[42] Newman to Miss E. Bowles, 19 May 1863, quoted by Ward, *Life of Newman*, I, 588. For the story of Newman's vindication in 1867, see *ibid.*, II, 165-179, 546-8.

[43] Bokenkotter, *Newman as an Historian*, p. 138.

[44] Manning to Talbot, 17 June 1859, quoted by Edmund Sheridan Purcell,

The bishops had chosen to snub the intellectual laymen and to remove Newman's direction of their efforts. With Newman "a great influence disappeared to which men of very divergent opinions look for guidance."[45] The position which Newman had held, as a bridge between Liberal Catholics and Ultramontanes, was no longer tenable.

Life of Cardinal Manning, Archbishop of Westminster, 2 vols. (New York, 1896), II, 140-1.
[45] Acton to Newman, June 1860, Newman MSS.

CHAPTER VII

RAMBLER, NEW SERIES, 1859-1860

NEWMAN'S editorship had accomplished one thing: it had preserved the *Rambler* for Acton and Simpson. Newman gave up the *Rambler* as quietly as he had taken it, making no public announcement of the fact.[1] He continued to serve as an unofficial adviser and occasional contributor. It was some time before his resignation became generally known, and meanwhile his association with the *Rambler* "made him for a time appear as the leader and guide of a Catholic opposition."[2]

This popular view was not justified by the facts. Newman's continued association with the *Rambler* was hedged about with conditions and uncertainties. His assistance was not as great as Acton and Simpson had expected: Newman did not wish to become too much involved in the conduct of the magazine. He would, upon request, advise on the admissibility of specific articles or letters; but he refused to act as a general censor, and returned unread the proofs which the printer sent him. Newman agreed to allow his name to be associated with the *Rambler* as one of its patrons, but only on condition that he would be joined by other eminent priests, Döllinger, the Belgian Jesuit de Buck (one of the editors of the *Acta Sanctorum*), and the French Oratorian Gratry. It was more important to secure their names than their assistance, and in fact only de Buck ever contributed any articles. Newman hoped that the use of their names would relieve him of some of the odium which the *Rambler* might incur and, by giving evidence that it was under priestly supervision, increase its acceptance by the Catholic public. It is doubtful to what extent these names would have served the latter

---

[1] "I have refused all along to recognize any change of Editors." Newman to Simpson, 29 June 1859, Newman MSS.
[2] CUL Add. MS. 4988.

purpose: Newman and Döllinger had already been delated to Rome, and de Buck and Gratry were eventually to be denounced. Newman was more interested in ensuring the existence of theological supervision than in the quality or repute of the supervisors. The *Rambler* had fallen into disfavour, Newman thought, because it had become involved in questions of theology; therefore he demanded, as another condition of his assistance, that it abstain from theology and theological allusions. It was for this reason that he welcomed the proposal to make the *Rambler* mainly political in its emphasis. Even though his own politics were rather different from Acton's,[3] Newman urged Acton to concentrate on political articles, so as to keep the *Rambler* away from theology. Acton was in full agreement on the necessity for the *Rambler* to become "secular"[4] and political in order to keep out of trouble.

Simpson recognized the necessity of avoiding theology, but he was not happy about it. He had been trained as a minister in the Church of England, and he had not abandoned his theological interests on his conversion. It was natural for him to write in theological terms; and when Acton insisted on his abstaining from theology "he felt as if he was beginning to write for the first time."[5] Simpson was to continue on the staff of the *Rambler* as a proprietor and contributor; but Newman was determined that he should not share in the editing of the magazine and made it a further condition of his support that Simpson should not be sub-editor. Simpson's name would prejudice conservative Catholics against the *Rambler*; more important, his style of writing was bound to give offence. Newman did not disapprove of Simpson's theology in itself, but rather of his habit of making theological allusions and writing on theology without revision or censorship by a priest. "I have the greatest opinion of Simpson as an able and honest man, and sincere gratitude for the way in which he has ever spoken of myself; but I deliberately thought

---

[3] For an interesting discussion of their differences, see Terence Kenny, *The Political Thought of John Henry Newman* (London, 1957), pp. 153-4. I cannot, however, subscribe to all of Mr. Kenny's conclusions.

[4] Acton to Newman, 23 June 1859, Newman MSS.

[5] Acton to Newman, 15 Aug. 1859, Newman MSS.

him unfitted for the office of conductor of a work which was necessarily exposed to such jealous criticism."[6] Simpson unselfishly accepted the necessity of a public self-effacement, but he had no intention of relinquishing his active role as a conductor of the *Rambler*. A nominal sub-editor might be appointed to satisfy Newman and the Catholic public, but he desired to do the work himself.[7]

Newman, however, insisted that the sub-editorship should not be a sinecure, but should be filled by some responsible person. Acton could not edit the *Rambler* without assistance. His responsibilities as a member of Parliament, his active social life, and his frequent travels on the Continent would prevent him from exercising continuous supervision over the conduct of the magazine. In fact, Acton left at the beginning of September 1859 on a Continental journey which was to keep him abroad until the beginning of 1860. If an active sub-editor could not be found, Simpson would necessarily be left in charge of the *Rambler*.

To avoid this, Newman busied himself in finding a sub-editor. His choice fell on a young convert, Thomas F. Wetherell. Wetherell, an Oxford graduate, had been converted in 1855; his conversion had cost him the loss of an inheritance and resulted in serious financial difficulties.[8] His friends had secured him, in 1856, a post as a clerk in the War Office. In 1857, he had performed a useful service to Cardinal Wiseman. The "corporate reunion" movement, a group of Anglicans and Catholics who discouraged individual conversions in favour of remaining in the Church of England to effect its reunion as a body with the Roman Catholic Church, had made use of some early writings of Wiseman in support of its position. Wiseman arranged for Wetherell to write an article in the *Dublin Review* to show that his writings did not support the "unionist" position and that it was

---

[6] Newman to Acton, 20 June 1859, cited in Wilfrid Ward, *Life of John Henry Cardinal Newman*, 2 vols. (London, 1912), I, 636.

[7] Simpson to Newman, 8 July 1859, Newman MSS. The nominal sub-editorship was suggested by Acton: Acton to Simpson, July 1859, Abbot Gasquet, *Lord Acton and his Circle* (London, 1906), p. 75.

[8] See Wiseman to Patterson, n.d. [1855], cited in Wilfrid Ward, *The Life and Times of Cardinal Wiseman*, 2 vols. (London, 1897), II, 191.

disapproved by the Church.[9] Newman was aware of
Wetherell's association with Wiseman and believed that this
would provide a safeguard against the *Rambler's* getting itself
into further trouble with the hierarchy. Newman knew, also,
that Wetherell's main interests were political: he had written,
in Newman's first issue of the *Rambler*, an article against the
policies of Napoleon III. Newman, himself favourable to
Napoleon, knew that Acton was opposed to him and thought
that this would make Wetherell a congenial sub-editor.
Wetherell had briefly acted as editor of the *Weekly Register*
during Henry Wilberforce's absence earlier in the year, but a
disagreement with Wilberforce left him free to join the
staff of the *Rambler*.

Actually, Newman knew rather little of Wetherell. At first
a Tory, Wetherell was a great admirer of Gladstone and had
followed him into the Liberal camp.[10] He supported the
cause of Italian nationalism and had proposed in 1857 to
dedicate to Gladstone a translation of Gualterio's *Gli ultimi
rivolgimenti italiani*.[11] In both home and foreign politics,
Wetherell's position was more advanced than that which
Acton was then ready to take. Newman was unaware that he
was introducing onto the staff of the *Rambler* one who might
lead it further into opposition to Rome; he was interested
only in keeping Simpson out of the sub-editorship by putting
Wetherell in.

Acton was willing to have Wetherell as sub-editor: "We
want him for show and we want him to help us."[12] Wetherell,
however, was reluctant to be associated with the *Rambler*,
about whose conductors he knew little and with whose
previous conduct he did not sympathize. He was afraid of
getting himself into a false position by associating with it:
"I should dislike to find myself involved in a sort of systematic
antagonism to established authorities and prejudices."[13]

[9] Thomas F. Wetherell, "Catholic Unity and English Parties," *Dublin
Review*, XLIII (Sept. 1857), 172-206. See also Ward, *Life of Wiseman*, II, 483.
The *Rambler* had taken a similar position.
[10] Acton to Gladstone, 1 Jan. 1867, BM Add. MS. 44093 ff. 55-8.
[11] Wetherell to Gladstone, 7 Sept. 1857, BM Add. MS. 44388 ff. 157-8. He
could not, however, secure a publisher.
[12] Acton to Simpson, 10 Aug. 1859, Downside MSS.
[13] Wetherell to Newman, 2 Aug. 1859, Newman MSS.

Wetherell stated that he would be reassured about the *Rambler* provided Newman retained a connection with it and could assure him that its policies would not be hostile to the general opinions of the English Catholics. Newman wrote back: "I think you will find yourself able to give your confidence to Sir John Acton, the editor. I am sure he wishes to keep clear of what is likely to give offence to Catholics, and has no wish to make the *Rambler* the organ of a party."[14] This removed Wetherell's doubts, and, after some further persuasion by Acton and Simpson, he agreed to become subeditor.

Acton stated the principles on which he would conduct the *Rambler* in a letter to Northcote: "peace among Catholics; for Protestants of good will a golden bridge; polemics to be directed chiefly against freethinkers."[15] The motto which he eventually selected for the *Rambler*, at Döllinger's suggestion, was *Seu vetus est verum diligo, sive novum* (I seek the truth, whether it is old or new). Acton accepted Newman's advice to emphasize politics, because it appeared to be a less sensitive subject than theology and also because there was much useful work to be done in that field: "The great point is to open men's minds—to educate them—and to make them logical. . . . If you make them think in politics, you will make them think in religion."[16] Acton's first issue, September 1859, was predominantly (though not exclusively) political. Newman was pleased with it: "The whole number seems to me a good one—and quite inoffensive—though there are persons who can make anything a difficulty."[17]

The most important article in the issue was one by Simpson on English parties, with reference to the political conduct of Catholics. While there was little to choose from between Liberals and Conservatives, Simpson said, the two parties were necessary to the parliamentary system and balanced

---

[14] Cited in Gasquet, "Introduction" to *Lord Acton and his Circle*, p. liii.
[15] Acton to Northcote, 28 Aug. 1859, cited in Gasquet, *Lord Acton and his Circle*, p. 85 n.
[16] Newman to Acton, 9 Aug. 1859, Woodruff MSS.
[17] Newman to Acton, 6 Sept. 1859, Newman MSS. It also received "a flamingly favourable notice" in the *Saturday Review*: Simpson to Acton, 4 Nov. 1859, Woodruff MSS.

and complemented each other. Catholics should not form a party of their own, but should join one of the existing parties. There were no essential political differences between Catholics and Protestants which warranted the formation of a distinctively Catholic party, and it was the duty and interest of Catholics to remove all religious passions from the political sphere: "The separation of religion from politics can do no harm to the Catholic mission in England."[18] Catholics sought only the redress of particular grievances and disabilities, and for this they should work through the existing parties rather than risk an outbreak of anti-Catholic prejudice by forming one of their own. These arguments of Simpson were so close to Acton's views that, when Acton was credited with the authorship of the article, he did not disclaim it.

Simpson's article had a special reference to the actual political situation of the English Catholics. Their traditional alliance with the Whigs had been broken, and it could not be restored because of the Italian policy of Palmerston and Gladstone, which menaced the existence of the States of the Church. The Catholics had for a time flirted with a policy of "independent opposition"; but this had become entangled in the snares of Irish politics and had collapsed by 1859. Attracted by the promises of Derby and Disraeli to redress Catholic grievances, Wiseman had given his support to the Tory government in 1858 and 1859. Catholic support helped the Tories win a majority of the Irish seats in 1859, but it did not help them in the election generally, as the Liberals won a narrow majority. Only three English Catholics were elected, two of them—Acton and Sir George Bowyer—for Irish constituencies. Nearly all the Catholic members, Irish and English, were nominal Whigs, but few had any genuine allegiance to the party. With parties so delicately balanced, there was much temptation for the Catholic members to organize themselves into an independent group, shifting their support from one party to the other as might best serve Catholic interests.

The danger to the Pope's Temporal Power after the

[18] Simpson, "The Theory of Party," *Rambler*, n. s., I (Sept. 1859), 347.

Italian War of 1859, and the support given by the government to Italian nationalism, affected the position of the Catholic members. Wiseman, still sympathetic with the Tories, encouraged Bowyer, his spokesman in Parliament, to embarrass the government at every opportunity. Acton opposed this policy. Although he distrusted Palmerston and Gladstone and opposed the government's Italian policies, he rejected the notion that Catholic members should oppose the Liberal government as a matter of general policy, merely because they disagreed with it on particular matters of Catholic interest. "It is a precarious experiment," the *Rambler* warned, "for Catholic members of Parliament to exhibit themselves professionally as mere Catholics instead of English or Irish statesmen and gentlemen."[19] Catholic members should be guided, not by the immediate interests of their Church, but by the political principles which they shared with all Englishmen.

Acton was not an especially prominent member of Parliament. Henry Wilberforce told Gladstone that "his religion and that alone excludes him from all chance of political distinction."[20] It was his religion which determined the course of Acton's Parliamentary career, despite his differences from the other Catholic members. He confined his activity to issues of Catholic interest: Catholic schools, the legalization of bequests for Catholic charities, and the provision of chaplains for Catholics in workhouses and prisons. Perhaps because of his connection with Granville, Acton preferred to negotiate privately for concessions rather than to make speeches and present petitions. For this reason he rarely spoke in Parliament—only three times in seven years.

When the session of Parliament ended in September 1859,

[19] *Ibid.*, 345.
[20] Wilberforce to Gladstone, 13 June 1859, BM Add. MS. 44391 f. 344. For a more detailed study of his Parliamentary activity, see James J. Auchmuty, "Acton as a Member of the House of Commons," *Bulletin of the Faculty of Arts*, Farouk I University [Alexandria, Egypt], V (1949), 31-46. A later article by Auchmuty, "Acton: The Youthful Parliamentarian," *Historical Studies, Australia and New Zealand*, IX (May 1960), 131-139, is critical of Acton's conduct.

J

Acton went abroad and was therefore unable to take part in the preparation of the November issue of the *Rambler*. The issue was to be edited by Wetherell, but he found himself overworked at the War Office, where he had charge of the Volunteer movement. The result was that Simpson was practically left in charge of the magazine, with only a very general supervision by Wetherell. On Acton's advice, Simpson had begun to write frequently for the *Weekly Register* and the *Correspondant*; but his main interest was still the *Rambler* and he had no hesitation in accepting the unexpected opportunity to edit it again. Newman was not told about this: "He so fears my want of prudence that I doubt if he would have his articles published in a number for which I alone was practically responsible."[21]

Simpson had prepared an article on toleration, which he admitted that Newman would probably dislike, because it would necessarily deal with controversial topics; this prompted Acton to some remarks about Simpson's "perverse ingenuity" and the "perilous ardour"[22] of his pen. However, when Acton saw Simpson's draft of the article, he liked it, and even wanted it to be published as "editorial," an honour which Simpson declined.[23] Newman had contributed an article on St. Chrysostom for the November issue, and when the proofs were sent to him in mid-October, he saw on the back of them the first page of Simpson's article on toleration. It contained a criticism of Pope Gregory XVI's condemnation of Lamennais in the encyclical *Mirari vos*, and seemed to revive the controversy about "the famous questions which he made so much excitement with, several years ago, in the article about the future state of Non-Catholics."[24] Newman did not object to the theology of the article itself: "I should myself hold your conclusions under correction of the Church —but in working them out I cannot say for certain that you

---

[21] Simpson to Acton, 27 Aug. 1859, Woodruff MSS.

[22] Acton to Simpson, 28 Aug. 1859, Gasquet, *Lord Acton and his Circle*, p. 84. Acton feared that Simpson would make some references to the possibility of an episcopal censorship over the *Rambler*.

[23] Simpson to Newman, 22 Oct. 1859, Newman MSS.

[24] Newman to Acton, 24 Oct. 1859, cited in Ward, *Life of Newman*, I, 506. The reference is to the letters on Original Sin in 1855-6.

have not run aground."[25] What he objected to was Simpson's writing on theological subjects at all, and especially his doing so without submitting to revision by a priest: "my immediate and critical difficulty with that article was . . . that, wherever theological, it had not been submitted to any censor. I have never made anything but the censorship a *sine qua non*, and that rule I have ever observed myself."[26]

Newman wrote to Simpson to ask if the article had been submitted to censorship. Simpson said it had not, and sent Newman the proofs. Newman declined to revise it himself, but wrote back: "If the new article on Toleration appears in the *Rambler* without a *bona fide* revision, I must ask you to be so good as not to publish mine."[27] He later explained that "I could not, consistently with my understanding with the Bishop or my responsibilities as head of the Oratory, let any writing of mine appear with a theological article which had not had revision."[28] This ultimatum placed Simpson in a difficult position. The November *Rambler* was already in print, and was to be distributed within the week; it would be difficult to recast it without the article on toleration. On the other hand, it was still considered necessary to keep Newman's goodwill for the *Rambler*, and Simpson had no wish to offend him. Simpson therefore suppressed his article on toleration.

Simpson was unhappy and somewhat embittered about the incident. He still revered Newman, and told him that "as proprietor of the *Rambler* . . . I had rather suppress it, than carry it on against your deliberate judgment, whatever pain it may give me to destroy it";[26] but he resented Newman's last-minute ultimatum to the *Rambler*. He insisted that the article was not theological, but rather dealt with the mixed area between theology and politics. "It seems to me that it is just on that debateable land between theology proper and life that we are called on to debate. If we may not, it would be better to give up all pretence of Catholic

---

[25] Quoted in Simpson to Acton, 4 Nov. 1859, Woodruff MSS.
[26] Newman to Acton, 20 Feb. 1860, Woodruff MSS.
[27] Newman to Simpson, 24 Oct. 1859, cited in Ward, *Life of Newman*, I, 506.
[28] Newman to Acton, 20 June 1860, Woodruff MSS.
[29] Simpson to Newman, 27 Oct. 1859, Newman MSS.

literature at once.''[30] It appeared to him that Newman's prohibition against theology was unlimited in extent: "If I am not to meddle with education because it is the question which the bishops decide upon, the same rule will apply to politics, for they are certainly prescribing opinions and actions. . . . Where is that *indifferent* common ground on which I may expatiate, when you deny altogether . . . the indifference of any secular functions at all?''[31] Even the cautious Wetherell had not supposed "that anything so obvious could possibly give offence.''[32] But Newman maintained that the article "would simply have dished us,''[33] and regretted that Simpson could not keep clear of theology.

Newman later said that he was "all along in a state almost of hostility to Simpson.''[34] It seemed to him that neither Acton nor Wetherell was fulfilling the duties of the editorship, and that, "after all that had been said, Simpson *was* Editor.''[35] Simpson assured Newman that he had only served in an emergency as Acton and Wetherell's delegate, and that such an occasion would not arise again; but Newman was suspicious of Simpson's intentions and believed that he was using Wetherell's name to conceal his own editorship. He wrote to Wetherell "to say that I could not let my name be longer associated with the Magazine, while its arrangements were so incomplete.''[36] From this time, although he continued to contribute to the *Rambler* and to advise its editors, Newman assumed a position external to it and acted more as a critic than as a collaborator.

When Simpson's article was withdrawn, it was necessary to replace it with another article, a review of John Stuart Mill's essay *On Liberty* by Thomas Arnold, Jr., the convert son of the headmaster of Rugby. Arnold's article also dealt

[30] Simpson to Acton, 4 Nov. 1859, Woodruff MSS.
[31] Simpson to Newman, 25 Oct. 1859, cited in Ward, *Life of Newman*, I, 508.
[32] Simpson to Newman, 22 Oct. 1859, Newman MSS.
[33] Newman to Acton, 24 Oct. 1859, Woodruff MSS.
[34] Newman to Canon Oakeley, 18 Aug. 1867, quoted by Edmund Sheridan Purcell, *Life of Cardinal Manning, Archbishop of Westminster,* 2 vols. (New York, 1896), II, 335. Newman's letter contains a number of extracts from his correspondence with Simpson, Wetherell and Acton, designated respectively as A, B and C.
[35] Newman to Acton, 20 June 1860, Woodruff MSS.
[36] *Ibid.*

with the subject of toleration, but its tone was political rather than theological. While he did not accept Mill's rationalist viewpoint, Arnold gave a general adherence to his criticism of persecution. In the existing state of European civilization, persecution would do more harm than good. "Once for all, coercion is an educational instrument which Western Europe has outgrown; and the citizens of her commonwealth are all bound to assume, and must be permitted to assume, the burdens and the dangers of freedom."[37] The article was safe theologically, since it dealt with actual political needs rather than with doctrine; and Newman let it pass.

Simpson's acceptance of Newman's demands did not result in any improvement of the relations between Newman and the *Rambler*. A new difficulty soon arose. The *Dublin Review*, still under the feeble editorship of Bagshawe, was in a precarious condition, and the rumour became current that it was about to be discontinued. Bagshawe wrote to *The Tablet* denying this. In his letter he referred to Newman as if he were still editor of the *Rambler*. Newman felt that he could no longer keep his resignation a secret, now that it had been openly stated that he was responsible for the *Rambler*. "I could not in honour or in duty, after I had given up the Editorship at the Bishop's wish, allow this to pass without contradiction. Not to have denied it, would have been to have implied the affirmative."[38] Newman therefore caused the following notice to be published in *The Tablet* of 16 November 1859:

> We are requested to state that the reference to Dr. Newman as Editor of the *Rambler*, contained in the recent letter of the respected Editor of the *Dublin Review*, which has appeared in our columns, is founded on a misconception, as Dr. Newman has no part in conducting or superintending that able periodical.[39]

The language of this notice was strictly correct, but it

---

[37] Thomas Arnold, Jr., "Mill on Liberty," *Rambler*, n.s., II (Nov. 1859), 75. The article was concluded in the March 1860 issue, pp. 376-385. It was signed "A," which has misled some into attributing it to Acton, but Simpson's letters to Newman establish it as Arnold's.

[38] Newman to Acton, 20 June 1860, Woodruff MSS.

[39] Cited in Ward, *Life of Newman*, I, 511.

implied, what was not the case, that Newman had completely dissociated himself from the *Rambler*. The result was that the circulation of the *Rambler*, which had increased in previous months, fell by forty per cent between November and January. Acton, on the Continent, was unable to believe that the notice had been authorized by Newman, as it seemed to be in contradiction to the arrangements that he had made. When he later learned that Newman had authorized the statement, Acton was very indignant.[40]

Acton was detained in Germany by his mother's illness there, and Wetherell was still busy at the War Office; therefore Simpson had to undertake the January 1860 issue of the *Rambler*, despite Newman's warnings and his own reluctance to place himself again in an awkward position. Simpson kept clear of theology in the issue, which was largely political. Acton contributed two articles. One of these contained Acton's first public expression of opinion on the question of the Temporal Power of the Pope. Recent events in Italy had placed the Temporal Power in serious danger, and Catholics in all countries were called upon to take a position in favour of preserving it.

Acton also called upon Catholics to support the Temporal Power; but he did so with a difference. He regretted that many Catholics should set their religious doctrines at variance with their political ideals, and proclaimed himself an adherent of that "Ultramontanism" which "signifies the conscious harmony of all our opinions with our belief; the habit of viewing profane things through the medium of religion, and of judging them by the standard which it supplies."[41] It was unfortunate that many Catholics failed to support the Temporal Power for political reasons; but equally unfortunate was the policy of those Catholics who supported it merely because of their religion:

> This line of thought is not only false, but also eminently injudicious and unsafe. It narrows the ground on which the cause can be defended. . . . It would be an act of the greatest

[40] Acton to Newman, June 1860, Newman MSS.
[41] Acton, "The Roman Question," *Rambler*, n.s., II (Jan. 1860), 139.

injustice, to deny the subjects of the Pope, on account of a religious interest which they do not consider paramount, a right which is acknowledged to belong to the rest of mankind. It is invidious to assert that the subjects of the Pope must be necessarily less free than those of other princes. Can any spiritual necessity be an excuse for so gross a political wrong? On the contrary, the cause of the temporal power is the cause of other religions and of all other states, and it is in the interest of them all to preserve it.[42]

The Temporal Power must be defended on the same political grounds on which all other governments are defended, for "the revolution" which menaced it ultimately menaced all lawful authority. The essential question was not whether the Pope governed Rome well or badly, but whether he should continue to govern Rome at all; therefore Acton did not attempt either to conceal or to justify the defects of the Pope's government. The Temporal Power was founded on the sacred rights of property and sovereignty. It had arisen under historical conditions which made those rights the only security for the liberty of the Church, and was justified by the necessity of preserving the independence of the Pope and the freedom of the clergy. But "it is not absolutely essential to the nature and ends of the Church; it has its source in causes which are external to her. . . . It is not so much an advantage as a necessity, not so much desirable as inevitable."[43]

The politics of this article, as Acton admitted, were rather "antiquatedly conservative" and Burkeian: "I am afraid I am a partisan of sinking ships, and I know none more ostensibly sinking just now than St. Peter's." But the Temporal Power could not be defended on religious grounds, for the argument from religion would raise up more enemies than friends in Protestant England and was unsound in principle: "We cannot absolutely identify an accident with the essence of the Church, and if all at once the Temporal Power goes, one would look foolish." Therefore it must be defended on political grounds, for the sake of the states which would be menaced by "the revolution" once it had

[42] *Ibid.*, 140.
[43] *Ibid.*, 149.

overthrown the government of the Pope. "But who has political instruction enough to comprehend this?"[44]

The English Catholics, it soon appeared, had not. The only argument that appealed to them was the religious one. They had no patience with a complex argument which treated the Temporal Power as a political necessity rather than as a religious essential, envisioned the possibility of its termination and spoke of the denial of self-determination to the Roman people as a gross "political wrong." In political as in intellectual matters, Acton was out of harmony with the English Catholics.

For different reasons, the article on the Roman question also displeased Wetherell. Wetherell's support of Italian nationalism did not involve direct opposition to the Temporal Power, which he had called "the rock on which great principles of social wrong have split."[45] But he could not agree with Acton's Burkeian conservatism. He thought that Acton had maintained the abstract principles of legitimism, denying the propriety of any change of government and asserting that the Temporal Power possessed a sacred quality as well as a merely political justification. He had seen little of Acton since he accepted the sub-editorship, and he was not fully acquainted with Acton's views. "In consequence of this, and of the obscurity of what he wrote in the January number, he understood him to be supporting the Temporal Power to a degree to which he was not prepared to go with him. Wetherell consequently thought it best, as his official work left him no time for discussion, to withdraw from editorial responsibility."[46] He submitted his resignation to Acton.

Acton wished to retain Wetherell as sub-editor, but for several months Wetherell refused to withdraw his resignation. In July of 1860, the misunderstanding was finally

[44] Acton to Simpson, 7 Dec. 1859, Gasquet, *Lord Acton and his Circle*, pp. 113-4. Simpson had induced Acton to withdraw an earlier article on the subject, prepared for the September issue; Acton at that time was still unsure of his position. Acton to Döllinger, 29 Sept. 1859, Woodruff MSS.

[45] "Sigma" [Wetherell], "Napoleonism and its Apostolate," *Rambler*, n.s., II (Nov. 1859), 86.

[46] Gasquet, *Lord Acton and his Circle*, p. 115n. Gasquet consulted Wetherell before writing, and this passage may have been suggested by Wetherell.

cleared up: "as it turned out that he had not meant what I thought he had," said Wetherell later, "and that we were substantially in agreement on the subject, I willingly withdrew my withdrawal, and all went on as before."[47] But in fact all did not go on as before. Wetherell required Acton "to give up the right of publishing all his own opinions editorially,"[48] that is, to place himself in the position of an ordinary contributor with regard to his political articles, unless Wetherell approved them. Wetherell seems to have regarded himself not as a sub-editor but as joint editor "with a full equal share of authority, responsibility and management."[49] There was a source of further misunderstanding here, for neither Acton nor Simpson acknowledged Wetherell's assumed status; but the difficulty did not arise for some time, as Wetherell soon learned to get along with Acton. Meanwhile Acton, who had returned to England, had edited three issues without him in the first half of 1860.

These first months of 1860 were an unhappy period for Acton. His mother died, after a long illness, in March; and personal difficulties were superimposed upon his other problems as editor and politician. The result was a transient mood of bitterness which is reflected in his correspondence with Newman.

In February, Acton went to the Birmingham Oratory to remonstrate with Newman for his apparent abandonment of the *Rambler*. Newman explained that he had not renounced his connection with it and differed from Simpson on the question of prudence rather than of principle. But other things were troubling Newman, Acton found. "I have never heard him speak openly on affairs as in the bitterness of his spirit he spoke during the half-hour I was with him, and his language was—more vehement indeed—but in substance the same that I have been hearing and imbibing these nine

[47] Note by Wetherell, Downside MSS.
[48] Wetherell to Newman, 9 Aug. 1860, Newman MSS.
[49] Note by Wetherell, Downside MSS. Wetherell says that he had always been "co-Editor" and had never accepted any other position. Yet in the letter to Newman of 9 Aug. 1860, Wetherell stated that he has "again taken the Subeditorship": Newman MSS.

years from Döllinger."[50] The occasion for Newman's bitterness appears to have been the news which he had just received that his article "On Consulting the Faithful" had been delated to Rome. Because of this, he decided to suspend his contributions to the *Rambler* for a while.

Acton, convinced that the *Rambler* could not survive without Newman's assistance, talked of giving it up altogether. Newman urged him to carry it on, but to "eschew absolutely the treatment of theological questions and the theological treatment of questions."[51] This Acton agreed to do, "but without any hope."[52] He sought to reconcile Simpson to Newman and to obtain from Simpson "the comfortable assurance that in an emergency which may disable me for a time, a number can be brought out without overworking you."[53] Acton also proposed to advance two hundred pounds to the funds of the *Rambler*, and an additional ten pounds per number, to pay contributors. But he was still unhappy about the situation. He had to face the continued opposition of the *Dublin Review* and *The Tablet*, and even the *Weekly Register*, which he had helped to revive and for which Simpson wrote regularly, failed to support the *Rambler*. The theologians whom Newman had proposed as censors for the *Rambler* were of no help. Acton had to reject a letter by de Buck for theological reasons, and Gratry offered an unacceptable paper on the difference between "Papism" and "Catholicism" of which Gratry himself said that if it were published with his name he should immediately be obliged to leave the Oratory. If even its chosen theologians could not be relied upon, the *Rambler* would have to avoid all discussion of the most important intellectual questions of the day. "This was a losing game,"[54] Acton decided.

By June he was again writing despondent letters to Newman. Newman pointed out that his chief complaint against the *Rambler* had not been removed, for Simpson was

---

[50] Acton to Simpson, 11 Feb. 1860, Gasquet, *Lord Acton and his Circle*, p. 117.
[51] *Ibid.*, p. 118.
[52] Acton to Newman, 29 June 1860, cited in Ward, *Life of Newman*, I, 510.
[53] Acton to Simpson, 11 Feb. 1860, Gasquet, *Lord Acton and his Circle*, p. 119.
[54] Acton to Newman, 29 June 1860, cited in Ward, *Life of Newman*, I, 570.

still doing the work of the editorship. "I am exceedingly desirous for the success of the *Rambler*, and to contribute to it, but I cannot . . . give my name to it (though for its talent and information it would do credit to anyone to be connected with it) unless it had a responsible Editor, and the countenance of such theologians as I have mentioned."[55] Acton argued that he had done all that Newman required, and it still had not availed to keep the *Rambler* out of difficulty.

> I beg of you, remembering the difficulties you encountered, to consider my position, in the midst of a hostile and illiterate episcopate, an ignorant clergy, a prejudiced and divided laity, with the cliques at Brompton, York Place, Ushaw always on the watch, obliged to sit in judgment on the theology of the men you selected to be our patrons, deserted by the assistant whom you obtained for me, with no auxiliary but Simpson.[56]

This mood of bitterness did not last. Newman resumed his contributions to the *Rambler*, and Wetherell agreed to come back to its staff. But the high spirits with which Acton had begun his work on the *Rambler* were gone. The editorship of the *Rambler* had become a more serious task than Acton had expected.

[55] Newman to Acton, 20 June 1860, *ibid.*, 636.
[56] Acton to Newman, 29 June 1860, cited in David Mathew, *Acton: The Formative Years* (London, 1946), p. 122. "Brompton" was Faber's London Oratory; "York Place" was the residence of Cardinal Wiseman.

Chapter VIII

CATHOLIC POLITICS AND CATHOLIC INTELLECT, 1860-1861

THE Liberal Catholics had to maintain the struggle for their principles on two fronts. In politics, the Temporal Power of the Papacy became the preoccupation of Catholics throughout Europe. At the same time, new developments in science and scholarship demanded an intelligent Catholic response. The Liberal Catholics attempted to meet both challenges, but their efforts to do so brought them into conflict with important elements in English Catholicism.

The 1860s were, for the Catholic Church, years of crisis. Italian nationalism threatened to put an end to the rule of the Pope as a temporal sovereign in Italy. Pius IX, refusing to distinguish his temporal from his spiritual authority, called upon the resources of the Church in the defence of his political power. Catholics in all countries were expected to demonstrate their sympathy for the beleaguered Pontiff and to exercise their political influence to secure the preservation of his sovereignty. The Temporal Power, however, became a party question within the Catholic Church itself. The division of parties on political issues paralleled that on intellectual issues. The extreme advocates of the prerogatives of the Papacy, the new Ultramontanes, were the dominant party. Convinced of the absolute opposition between the principles of Catholicism and the ways of the modern world, they fostered a spirit of withdrawal from modern society and thought. Both in politics and in philosophy, the leading principles of this Catholic reaction were opposed to the tenets of Liberal Catholicism.

In England the new Ultramontanism received the sanction of Cardinal Wiseman, who sought to employ the political resources of English Catholicism against a government which favoured the Italian revolution. Wiseman was less affected by the intellectual intolerance of the Ultramontanes; but in the 1860s he was enfeebled by illness and allowed the leadership of English Catholicism to pass into the hands of more extreme men, notably Manning, Provost of Westminster. Manning had earlier devoted his energies to the struggle against the recalcitrant old Catholics led by Errington; by 1860 Errington had been defeated and removed, and Manning took up the cause of the Temporal Power. His sermons on the Temporal Power were regarded as extreme even by his own party and were delated to the Index; but he possessed a powerful friend at Rome in Monsignor Talbot, a Papal Chamberlain, and he was favourably regarded by the Pope himself. Manning was prepared to make the Temporal Power a dogma of faith; to him it was "providentially the centre of the Christian order of Europe."[1] He had the enthusiastic support of Father Faber of the London Oratory, who emphasized the emotional side of Ultramontanism, personal devotion to the Pope and imitation of Roman practices. The intellectual leader of the Ultramontanes was W. G. Ward, who urged that all problems be solved by recourse to Rome and that every intimation of the will of the Pope was as binding on Catholics as dogma itself. Ward's too logical mind was delighted by the most absolute and extravagant statements. In the tense atmosphere of the 1860s there was little room for balanced views. The Church was regarded as being in a "state of siege," and the Ultramontanes sought to foster the mentality of inflexible resistance appropriate to a besieged army. This attitude pressed hard upon those who held that the Church should emerge from its isolation into freer contact with the modern world, and it was particularly uncomfortable for Newman and Acton.

Newman concealed his thoughts from the public, but he was evidently cool towards the Temporal Power and declined to speak out in favour of it or to give any assistance to its supporters. He opposed the attempt to make the Temporal Power a doctrine of faith or a test of Catholic loyalty. This

[1] Manning to Gladstone, 24 October 1864, BM Add. MS. 44248 ff. 222-7.

was sufficient to cause the Ultramontanes to brand him as disloyal; and the question of the Temporal Power completed what the article on "Consulting the Faithful" had begun, in rendering Newman an object of suspicion among Catholics. In private, Newman went still further; he had a distaste for the Temporal Power as it affected the spiritual life of the Church.

> The Temporal Power had according to him a distinct tendency to strengthen the spirit of the world in the Church. The T[emporal] P[ower] was not a thing either to be attacked absolutely or to be defended absolutely. It was perhaps according to him productive in our time of more harm than good; at all events it was not to be defended in the wild way Manning defended it.[2]

But Newman refused to speak out, partly from timidity and partly out of a personal reverence for the Pope. The public never realized how great was his dislike of the Temporal Power.[3] In 1860 Newman's aversion to it was greater than Acton's.

Acton was convinced of the necessity of some temporal sovereignty for the Pope as a safeguard for his liberty of action and the independence of the Church. But he acknowledged the faults of the Papal government of Rome and had no hope for the success of any reforms. More important, he had come to believe that the Temporal Power was in fact a hopeless cause. As early as 1857, Döllinger had spoken to Acton of the certainty of the fall of the Temporal Power. Acton himself had observed that if the Temporal Power should ever come to be considered an impediment to the spiritual mission of the Church "then the last hour of the papal state would have sounded. The Church was 700 years without a territory, and might be so again for 7000 years.

---

[2] Sir Rowland Blennerhasset to Acton, 16 Oct. 1890, quoted in CUL Add. MS. 4989. For Newman's own re-statement of his views, see his memorandum, 22 May 1882, in Wilfrid Ward, *The Life of John Henry Cardinal Newman*, 2 vols. (London, 1912), I, 521.

[3] Terence Kenny, *The Political Thought of John Henry Newman* (London, 1957), p. 26. See also Acton to Gladstone, 1 Feb. 1892 and 28 Jan. 1895, in *Selections from the Correspondence of the first Lord Acton*, ed. J. N. Figgis and R. V. Laurence (London, 1917), pp. 74, 80. For the reasons for his silence, see Newman to Acton, 7 June 1861, *ibid.*, pp. 31-3.

As things now are it cannot be, but such a state of things might be possible."[4] At the beginning of 1860 Acton still defended the Temporal Power, but without enthusiasm and without hope.

Acton's writings in the *Rambler* showed the limitations of his zeal for the Papal cause. He called history to its defence and in a series of articles sought to justify the political conduct of the Popes during the Middle Ages.[5] But history was an uncertain ally: "Every record older than the thirteenth century which could be quoted as an authority for the full territorial rights of the Holy See is almost certainly spurious, whilst all those documents by which those rights were actually created have been lost." Acton admitted that the Papal States were badly governed. The only plea he raised on behalf of the Temporal Power was its necessity, "the conservation of the independence of the Holy See through the integrity of its territory."[6]

As a member of Parliament Acton showed that he would not sacrifice his political principles to the cause of the Temporal Power. "I find everybody saying that the interests of religion must override the precepts of politics, which seems to me a contradiction."[7] He was not a confirmed Liberal, but he would not oppose a Liberal ministry whose principles were generally sound merely because of a disagreement with its Italian policy. Neither would he conceal the faults of the Papal government or the weakness of its advocates. The Catholic members of Parliament were anxious to make public information which would reflect favourably on the Papal government of Rome, and thought that a certain despatch of Mr. (later Lord) Lyons, a former British diplomatic agent at Rome, would support their case. Acton, however, asked that not only this particular document, but all of Lyons' despatches, be made public.

[4] CUL Add. MS. 5751. See also J[ohann] Friedrich, *Ignaz von Döllinger*, 3 vols. (München, 1901), III, 184-5.
[5] Acton, "The Political System of the Popes," *Rambler*, n. s., II (Jan. 1860), 154-165; III (May 1860), 27-38; IV (Jan. 1861), 183-193. Reprinted in *Essays on Church and State*, ed. Douglas Woodruff (London, 1952), pp. 123-158.
[6] Acton, "The States of the Church," *Essays on Church and State*, pp. 86-7. Reprinted from the *Rambler*, n.s., II (March 1860), 291-323.
[7] Acton to Simpson, July 1860, Downside MSS.

I ask for it not because I expect that it will be favourable, but because I hope that it will be authentic. It is impossible at present for any impartial persons to distinguish truth from falsehood in the midst of so much conflicting testimony and of so many conflicting passions. We have plenty of unscrupulous attacks on one side, and a good deal of not very discriminating eulogy on the other. . . . All Catholics are, or ought to be, anxious to know all the truth concerning the accusations brought against the Roman Government. We do not wish to be open to the accusation that we are arguing from imperfect knowledge, or defending that which does not deserve to be defended. We do not wish that it should be believed that the Catholics of this country . . . are indifferent to the political welfare of their fellow-Catholics abroad, or that we are blinded by attachment to our religion to facts by which, if they are true, that religion is injured and disgraced.[8]

Acton had turned an attempt to embarrass the Government into an occasion for criticism of the Catholics themselves for their undiscriminating advocacy of the Temporal Power. Sir George Bowyer, the leading Catholic spokesman in the House, was caught by surprise. "The fun was that Bowyer, expecting something in his line, began cheering aloud at first, but pulled a very long face before I had done."[9] Acton rather enjoyed the situation, and compared himself to De Decker, the Belgian Liberal Catholic statesman: "An enemy said of De Decker that he is a double-barrelled gun, one barrel to shoot at his enemies, the other at his friends. *Rambler, tout pur.*"[10]

The Lyons despatches were made public in July. Acton found them satisfactory, "confirming, thank God, all I said."[11] While Lyons criticized the efficiency of the Roman administration, he gave no support to the more extreme charges against it and showed that reforms had been made impossible by the Italian liberals. If Acton had little sympathy for the Papal administration, he had none at all for the Italian liberals, holding that their nationalism was opposed

---

[8] *Hansard's Parliamentary Debates*, 3rd ser., CLVIII (1860), 679-681.
[9] Acton to Simpson, June 1860, Abbot Gasquet, *Lord Acton and his Circle* (London, 1906), p. 139.
[10] Acton to Simpson, July 1860, *ibid.*, p. 145.
[11] Acton to Simpson, 9 July 1860, *ibid.*, p. 140.

to true liberty. Some of the other Catholic members, however, were disturbed by Lyons' criticism of the Roman government.[12]

Acton was still closely associated with the other Catholic members. He was on particularly good terms with certain Catholics who were supporters of the Liberal Government, notably William Monsell (later Lord Emly), an Irish gentleman educated at Oxford and converted in 1850, who was a friend of Newman. Acton was unconsciously drawing closer to the Liberal party. On Catholic issues, however, the Catholic members operated independently of party affiliation. In August, during a debate on Italy, the Whig Catholics rose in a body and left the House in protest against the party's Italian policy. The Roman question had already caused a breach between Acton and his stepfather Granville, a member of the Government; and Granville complained that "Johnny Acton has thrown us over."[13]

Acton was still maturing his position on the Temporal Power. In February, he had taken pains to avoid appearing at a great Catholic rally in Birmingham, in order not to be committed to the resolution voted by the meeting in favour of the Temporal Power.[14] He was aware that his position on so difficult a subject was liable to misrepresentation, and secretly wrote an article for the *Weekly Register* to explain his speech on the Lyons despatches. Still convinced of the necessity of the Papal sovereignty, he had come to believe that it was doomed to fall. "The inquiry seems to me nearly superfluous, as I cannot believe that the Temporal Government has any future before it."[15] It was necessary above all for Catholics not to be committed to an untenable position. To Simpson, who had become the regular writer on foreign affairs for the *Weekly Register*, Acton sent notes on the

[12] See E. E. Y. Hales, *Pio Nono: A Study in European politics and religion in the nineteenth century* (London, 1954), pp. 343-4.

[13] Granville to Lord Canning, 4 Aug. 1860, cited in Lord Edmond Fitzmaurice, *The Life of Granville George Leveson Gower, Second Earl Granville*, 2 vols. (London, 1905), I, 387. See Gertrude Himmelfarb, *Lord Acton: A Study in Conscience and Politics* (Chicago, 1952), pp. 91-2.

[14] Acton to Simpson, "Friday" [prob. Feb. 1860], Gasquet, *Lord Acton and his Circle*, p. 115.

[15] Acton to Simpson, 12 July 1860, *ibid.*, pp. 147-8.

K

Roman question, but he warned: "don't speak decisively on the character or future of the Roman Government."[16]

Simpson wrote on "The Roman Question" in an appropriately indecisive fashion in the November *Rambler*: "The events of the day seem to render it probable that the complication may be ultimately solved by the development of some new arrangement of the temporal guarantees of the spiritual liberty of the Pope."[17] The *status quo* should be supported as long as possible, but it was likely to fall. The revolution which menaced Rome ultimately threatened the entire political system of Europe; but if the Temporal Power was to be preserved by French troops in Rome, there was an equal danger of the loss of the liberty of the Church by means of French domination. Simpson concluded that "no Catholic can be justified in consenting to the spoliation of the Papal States; yet every believer will be sure that, in any case, if a new system should arise on the ruins of the present one, it will be better adapted than its predecessor to secure the spiritual independence of the Church amid the complications of the coming centuries."[18] The Liberal Catholics were moving hesitantly towards a position of criticism of the Temporal Power. A review written by Acton spoke of the Italian revolution having been provoked by the "orthodox party" and its "too exclusive reliance on foreign bayonets."[19] In the *Weekly Register* Simpson was taking a more critical line, somewhat to the distress of the timid Wilberforce.[20]

The decisive change in Acton's attitude came in December 1860, after a meeting with Döllinger in Munich. Döllinger talked of the fall of the Temporal Power as a certainty, and Acton adopted his views. "We must certainly be prepared to see the Pope leave Rome and take refuge in Spain or Germany. . . . a restoration of the old regime and of the position of the Pope as a ruler of millions is, I am persuaded, out of the question." Döllinger was hopeful that the removal

[16] Acton to Simpson, 9 July 1860, *ibid.*, p. 141.
[17] Simpson, "The Roman Question," *Rambler*, n.s., IV (Nov. 1860), 13.
[18] *Ibid.*, p. 27.
[19] *Rambler*, n.s., IV (Nov. 1860), 127.
[20] Acton to Simpson, 9 Jan. 1861, Downside MSS.

of the Pope to Germany would lead to a reunion of German Protestants with the Church and at the same time effect a needed change in Catholicism itself: "the Romanism of the Church was destroyed for good."[21] Yet Döllinger did not oppose the Temporal Power itself, and he rejected Cavour's dream of a "free Church in a free State": he was more liberal in religion than in politics. Döllinger and Acton looked forward to the impending fall of the Temporal Power, not for the sake of the State, but for the sake of the Church which would thereby be purged of its greatest defects.

On his return to England, Acton found that his fellow Catholic members of Parliament were still determined to uphold the Temporal Power and make it a public issue between themselves and the Government. Acton, convinced of the hopelessness of the cause, thought this bad policy. Fearing that the too evident commitment of the English Catholics to the Papal cause would provoke a Protestant reaction, he meditated a speech on the Temporal Power "to save us, as far as I can, from a no popery excitement."[22] He eventually decided not to deliver the speech, feeling that it would have no useful effect;[23] but the incident showed clearly the extent of his political differences with his fellow Catholics.

The years from 1859 to 1861, during which the English Catholics were occupied with the crisis of the Temporal Power and their own internal dissensions, were notable in English intellectual history for the outbreak of a conflict between the forces of science and religion. Darwin's *Origin of Species* in 1859 and *Essays and Reviews* in 1860 signified that the conventional formulations and interpretations of the Christian revelation were to be challenged by the new

[21] Acton to Simpson, 6 Dec. 1860, Gasquet, *Lord Acton and his Circle*, pp. 153, 155.

[22] Acton to Simpson, 14 Feb. 1861, Downside MSS. Acton feared that the Catholics would join with the Tories to defeat the Liberal government and that the ensuing election would be fought on the Catholic issue. Acton to Döllinger, 25 Feb. 1861, Woodruff MSS.

[23] Acton to Simpson, March 1861, Gasquet, *Lord Acton and his Circle*, p. 172: "I will not waste powder, make enemies and get into so much trouble without an object and an occasion."

theories of natural science and Biblical criticism. While outraged Protestants defended the citadel of Biblical literalism,
the English Catholics took little part in the struggle. This
was largely due to their preoccupation with other concerns
and to an ignorance of science and scholarship which prevented them from formulating a response to the new
challenge. Although Wiseman, in his younger days, had
been a Biblical scholar of some repute, the dominant intellectual force among the English Catholics in the 1860s was
the Ultramontanism of Ward and Faber, which emphasized
inward sanctification rather than scientific investigation.

Acton recognized the desirability of a greater spirituality
among the English Catholics, but he regarded Ward's
exclusive asceticism as a dangerous remedy.

> The idea of cultivating devotion on a new scale without
> promoting at the same time philosophy and literature is in
> reality very dangerous. Rather less devotion than more so
> long as there is so little reasoning and learning. Piety is a
> respectable and impenetrable cloak for all kinds of errors and
> false tendencies.[24]

Asceticism without knowledge was dangerous to belief: it led
to a "one-sided view of things, ignorance of the world,
ignorance of proportion and perspective in things purely
religious, ignorance of the borderland where religion touches
the outer world of life and ideas. There have been heresies
of false asceticism just as there have of false speculation."[25]
Catholics should be prepared to respond to the intellectual
challenges of the age with the best weapons of the day, to
meet scientific objections by a more perfect science and
critical scholarship by a more acute criticism.

This required an improvement in the education of
Catholics. Acton desired that a Catholic university should be
founded in England, under the guidance of Newman.[26] For
this reason he supported the Oratory School founded by

---

[24] Acton to Simpson, 8 March 1859, quoted by [Dom] A[elred] Watkin and
Herbert Butterfield, "Gasquet and the Acton-Simpson Correspondence,"
Cambridge Historical Journal, X (1950), 82.
[25] Acton to Simpson, 23 Jan. 1861, Gasquet, *Lord Acton and his Circle*, p. 167.
[26] Newman at first entered into this idea, regarding it "as the last great work
of his life": Acton to Döllinger, 10 Feb. 1860, Woodruff MSS.

Newman at Edgbaston, which trained lay students up to the university level; he felt that it would inevitably lead to a demand for university education.[27] This did not materialize; but the Edgbaston School, the first of the English Catholic public schools, represents the most lasting institutional accomplishment of the Liberal Catholic movement in England.

To a large extent Newman shared Acton's views. He was conscious of the urgency of preparing men's minds for the fundamental questions being posed by scientists and scholars. Newman believed that Catholics need not fear the discoveries or theories of science: "If anything seems to be proved . . . in contradiction to the dogmas of faith, that point will eventually turn out, first, *not* to be proved, or secondly, not *contradictory*, or thirdly, not contradictory to anything *really revealed*, but to something which has been confused with revelation."[28] Therefore Catholics could be fearless in their use of the scientific method, recognizing the necessity of free discussion and debate in the scientific process. This was precisely the spirit of the *Rambler;* but Newman was too cautious to give his full support to the Liberal Catholics. He feared that their freedom of inquiry and statement might raise doubts in the minds of pious Catholics unprepared for critical thought, or that some rash speculation might step beyond the limits of orthodoxy. In the *Rambler's* attempt to formulate a Catholic response to natural science and Biblical scholarship, Newman was of little assistance.

That task was largely left to Simpson. Simpson's review of Darwin's *Origin of Species* was written in an "exceptionally impartial spirit for the time."[29] He questioned Darwin's

[27] Acton to Döllinger, 20 Jan. 1861, Woodruff MSS; Acton to Simpson, 1 Jan. 1862, Downside MSS. Acton had expressed these hopes when the school was being planned in 1858. He placed one of his Italian cousins, Paolo Beccadelli, as a student at the school.

[28] Quoted in Ward, *Life of Newman,* I, 407.

[29] Charlotte Lady Blennerhasset, "The Late Lord Acton," *Edinburgh Review,* CXCVII (April 1903), 505. Simpson's article should be compared with Canon W. Morris, "Darwin on the Origin of Species," *Dublin Review,* XCV (May 1860), 50-81. Morris praised Darwin's research and accepted the doctrine of the mutability of species; he rejected as absurd the application of

conclusions on scientific grounds, arguing that Darwin's facts did not justify the treatment of evolution as anything but an unproved hypothesis. Here Simpson showed himself dependent upon the erroneous theories of anti-evolutionary scientists such as the paleontologist Owen.[30] Simpson's criticism, however, was directed equally against those who rejected Darwin's work in its entirety. Catholics, he said, may appreciate the facts gathered by Darwin and might even regard his theory as a useful hypothesis. There was no incompatibility between creation and natural law. "Creation is not a miraculous interference with the laws of nature, but the very institution of those laws. . . . The law of creation is no exceptional rule that acts by fits and starts, by catastrophes and miraculous interpositions; but an equable ever-present force."[31] Darwin's infidelity was to be met by argument, not by ignorance. Catholics ought not to attempt to suppress the discussion:

> There is a tendency in all religious bodies towards intolerance in matters of opinion, towards an unwillingness to allow the few to hold sentiments which differ from those of the many; there is a tendency to force all thought into the mold of the average mediocrity. There could be no surer way of offending men of original views, or of tempting them to degrade opinions that are at first only novel or paradoxical into real and conscious attacks upon religion.[32]

Simpson had succeeded in formulating at least a temporary Catholic response to Darwin; at the same time he had scored a hit upon the Catholic opponents of the *Rambler* with his argument for free debate. The argument was carried one stage further in May 1860, with an article by the Baron d'Eckstein on "The Church and Science." Eckstein urged religious men not to despise science, which shows the great-

the doctrine to the descent of man, but thought that this was no essential part of Darwin's argument.

[30] Review of Owen's *Paleontology*, *Rambler*, n.s., III (May 1860), 128: "We confirm by the high authority of Mr. Owen the arguments which we ventured to put forward . . . in reply to Mr. Darwin's theory."

[31] Simpson, "Darwin on the Origin of Species," *Rambler*, n.s., II (March 1860), 372, 374. This is an extension of Newman's concept of Development.

[32] *Ibid.*, 376. For a different account of this article, see Basil Willey, "Darwin and Clerical Orthodoxy," *1859: Entering an Age of Crisis*, ed. Philip Appleman, William A. Madden and Michael Wolff (Bloomington, Ind., 1959), pp. 58-9.

ness of God. Theology must not overstep its limits and pretend to lay down the law for science, and it must clear and simplify its language in order to deal with scientific discoveries.[33] A second article by Eckstein, however, proved too bold for Wetherell and Newman, and was not published. Yet even Newman, in urging the rejection of the article to avoid conflicts with authority, admitted that the *Rambler*, "do what it will, is sure to give offence."[34] The work of formulating a Catholic response to scientific criticism had to be carried on simultaneously with the defence of the right of free inquiry.

The Biblical criticism of *Essays and Reviews* was dealt with in the same spirit. The *Rambler*'s review of the book was written by Henry N. Oxenham, a former Anglican minister who had been converted in 1857. Oxenham was somewhat of an eccentric: he had studied at a Catholic seminary but, believing his Anglican orders still valid, did not proceed to the priesthood. He was an admirer of Newman; he was also a friend of Döllinger, whose later works he translated. He was active in the "reunion" movement and retained many of his Anglican friendships. Oxenham's Anglican connections and his competent scholarship made him a suitable reviewer for *Essays and Reviews*. Acton had called the book "a weak reproduction"[35] of German scepticism and was not impressed with it. Oxenham gave it a more respectful treatment, calling it the most remarkable contribution to English Protestant theology since Newman's tracts; but he condemned the work as undermining the foundations of all religious belief. Biblical criticism, he said, will dissolve ordinary Protestant belief; only Catholicism can defend the cause of religion against rationalism and scepticism. Biblical criticism pre-

[33] Baron d'Eckstein, "The Church and Science," *Rambler*, n.s., III (May 1860), 68-83.
[34] Newman to Wetherell, 12 Aug. 1860, Newman MSS; partly quoted in Ward, *Life of Newman*, I, 505-6. Wetherell, alarmed by Eckstein's language, had sent his article to Newman, who rejected it because it seemed to teach as fact what was merely unproved opinion and disregarded the prepossessions of the majority of Catholics.
[35] Acton to Döllinger, 25 Feb. 1861, quoted by E. L. Woodward, "The Place of Lord Acton in the Liberal Movement of the Nineteenth Century," *Politica*, IV (1939), 254. Prof. Woodward describes Acton as being "in fundamental things, a believing Catholic, a *croyant* of a simple kind."

sented a challenge which the Catholic Church should be anxious to meet:

> It is clear that we shall have to deal hereafter rather with the fundamental principles of Revelation than with the specialities of the Evangelical or Anglican creeds. And we do not regret that it should be so. It will demand from us a firmer grasp of ascertained principles, a wider range of speculation, a nicer discrimination of what is essential and what is accidental, a more generous estimate of an adversary's position, and bolder proclamation of our own.[36]

Oxenham found it better to deal with sceptics who denied revelation altogether than with adherents of other denominations who differed only on particular points. As Protestantism showed that it could no longer defend the cause of religion, men would turn to Rome.

This notion that the progress of scholarship would demonstrate the failure of Protestantism and the necessity of Catholicism was one of Döllinger's ruling ideas. It was the basis of the Liberal Catholics' willingness to accept the risks of free scientific inquiry. They held that Catholic theology, founded on the living Church rather than the letter of the Bible, was invulnerable to scholarly criticism: "We differ from the Protestant supernaturalists because the critical examination of the Bible, conducted in the spirit of religion, does not equally affect the foundations of our faith."[37] The real danger came from the tendency among Catholics to confuse the actual substance of revelation, the dogmas of faith, with a variety of supplementary beliefs, analogies and explanations which had become accidentally bound up with dogma in men's minds. "Real faith," said Simpson,

> keeps divine dogma in its proper isolation from all earthly things. Sham faith brings it down, mixes it with false conceptions of these things, and places orthodoxy in strict adherence to these falsehoods. This is the real reason why faith is so supremely indifferent to speculation—because speculation

[36] Henry Nutcombe Oxenham, "The Neo-Protestantism of Oxford," *Rambler*, n.s., IV (March 1861), 298-9.

[37] Acton, "Döllinger's History of Christianity," *Rambler*, n.s., IV (Jan. 1861), 168.

cannot really touch it, however much it may seem to do so.[38]

The opposition between reason and faith, Simpson argued, was an unnatural one. If Christians have been overcome in conflicts with science, it was "because they have always fought for more than the Christian dogma; because . . . they have failed to recognise that all except the central core of revealed truth is human addition, and therefore fallible, changeable, and obnoxious to decay; and because they have defended the accidental and temporary vestment of truth with as much obstinacy as they defended truth itself."[39] To rescue the Catholic cause from its unworthy defenders and to demonstrate the harmony of faith and reason, Simpson wrote two articles on "Reason and Faith" which were published in the summer of 1861.

The danger of conflicts between religious authority and inductive science might be avoided, Simpson said, if each were confined to its proper sphere. The sphere of science is the world of phenomena; the sphere of faith is the world of spirit. Even in matters of faith, the mind must operate according to its own laws, and it is a requisite of faith that its articles should not contradict the laws of reason. Faith is not a distinct faculty of the soul opposed to reason, but "is only a function of reason, one of its modes of working."[40] There would be no contradiction between faith and reason, were it not for the failure to distinguish the internal element of faith, the dogmas, from the external element, their evidences. The latter element is not the object of faith; therefore Biblical criticism, while it may affect the proof of dogmas, can never affect the dogmas themselves. Hence the Christian may "hold fast to the faith, while all else is in a state of confusion and transition, because the dogmas of the faith are addressed to those powers of the intellect which transcend the sphere of phenomena in time and space, to which science is confined."[41]

---

[38] Simpson to Acton, n.d., Woodruff MSS. It is significant in this connection that Simpson had favourably reviewed Mansel's controversial Bampton lectures on the limits of religious thought in 1858. "Mansel's Bampton Lectures," *Rambler*, 2nd ser., X (Dec. 1858), 407-415.

[39] Simpson, "Reason and Faith," *Rambler*, n.s., V (July 1861), 182.

[40] *Ibid.*, 172.

[41] *Ibid.*, 184.

Simpson spoke of the Catholic faith as "limited to the invisible substance, and the few individual facts in which this substance was manifested."[42] The Church's infallibility is restricted to questions which are wholly religious, or to the religious element of mixed questions. In matters not of faith or morals, such as history, politics or science, Simpson did not regard himself as bound by the decisions of the Church. He acknowledged that the Church possessed a practical right to interfere in such matters, by virtue of her function as the guardian of faith. Nonetheless, such disciplinary prohibitions, though binding in practice, make no claim to the interior assent of Catholics but only require "a silent acquiescence."[43] The danger of such interferences lies in the fact that the Church is frequently involved in the prejudices of the ignorant.

> If students in theology are forced to suck in the theories which ages of ignorance have foisted on Moses, when they have to work as clergymen they will experience in their own persons the way in which Church and Scripture have been exposed to the contempt of intelligent infidels who, after hearing divines teaching physical falsehoods as Bible truths, have mocked at the same men when they claimed credence for biblical faith and morals; for most people have at least biblical knowledge enough to be aware that those who are found unfaithful in what men can see, are not to be believed when they speak of heavenly things that men cannot see.[44]

The divine character of the Church may be overshadowed by the human weaknesses of its leaders. "There is danger in all cases of interference with secular science or progress on the ground of its supposed ill-effects on faith, lest the interfering authorities should mistake their own irritation for a scandal growing up in the minds of the masses." The Church should cultivate versatility and extend its patronage to all knowledge, allowing freedom in doubtful matters. "In intellectual encounters the Church and the world must always use the same weapons; they must argue upon the

---

[42] Simpson, "Reason and Faith" (2nd article), *Rambler*, n.s., V (Sept. 1861), 329.

[43] *Ibid.*, 337.

[44] *Ibid.*, 338.

common principles of reason, and assume the same uni-versally-accepted truths. In her battle with successive schools of philosophy, she has ever fought with their arms: they have passed away, and she remains."[45]

In later years Simpson's articles were to provide the sub-stance for the charge of Modernism often made against the Liberal Catholics. Simpson's emphasis on the "central core" of faith sounds Modernistic, but it meant something different from the Modernist viewpoint. The Modernists were prepared to see dogmas changed or abandoned in conformity with the progress of scientific criticism. Simpson, on the other hand, regarded dogma as the essence of that inward core of religion which he declared to be immutable. Liberal Catholicism cannot be held responsible for the errors of Modernism. It stands by itself as a response to the intellectual challenges facing the Catholic religion in the middle decades of the nineteenth century.

"Beyond the theological arguments involved, lay the decisive issues of freedom versus authority."[46] It was the persistent independence of the *Rambler*, more than its questionable theology, which made it a source of contro-versy. In 1859, it had come into conflict with ecclesiastical authority on a question of education. In 1860 another contro-versy arose on the same subject.

The controversy was started by a letter, signed "X.Y.Z.," written by Oxenham in the July *Rambler*. Oxenham was at the time an instructor at St. Edmund's Seminary, Old Hall, where he had come into conflict with some of his superiors by his criticisms of Catholic seminary education.[47] In the "X.Y.Z." letter, he objected to the separate training from boyhood of candidates for the priesthood, the restrictions on their general reading, and the system of "surveillance" by which their behaviour was rigidly supervised. This amounted to a denunciation of the whole seminary system which had

---

[45] *Ibid.*, 339.
[46] Stephen J. Tonsor, "Lord Acton on Döllinger's Historical Theology," *Journal of the History of Ideas*, XX (June-Sept. 1959), 352.
[47] See letters from Thomas MacDonnell to Wiseman, 9 Nov. 1860, and Wiseman to Dr. Weathers, 10 Nov. 1860, Westminster Archives.

been established by the Council of Trent. Oxenham sought
to replace it with a more general education which would tend
to intellectual refinement. In support of his arguments he
cited Newman's Dublin lectures to the effect that general
knowledge was the best preparation for a professional career.
The letter was temperate in tone, "seeking rather to ventilate
the question than to lay down the law."[48]

Acton thought that Oxenham's "general view requires
and deserves support."[49] Having been educated at Oscott,
Acton knew the weaknesses of the Catholic colleges; and his
opinions had been confirmed by Northcote, the former editor
of the *Rambler*, who had recently become president of Oscott.
Acton told Simpson:

> What is most wanted is a high standard of education in the
> clergy, without which we can neither have, except in rare
> cases, good preachers or men of taste or masters of style, or
> up to the knowledge, the ignorance and the errors of the day.
> They will have neither sympathy nor equality with the laity.
> . . . It is no answer to say that an ignorant clergy is good
> enough for an ignorant laity. They must be equal not only to
> lay Catholics, but also to Protestants, both lay and clerical.
> They must be educated with a view to the clever enemy, not
> only to the stupid friend.

Above all, Acton believed, questions of this kind "require
ventilation" to enlighten those who have to decide about
them and to inspire confidence in others: "nothing is safe
that does not show how it can bear discussion and publicity."[50]

Oxenham's educational views met a hostile reception.
Ward, who had penetrated the pseudonym of "X.Y.Z.,"
strongly attacked him in *The Tablet* under the signature of
"A.B.C." But the sharpest criticism of Oxenham came from
an unexpected quarter. Newman felt it necessary to speak
out, lest it be suspected that he had acquiesced in the use of
his Dublin lectures to buttress Oxenham's arguments.
Newman regarded the question of seminary education as
having been settled by the Council of Trent. To discuss such

---

[48] "X. Y. Z." [Oxenham], "Catholic Education," *Rambler*, n.s., III (July
1860), 253.
[49] Acton to Simpson, 12 Jan. 1861, Gasquet, *Lord Acton and his Circle*, p. 162.
[50] Acton to Simpson, 23 Jan. 1861, *ibid.*, pp. 166-7.

matters in public was to court ecclesiastical censure for the *Rambler*. But the discussion annoyed Newman "not only for the sake of the *Rambler*, but for itself."[51] It seemed to him that "X.Y.Z.," and by implication the *Rambler*, represented an excessively secular outlook, an "intellectualism," which was ultimately subversive of religion. It was in regard to this question of the emphasis to be placed on the intellect that Liberal Catholicism seemed to partake of that "liberalism" which it was the mission of Newman's life to oppose.

Newman replied to "X.Y.Z." in a letter in the *Rambler*. Not knowing that Oxenham was the author of the "X.Y.Z." letter, Newman chose by accident Oxenham's own initials, "H.O.," for his signature.[52] He complained of "X.Y.Z." that "in a lay magazine he has discussed a purely clerical subject."[53] The Council of Trent had set up a professedly narrow system that cultivated holiness rather than intellectual attainments. Newman argued that the Dublin lectures had been misunderstood by "X.Y.Z.," and he cited passages to prove that his praise of general education had not been intended to cover the special case of the education of the clergy.

Oxenham was greatly annoyed by this letter. Not suspecting that it had been written by Newman, he thought that "H.O." was the "A.B.C." who had written in *The Tablet*; and the use of his own initials appeared to him to be a personal attack. He replied with a sharp letter in the November *Rambler*, saying that "H.O." (i.e., Newman himself) had misunderstood Newman! Oxenham argued that the decrees of Trent had never been formally received in England; they were merely disciplinary and might be changed. Laymen were intimately concerned with the education of their clergy and were entitled to discuss the subject. The constitution of the Church contained elements

---

[51] Newman to Acton, 5 July 1861, Ward, *Life of Newman*, I, 528.

[52] It is possible that the "H" represented Newman's middle initial and the "O" stood for "of the Oratory," which Newman usually appended to his signature. Newman's signatures in the *Rambler* contained the letter "O": "Ancient Saints" and "Consulting the Faithful" were signed "O," "Napoleonism not Impious" was signed "J.O." [J. for John?], and Newman's poems were signed "Omega."

[53] "H.O.," "Seminaries of the Church," *Rambler*, n.s., III (Sept. 1860), 398.

not only of monarchy but of aristocracy and democracy. Paraphrasing Newman's argument in "Consulting the Faithful," Oxenham urged that the *sensus fidelium* be consulted:

> The *sensus fidelium* was a plea among the preliminaries even of dogmatic definitions; nay more, . . . there have been periods in her history when, under the infliction of time-serving or heretical pastors, the Church has, humanly speaking, been thrown back on that *sensus fidelium* as . . . the main preservative of her faith. *A fortiori*, then, we may suppose that, in matters not of faith, but of practice, . . . our ecclesiastical rulers would desire to be conversant with the sentiments of the faithful. . . . But this is impossible without a free ventilation of such questions.[54]

Oxenham had turned Newman's arguments against him, particularly the arguments of the article "On Consulting the Faithful" which had caused Newman so much trouble. Acton thought that Oxenham had had the better of the controversy: "X.Y.Z. is really a treasure of knowledge, temper and sense. . . . His treatment of Newman is exquisite, quoting him against himself so often."[55] But Oxenham, learning that Newman, whom he admired, had been his antagonist, was completely crushed. He found himself in the ludicrous position of having asserted that Newman had misinterpreted his own words. Oxenham wrote to Wetherell to assure Newman that he would never have answered him as he did if he had known whom he was opposing. Newman answered that he had not been offended: "On the contrary, I was very much amused to find with what good will he laid on me, and with what simple good faith."[56] Nonetheless Oxenham determined to withdraw from the discussion.

The controversy was kept alive by the pertinacity of W. G. Ward. Ward, who had taught at St. Edmund's, was well aware of the weaknesses of the Catholic colleges. "The whole philosophical fabric which occupies our colleges is rotten from the roof to the floor . . . it *intellectually debauches*

[54] "X.Y.Z.," "Catholic Education," *Rambler*, n.s., IV (Nov. 1860), 103.
[55] Acton to Simpson, 28 Nov. 1860, Gasquet, *Lord Acton and his Circle*, p. 150.
[56] Newman's endorsement on letter of Wetherell to Newman, 21 Dec. 1860, Newman MSS.

the students' minds."[57] Nonetheless he violently opposed the theories of "X.Y.Z." In a letter in the *Rambler* for January 1861, Ward protested against the public discussion of an ecclesiastical question, which amounted to an indictment of the episcopate "before the miscellaneous readers of a lay periodical."[58] He defended the principles of the existing system. The main work of Christians was their own sanctification; Catholic education was based upon the principle that men must be trained for holiness and not for mere intellectual pleasure. In his attack on the worship of intellect, to which he ascribed no place in man's true perfection, Ward showed some sympathy with the theories of the Abbé Gaume, who wished to eliminate the classics altogether from Catholic higher education. Ward, less extreme than Gaume, argued that the free reading of general literature was dangerous.

Ward procured from Newman a statement of his views on clerical education. Newman described Oxenham's position as "unutterably strange" and "extravagantly novel" and supported Ward's general view that holiness was to be preferred above intellectualism: "The more a man is educated, whether in theology or in secular science, the holier he needs to be if he would be saved. . . . devotion and self-rule are worth all the intellectual cultivation in the world."[59] Newman's action in this case, an example of the way in which he balanced reason with faith, seemed to indicate greater sympathy with Ward than with the *Rambler*. He urged Acton to allow no reply to be published to Ward's letter.

Acton, however, thought that Ward's opinions were more dangerous than those of "X.Y.Z."[60] He was concerned to refute the notion that the subject of clerical education was excluded from public discussion. He wished to write an editorial article on the subject; but Wetherell was resolute that the *Rambler* should not be committed to a position opposed to Newman's, and Acton's views were eventually

---

[57] Ward to Simpson, n.d., cited in Gasquet, "Introduction," p. xxxvii.
[58] W. G. W[ard], "Catholic Education," *Rambler*, n.s., IV (Jan. 1861), 272.
[59] Newman to Ward, 8 Nov. 1860, quoted in Ward, *Life of Newman*, I, 516.
[60] Acton to Simpson, 23 Jan. 1861, Gasquet, *Lord Acton and his Circle*, p. 168.

represented by a letter.[61] Ward's letter had provoked several replies. Oxenham complained that Ward had misrepresented him. Frederick Oakeley, who had earlier written against Oxenham, now said that he had done good by ventilating the subject, which could not be kept sacred from discussion: "We English live in a land of liberty; and even the Catholic Church herself cannot keep on the outskirts of the national atmosphere."[62] Simpson, writing under a pseudonym, subjected Ward's arguments to an extended critique. Simpson expressed his preference for the public-school system of Protestant England over the un-English system of separate education, restricted reading and surveillance. A final exchange of letters in the May *Rambler* concluded the discussion.

The chief result of the controversy had been to produce an estrangement between Newman and the *Rambler*. The issue of September 1860, in which the "H.O." letter had appeared, had seen Newman's last contribution to the *Rambler*, the concluding article on "Ancient Saints." The course of the discussion led Newman to decide to contribute no more articles. Meanwhile Acton had given Newman further cause of offence. Father Bittleston of the Birmingham Oratory had written a letter in support of the arguments of "H.O." Newman forwarded this letter to Acton, who replied frankly that he would not have thought it worthy of publication but for Newman's recommendation. Newman withdrew Bittleston's letter; but, as he wrote later, "this episode clenched what the introduction of the discussion about clerical education had wrought in my feelings about the *Rambler*."[63]

In the midst of all the criticism to which the *Rambler* was being subjected, it received a token of respect from a most unexpected quarter. Ward, despite his opposition to the *Rambler*, retained his friendship with Simpson; and while the

---

[61] See "S.A.B.S.," "Catholic Education," *Rambler*, n.s., IV (March 1861), 392-6. There is no direct evidence to warrant assigning this letter to Acton; but it represents his views, and passages are taken almost *verbatim* from his letters.

[62] Oakeley, "Catholic Education," *Rambler*, n.s., IV (March 1861), 399.

[63] Note by Newman, cited in Ward, *Life of Newman*, I, 518. See also Acton to Simpson, 10 June 1861, Gasquet, *Lord Acton and his Circle*, p. 190.

"X.Y.Z." controversy was still raging he wrote the following letter:

> Amidst the differences which I recognize between the *Rambler* and myself . . . I am extremely grateful to you and it for many things. First, you have been bold enough to face much obloquy in refusing to "bow the knee to Baal," to join in the most disgusting chorus of self-laudation, which is the present fashion. I cannot indeed think your "croaking" at all up to mark; but it is refreshing to hear the "croaking" at all. Secondly, I think the *Rambler* has been *the only publication* which has shown the most distant perception as to the immense intellectual work incumbent upon us, in both theology and philosophy. Even your contributions on "Original Sin"— though I doubt if they contained two consecutive sentences in which I could concur—yet did this most important service (in my humble opinion): that they opened the way into a new ground which it is absolutely essential that we Catholics should occupy. . . . At least *we* agree that all these questions are most momentously important.[64]

[64] Ward to Simpson, n.d., quoted by Gasquet, "Introduction," pp. xxxvi-xxxvii.

Chapter IX

FRIENDS AND ENEMIES, 1861

THE year 1861 saw the final division of the English
Catholics into irreconcilable factions. The last occasion
when all groups came together in apparent harmony
was the founding of the "Academy of the Catholic Religion"
in June 1861. This was a project of Cardinal Wiseman, who
conceived of the Academy as an intellectual centre for the
English Catholics which would enable them to keep abreast
of current science and literature. Manning and Ward, however, did not share Wiseman's large views of the Academy.
To Ward, it represented a forum in which he could advance
his favourite ideas, the danger of intellectualism and the
necessity of submission to ecclesiastical authority. Manning
sought to transform it into an organ for propagating his
views on the Temporal Power. Acton and Newman viewed
these tendencies with alarm. Acton considered it "disgrace-
ful" that Manning and Ward should "turn the academy into
a field for disporting themselves on their peculiar hobbies,
stripping it of its scientific, honest, disinterested character,
corrupting men's minds with views instead of method."[1]
Newman went further, and wrote to Manning that, if
Wiseman should make his inaugural address an occasion for
a speech in favour of the Temporal Power, he would withdraw his name from the Academy. "From that day,"
Manning later wrote, "a divergence began between us."[2]
Manning henceforth sought to counteract the influence of
Newman, whom he regarded as the leader of the English
intellectual opposition to Rome.

[1] Acton to Simpson, 20 Nov. 1861, Downside MSS. Acton and Simpson were
members of the Academy; Acton was made one of the "censors," a post of some
distinction and no importance.
[2] Quoted in Shane Leslie, *Henry Edward Manning: His Life and Labours*
(London, 1921), p. 272. See also Wilfrid Ward, *Life of John Henry Cardinal
Newman*, 2 vols. (London, 1912), II, 525.

Wiseman's inaugural address did not, after all, deal with
the Temporal Power. It was a sketch of his ideal of the
Church guiding the energies of modern civilization. Catholics
might accept the facts ascertained by science, Wiseman said,
but they must be cautious about scientific deductions and
theories. The Church must be vigilant to ward off the danger
of superficial applications of scientific knowledge which may
mislead the weak.

Acton politely complimented Wiseman on his speech; in
private, however, he revealed his low opinion of the Cardinal's views. "He seems to think that Catholic science has
only a great victory to gain, not great problems to solve."[3]
Acton's conception of the dignity and obligations of science
was more exalted. His review of Wiseman's address in the
Rambler was an exposition of these views and a lecture to the
Academy on the conditions necessary for the progress of
science. The Cardinal himself was treated with somewhat
exaggerated respect; his statement that the Church en-
courages all that is good in the secular movements of the
age was interpreted in a Liberal Catholic sense. Acton
argued that conflicts between religion and science, or between
Church and State, arose because the proponents of one cause
failed to respect the independent authority of the other:
"In the domain of learning, as well as in civil society, there is
an authority distinct from that of the Church, and not
derived from it, and we are bound in each sphere to render
to Caesar the things that are Caesar's."[4] Political wrong and
scientific error are to be met by the advancement of sound
politics and valid science, not by retreat from secular to
purely ecclesiastical ground. Acton urged that the regula-
tions of the Academy, which had been devised to ensure strict
ecclesiastical control, be modified in the direction of greater
freedom. This hope was vain, for the Academy came to be
dominated by the spirit of Manning and Ward.

Ward's anti-intellectualism was subjected to a severe
critique by Simpson in the May *Rambler*. With the general

[3] Acton to Newman, 8 July 1861, Newman MSS.
[4] Acton, "The Catholic Academy," *Essays on Church and State*, ed. Douglas
Woodruff (London, 1952), p. 282. Reprinted from the *Rambler*, n.s., V (Sept.
1861), 291-302.

thesis of Ward's *Nature and Grace*, a refutation of J. S. Mill's philosophy, Simpson was in agreement; but he deplored Ward's methods of argument, "the unfairness and violence with which he treats his opponents."[5] If Simpson had little sympathy for Mill's doctrines, he had even less for Ward's refutation, and he objected to Ward's distrust of intellect and his subjection of science to theology.

The intellectual battlefield between Liberal Catholicism and Ultramontanism was, however, neither philosophy nor science, but history. The *Rambler* had had a foretaste of this in 1860. Its Belgian adviser, Father de Buck, in the course of his work on the *Acta Sanctorum*, had come to the conclusion that the accepted method of identifying the bodies of martyrs in the Roman catacombs was in error. The bodies were identified by the presence above their graves of glass vials containing a red substance supposed to be blood; de Buck believed that the substance was not blood, but the sediment of consecrated wine. His arguments were used by the *Edinburgh Review* to demonstrate that the Roman authorities were guilty of fraud. A controversy raged on the subject, several letters appearing in the *Rambler*.[6] Because he had brought forth facts which had been turned to the disadvantage of the Church, de Buck was severely criticized by many Catholics and even accused of heresy.

This tendency to sacrifice the integrity of history to the immediate interests of the Church was what Acton most deplored about Ultramontanism. Acton sang the praises of scientific history in a review of Döllinger's *Christenthum und Kirche* in January 1861. He contrasted the German love of knowledge for its own sake with the more partisan and literary spirit of English historical writing, and expressed his preference for the Germans, who acknowledged "the dignity, the freedom and the authority of learning." The Church had nothing to fear from the advancement of learning, "for to

[5] Simpson, "Dr. Ward's Philosophy," *Rambler*, n.s., V (May 1861), 75. See Ward to Simpson, 22 May 1861, cited in Abbot Gasquet, *Lord Acton and his Circle* (London, 1906), p. 171n.

[6] E.g., J. S. Northcote, "On the Signs of Martyrdom in the Catacombs," *Rambler*, n.s., III (July 1860), 203-222. An editorial note (pp. 222-3) supported de Buck's views and suggested that the controversial substance be examined microscopically.

her, who is the depositary and the protector of truth, truth alone is natural and congenial."[7] Acton added that scientific history would ultimately work to the advantage of Catholicism, as it would expose Protestant misrepresentations.

Acton's practice in these years was not up to the standard he had set. His historical articles in the *Rambler* were frequently written with the intention of vindicating Catholicism and correcting the historical misrepresentations of which its opponents had been guilty. In this apologetic spirit Acton wrote the most distinguished historical work of his early years, his article on "The Protestant Theory of Persecution." Acton explained away Catholic persecution as a necessary (if unfortunate) historical development, while he condemned Protestant intolerance as the product of abstract theory. The Reformers had adopted intolerance as an integral portion of their doctrines, while Catholic persecution was no essential part of the Catholic faith.[8] The article was a brilliant *tour de force*, a valid statement of half the case; but it was not objective history.

Simpson was also an historian. He had written numerous articles in the *Rambler* on the Catholic martyrs of the Elizabethan period. Acton, who desired to organize an English Catholic historical society, thought that Simpson would be the proper man to manage it. He urged Simpson to make a reputation for himself, independently of his connection with the *Rambler*, by writing a biography of the martyr Edmund Campion.[9] The first eight chapters of the book were published serially in the *Rambler*, beginning in January 1861. Simpson, however, was as little capable as Acton of perfect detachment in his historical writings; many passages in his work contain allusions to the problems of his day. Acton cautioned Simpson about this failing: "I beseech you not to

---

[7] Acton, "Döllinger's History of Christianity," *Essays on Church and State*, pp. 377-8. Reprinted from the *Rambler*, n.s., IV (Jan. 1861), 145-175.

[8] Acton, "The Protestant Theory of Persecution," *Rambler*, n.s., VI (March 1862), 318-351; reprinted in *The History of Freedom and other Essays*, ed. J. N. Figgis and R. V. Laurence (London, 1907), pp. 150-187. Gasquet (*Lord Acton and his Circle*, p. 258n.) says this article was by Simpson; but this is contrary to Wetherell's recollection (Downside MSS.).

[9] Acton to Simpson, 7 Oct. 1859 and 6 Dec. 1860, Gasquet, *Lord Acton and his Circle*, pp. 90-1, 155-6. Simpson's *Campion* was published as a book in 1867.

fill Campion with contemporary allusions. . . . It will look too like a pamphlet."[10] Acton urged that "in history the historian has to disappear and leave the facts and ideas objectively to produce their own effect."[11]

One passage in Simpson's *Campion* aroused considerable criticism. In a discussion of the problems of the English Catholics under Elizabeth, Simpson asserted that the popes of those times had encroached on the political rights of England and thereby exposed the Catholic faith to the hostility of patriotic Englishmen. Although his observations were relevant to his subject, the exercise of the deposing power by St. Pius V, Simpson's language might be interpreted as a veiled allusion to the conduct of Pius IX in his defence of the Temporal Power: "in endeavouring to preserve a temporal prerogative that had always been disputed . . . those Popes lost England to the faith."[12] Many Catholics were scandalized by Simpson's criticism of a pope and saint. It was rumoured that Faber had spoken against Simpson in a sermon, and that the *Rambler* was to be denounced to Rome.[13] Acton, however, regarded Simpson's comments as both relevant and just, and was prepared to make his *Campion* a test case of the independence of Catholic history.

The intellectual battles of Liberal Catholicism went on side by side with an equal concern with political affairs. Acton and Simpson regarded politics as being, like history, governed by principles which were scientifically determined and independent of religious authority:

> Political principles are as definite and as certain as those of ethics, of jurisprudence, or of any other science. It is no more lawful to forget them than to forget the principles of morality; and it is a contradiction to suppose that religious interests can supersede or set aside either one or the other. . . . What is politically right, not what seems advantageous to religion, must be our guide in public life.[14]

[10] Acton to Simpson, 15 Jan. 1861, Downside MSS.
[11] Acton to Simpson, Jan. 1861, Gasquet, *Lord Acton and his Circle*, p. 164.
[12] Simpson, "Edmund Campion," *Rambler*, n.s., V (May 1861), 91.
[13] Acton to Newman, 4 June 1861, Newman MSS.
[14] "Home Affairs—Catholic Policy," *Rambler*, n.s., II (Jan. 1860), 249.

Acton's political principles inclined him to the Liberals, but he preserved a certain independence of action. There were many issues on which a Catholic member of Parliament could not support the government of Lord Palmerston. In foreign affairs Acton opposed the principle of nationalism and democracy which the Liberal government encouraged abroad, and he disapproved of the support which Palmerston gave to the Italian enemies of the Temporal Power. Nonetheless Acton believed that, although the Liberals might be unfaithful to their principles, those principles were fundamentally sound and appropriate for Catholics. They were the principles of Emancipation: civil and religious liberty and equality, and fair treatment for Ireland. The Tories, on the other hand, were bound to the maintenance of Protestant ascendancy, and Catholics could not be justified in supporting them. "The policy, therefore, which recommends itself," said the *Rambler*,

> involves no abandonment of liberal principles, and no defection from the liberal party. They may turn out the government over which Lord Palmerston and Lord John [Russell] preside, but they will not become Tories. It would be madness to establish Orange ascendancy because, for a moment, under the influence of politico-religious excitement, the party with which we have been identified has been untrue to its principles.[15]

This policy of independent support for the Liberal party was not in favour among the English Catholics, who were primarily concerned with the issue of the Temporal Power. It was more popular among some of the Irish, whose special interests were bound up with the Liberal cause. The Liberal Catholics thus came to be closely associated with a group of Irish Whigs, two of whom, Monsell and John O'Hagan, were frequent contributors to the *Rambler*. The Irish Whigs drew Acton closer to the Liberal party.

Acton's rapprochement with the Liberals was made easier by his growing friendship for Gladstone. He had originally been suspicious of Gladstone's opportune conversion to Liberalism and had questioned his intellectual honesty.

[15] William Monsell, "Catholic Policy," *Rambler*, n.s., V (May 1861), 10.

Gladstone had greater respect for Acton, and consulted him on his scholarly hobby, the history of mythology and primitive religion. Acton came to know Gladstone better in the course of his Parliamentary activity. In May 1861, they breakfasted together, and Acton described the article he had written on the American Civil War. Acton's sympathies were entirely with the South: he regarded the issue of state sove-reignty as of greater significance than that of slavery and the Southern states as the defenders of liberty against revolution and centralization.[16] This coincided with Gladstone's views: "I have read your valuable and remarkable paper. Its principles of politics I embrace: its research and wealth of knowledge I admire: and its whole atmosphere, if I may so speak, is that which I desire to breathe. It is a truly English paper."[17] From this time Gladstone's admiration for Acton was unbounded.

Acton was beginning to develop a similar admiration for Gladstone. He learned to appreciate Gladstone's religious approach to politics and his ability to maintain the old Whig principles of Burke while making terms with the new electorate. The budget of 1861, notable for the repeal of the paper duties, confirmed Acton's newly-acquired respect for Gladstone: "he is not inclined to democracy or to class legislation, but tries to carry out true principles of economy."[18]

Acton's political affiliations in mid-1861 were still tenta-tive:

> You must not consider me a regular supporter of the Government. I should vote against their foreign policy, and I probably would not vote for them on a motion of confidence. But it seems to me equivalent to a falsehood to vote against the merits of a question, only from general sympathy or resentment towards a party.[19]

---

[16] Acton, "Political Causes of the American Revolution," *Rambler,* n.s., V (May 1861), pp. 17-61; reprinted in *Essays on Church and State,* pp. 291-338. See Acton to Simpson, 2 May 1861, Gasquet, *Lord Acton and his Circle,* pp. 188-9. Acton's letters to Döllinger, contemplating the possibility of war between Britain and the Northern States, reveal a distinctly martial spirit.

[17] Gladstone to Acton, 8 May 1861, *Selections from the Correspondence of the First Lord Acton,* ed. J. N. Figgis and R. V. Laurence (London, 1917), p. 158.

[18] Acton to Simpson, 15 April 1861, Gasquet, *Lord Acton and his Circle,* p. 187. See also Acton to Döllinger, 4 May 1861, Woodruff MSS.

[19] Acton to Newman, 29 June 1861, Newman MSS.

Except for the Temporal Power, there was no major question on the merits of which Acton was in disagreement with the Liberal party as represented by Gladstone; and he had too little faith in the Temporal Power to make it a reason for voting against the Liberals. In the crucial vote on the repeal of the paper duties, Acton voted for the Government.

This issue separated Acton from most of the English Catholics. Up to this time, he had managed to work together with the other Catholic political leaders, who met informally at the Stafford Club. Acton had been assigned to represent in Parliament the case for equal treatment of Catholic chaplains in prisons. Articles in the *Rambler* supported this and other Catholic claims. But Acton, because of his connections with Gladstone and Granville, relied on private negotiations with the Government to secure redress of grievances and refused to start a debate on the prison question in Parliament. He sought to avoid unnecessary provocation of the Protestant majority. This ran counter to the policy favoured by Wiseman and his spokesman Sir George Bowyer, who were prepared to sacrifice English Catholic matters for the sake of the Temporal Power. They sought to embarrass the Liberal Government at every opportunity. Manning worked actively in support of this policy, which was also urged by John Wallis, the Tory editor of *The Tablet*.

In the spring of 1861 attempts were made to force Acton to start a debate on the prison question, in which he would have to take a stand against the Government. On 7 May, an Irish member, MacEvoy, asked Acton in the House when he proposed to bring on his motion on the prison question. Acton evaded the difficulty by stating that he desired to wait until a similar question, relating to the treatment of Catholic inmates in workhouses, had been disposed of.[20] At the beginning of June another attempt was made to force Acton's hand. At a meeting of the Stafford Club, Manning and Bowyer proposed "a very peremptory resolution"[21] requiring Acton to bring on his motion at once. Acton declined to do so: he saw the larger issue of the Temporal

---

[20] *Hansard's Parliamentary Debates*, 2nd ser., CLXII (1861), 1652.
[21] Acton to Newman, 4 June 1861, Newman MSS.

Power in the background.[22] He countered by offering to resign his responsibility for the prison question. This proved effective: a second meeting of the Club "knocked under" to Acton's letter, and Manning offered him "a sort of apologetic explanation"[23] for the part he had taken in the affair. Acton's position had not been shaken, but he had been made to feel very uncomfortable.

A similar pressure had been applied more successfully to Henry Wilberforce, whose *Weekly Register* was an avowedly Liberal paper, in which Simpson had been able to write critical articles on the Temporal Power. The *Rambler* seemed now to be quite alone among Catholic periodicals in its independent policy. Acton found himself isolated politically. He had already lost the support of his constituency. "Nothing would induce me to stand for Carlow again after certain proceedings which came to my knowledge long after my election. Moreover they are in other ways a constituency I cannot well represent." He was unhappy with his political role: "I am resolved," he said, "to cling to my obscurity."[24]

It was difficult for a Liberal Catholic to cling to obscurity under the conditions of the 1860s; it was only possible at the price of keeping silent on the issue of the Temporal Power. The French Liberal Catholics were divided on that issue. Montalembert and Dupanloup upheld the Papal cause, joining in this with Veuillot. Their support of the Temporal Power was connected with their opposition to Napoleon III, who was charged with betraying the Pope to the Italians. Other Liberal Catholics, like Lacordaire, refused to sacrifice their principles to the cause of the Temporal Power; but Lacordaire protested only by his silence. In Italy, Passaglia, a Jesuit, left the Society, fled to Turin and published a

[22] Acton to Döllinger, 17 June 1861, Woodruff MSS.
[23] Acton to Newman, 9 June 1861, Newman MSS.
[24] Acton to Newman, 4 June 1861, Newman MSS. The "proceedings" presumably were incidents of violence or bribery during his election. Carlow was unhappy with Acton because he was an Englishman who did not visit his Irish constituents. A recent writer argues that Acton's indifference to his constituents was "irresponsible" and raises the question of the validity of his moral standard. See J. J. Auchmuty, "Acton: The Youthful Parliamentarian," *Historical Studies, Australia and New Zealand,* IX (May 1960), 131-9. Professor Auchmuty's judgment seems unduly harsh.

pamphlet which was placed on the Index; but few followed his example.[25] It seemed that the field would be left to the Ultramontanes. Then, in April, Döllinger gave public utterance to his views.

Döllinger had already come to the conclusion that the Temporal Power was destined to fall, and he was distressed by the Ultramontane attempt to commit Catholicism to the defence of a doomed institution. In March 1861, he read in the *Weekly Register* a report (later denied) that the Pope had said that he had "no illusions; the Temporal Power must fall."[26] This led Döllinger to deliver a series of lectures at the Odeon in Munich, to prepare the public for the impending blow. He argued that the Temporal Power, though legitimate and useful, was not essential to the Church. Catholics should not despair, nor Protestants rejoice, at its temporary collapse, for the Church would continue to function without it. The disaster which was overtaking the Papal States was the consequence of abuses in the Papal government; but the fall of the Temporal Power might be the means of purifying and regenerating the Church.

> The Papacy, with or without territory, has its own function and its appointed mission. . . . Let no one lose faith in the Church if the secular principality of the Pope should disappear for a season, or for ever. It is not essence, but accident; not end, but means; it began late; it was formerly something quite different from what it is now. It justly appears to us indispensable, and as long as the existing order lasts in Europe, it must be maintained at any price; or if it is violently interrupted, it must be restored. But a political settlement of Europe is conceivable in which it would be superfluous, and then it would be an oppressive burden.[27]

Döllinger had thought that, with the combined authority of a theologian and an historian, he could reconcile Catholics

---

[25] Acton believed that nine cardinals were in favour of giving up the Temporal Power. Acton to Döllinger, 4 May 1861, Woodruff MSS.

[26] J. Friedrich, *Ignaz von Döllinger: Sein Leben auf Grund seines schriftlichen Nachlasses*, 3 vols. (München, 1901), III, 236, 691 n.2.

[27] Döllinger's summary of his lecture, in the Preface to *Kirche und Kirchen, Papstthum und Kirchenstaat* (München, 1861); translated and quoted by Acton, "Döllinger on the Temporal Power," *The History of Freedom*, pp. 305-6; reprinted from the *Rambler*, n.s., VI (Nov. 1861), 1-62.

to the loss of the Temporal Power. Instead, his lectures provoked a hostile reaction. The Papal Nuncio walked out of the lecture hall as a sign of protest. The newspaper reports stressed the more sensational aspect of the lectures, the criticism of the Roman government and the prediction of its overthrow; this made it appear that Döllinger had simply come out in opposition to the Temporal Power. No authentic text of the lectures was published, and the public was left to form its conclusions from these misleading reports.

A very severe criticism of Döllinger's lectures was made by the *Dublin Review*. E. S. Purcell, Manning's protégé and future biographer, charged that Döllinger had given aid and comfort to the enemies of the Church by a half-hearted defence of the Temporal Power which was worse than outright opposition. Döllinger was criticized for being "hard, dry, and critical," for a "supreme and sovereign disregard" of the utterances of ecclesiastical authorities and for an "intellectual Protestantism which shrinks from or evades the supernatural character of the Papacy." Purcell concluded that Döllinger "had no business to give out an uncertain sound, or even to cast doubts upon the wisdom of the course which the Papacy is pursuing."[28]

The views which so offended the *Dublin Review* were welcome to Acton. Acton's dislike of the Temporal Power was perhaps greater than Döllinger's. Acton's letters in the spring of 1861 show how dissatisfied he was with the policies of the Papacy:

> Dante is condemned for saying in his time what I would say in ours. He did not stop at the consideration of what would suit the popes, but went on to think of the good of religion and of certain morals, rights and duties, beyond certain religious or rather ecclesiastical interests. The papacy had forfeited the leadership, and the life of the Church beat more warmly in other places than at the head. Have we not lived to see the same thing? The revival of faith in this century has left the papacy behind.[29]

---

[28] Edmund Sheridan Purcell, "Döllinger and the Temporal Power of the Popes," *Dublin Review*, XCIX (May 1861), 200, 215, 231. *The Tablet* was also severely critical of Döllinger.

[29] Acton to Simpson, 20 Mar. 1861, Gasquet, *Lord Acton and his Circle*, p. 180.

The outspokenness of Döllinger's lectures, as reported in the press, was a relief to Acton. He hastily prepared a summary of the lectures for the May *Rambler*.[30] It was made clear that the *Rambler* was in agreement with Döllinger's views.

The policy of the *Rambler* was regarded with suspicion and distaste by the authorities in Rome. This was largely due to the influence of Monsignor Talbot. As the Pope's chamberlain and favourite, consultor of Propaganda, and Wiseman's agent in Rome, Talbot exercised a great influence on English affairs. A convert who had adopted the most extreme Ultramontane views, Talbot was strongly opposed to any sign of an English national spirit within the Church and to any activity of the laity in ecclesiastical affairs: "What is the province of the laity? To hunt, to shoot, to entertain."[31] Talbot had long been suspicious of the *Rambler*; in 1859 he had arranged for copies to be sent to him regularly so that he could report on its conduct to the Roman authorities.[32]

In May 1861, Talbot learned of the *Rambler*'s favourable review of Döllinger's lectures. He wrote to Manning, proposing that the bishops should censure the *Rambler* and stating that he would probably be obliged to delate the article to the proper ecclesiastical authority.[33] Manning replied on 4 June that he hoped "before long to be able to report the cessation of the *Rambler*.[34] On 10 June Talbot wrote directly to Wiseman, denouncing the "detestable" tone of the *Rambler*, and singling out for criticism two articles in the last number, Simpson's criticism of St. Pius V and Acton's report of Döllinger's lectures. He concluded by expressing the hope that the *Rambler* would be suppressed.[35]

Meanwhile Talbot had brought the *Rambler* to the atten-

---

[30] *Rambler*, n.s., V (May 1861), 139-140. The summary was based on the newspaper reports but was not an inaccurate representation of Döllinger's views. See Acton to Döllinger, 4 May 1861, Woodruff MSS., for Acton's excitement over Döllinger's speaking "for the Church against the States of the Church."

[31] Talbot to Manning, 25 April 1867, quoted by Ward, *Life of Newman*, II, 147.

[32] Talbot to Canon Patterson, 22 Oct. 1859, Westminster Archives.

[33] Talbot to Manning, 10 May 1861, cited in Purcell, *Life of Cardinal Manning, Archbishop of Westminster*, 2 vols. (New York, 1896), II, 165.

[34] Manning to Talbot, 4 June 1861, *ibid.*, p. 384.

[35] Talbot to Wiseman, 10 June 1861, Westminster Archives.

tion of the Roman authorities. Cardinal Antonelli, the Secretary of State, had been unhappy about the failure of the Irish Catholic members of Parliament to vote against a government which was hostile to the Temporal Power; he now concluded that their behaviour was due to the influence of the *Rambler*.[36] In June Antonelli wrote a formal letter to Wiseman, "connecting the support given to government by Catholic members with things that have appeared in the *Rambler*."[37] Under pain of censure from Rome, the *Rambler* was required to come out unequivocally for the Temporal Power and to repudiate its support of the Liberal Government.

This was the first time that the *Rambler*, accustomed to conflicts with the English hierarchy, had been dealt with by the authorities in Rome. "It is worth observing," said Newman, "that the R[ambler] has been untouched, till politics came in."[38] It was the politics of the *Rambler*, and not its theology or philosophy, which first brought it into conflict with Rome.

On 18 June, Manning, acting as Wiseman's agent, informed Acton of Antonelli's letter. Manning warned Acton that a censure was impending from Rome and urged him to escape it by giving up the *Rambler*.

Then he said that the *Rambler* had appeared to him of late less Catholic in spirit and tendency, and was doing harm, and that it was highly desirable to put an end to it altogether. The points of difference were numerous enough, both as to history and metaphysics, but from his own statements as to my articles on the Roman question not being up to the mark, and Anglican in tone, and from the connexion I perceive in the minds of people in Rome between the *Rambler* and the support given to ministers in parliament, it is obvious that the present political question is the decisive cause.[39]

[36] The May *Rambler* had contained an article urging continued support of the Liberals ("Catholic Policy," pp. 1-17) and a criticism of Bowyer's conduct in the debate on the Temporal Power (pp. 126-9). The "significant silence" of most of the Catholic members during that debate was noticed by Oxenham, reviewing Döllinger's lectures in the *Edinburgh Review*, CXVI (July 1862), 264.

[37] Acton to Newman, 19 June 1861, cited in Ward, *Life of Newman*, I, 522.

[38] Newman to Acton, 20 June 1861, Woodruff MSS.

[39] Acton to Newman, 19 June 1861, portion cited in Douglas Woodruff, "Introduction" to Acton, *Essays on Church and State*, p. 26.

Acton declined to give up the *Rambler*, and explained his position to Manning. He thought that Manning's "personal kindness was extreme."[40] But Manning had no personal sympathies where the will of the Pope was concerned; and Acton's refusal to submit made him an enemy for life.

Engaged in controversy over history, philosophy and politics, under attack both in England and in Rome, Acton was now made to feel the isolation of his position. Outside the small group of writers for the *Rambler*, there was only one English Catholic to whom he might turn for sympathy—Newman. Although Newman had dissociated himself from the *Rambler* after the X.Y.Z. affair, he still maintained a friendly correspondence with Acton. He had never fully explained to Acton and Simpson the extent to which he differed from them; he did not wish to inflict pain or to add to their troubles. On the question of the Temporal Power Newman was in full agreement with the Liberal Catholics. Acton was impatient at his silence: "He ought to be ashamed not to pronounce himself."[41]

On 4 June, Acton wrote a plaintive letter to Newman, reciting the troubles with which he was beset: criticism of Simpson's *Campion*, denunciations in Faber's sermons, rumours of delation to Rome and of Antonelli's letter to Wiseman, attempts to embarrass him politically, and his isolation in Parliament. There were many who agreed with him, Acton said, but they were intimidated and would not speak out. Acton called upon Newman to take the leadership of the Liberal Catholic cause: "I feel very painfully that I am altogether unworthy to be regarded as the champion in this country of the cause which is yours. . . . We are still listening in vain for the voice we most reverence and most love to hear."[42]

[40] Acton to Newman, 19 June 1861, in Ward, *Life of Newman*, I, 523. Up to this time Acton's relations with Manning had been friendly.

[41] Acton to Simpson, 2 May 1861, Gasquet, *Lord Acton and his Circle*, p. 188. Acton told Döllinger that he found Newman tired and unhappy, and hoped that Döllinger would encourage Newman to undertake some scholarly project that would banish his *Lebensabendstimmung*. Acton to Döllinger, 4 May 1861, Woodruff MSS.

[42] Acton to Newman, 4 June 1861, *Selected Correspondence of Lord Acton*, p. 31. This was before Manning had formally notified Acton of the Antonelli letter.

Newman was now forced to make his position clear, and he emphatically repudiated the role in which Acton had cast him. He explained the reasons why he would not speak out on the Temporal Power. There was no call on him to speak, and he refused to speak without a call. He had to consider the welfare of the Birmingham Oratory, and he was bound in gratitude to the Pope. "Acordingly I think I fulfill my duty in keeping silence. You may be sure that people wish me to speak on the other side, and to maintain the Temporal Power. That I have not done, and the omission itself is going a great way."[43] Newman agreed with Acton's remarks on the Temporal Power in the May *Rambler*; but Acton's association with the *Rambler*, he said, was an impediment to his parliamentary career, embarrassing his position as a representative of English Catholicism. This was due to Simpson's writings, and especially to his life of Campion. Newman thought that Simpson's comments on St. Pius V were unjustified, as "a wanton digression from Campion," an "underhand hit at Antonelli," and "an abrupt, unmeasured attack upon a Saint." Simpson's articles were doing a great disservice to a good cause. "I don't wonder at a saying which I hear reported of a Dominican, that he would like to have the burning of the author."[44]

This letter deeply troubled Acton. He could appreciate Newman's reasons for keeping silent on the Temporal Power; but Newman's attitude to Simpson, and his views on history, surprised and dismayed Acton. He defended Simpson's comments on Pius V, saying that not his sanctity but his judgment was impugned and that in matters not of faith saints and popes were subject to criticism like other men. What distressed Acton most was Newman's apparent approval of the Dominican's wish to burn Simpson: "In the saying of your Dominican friend I discern nothing but a dread of that which is one of the foundations of religion and holiness, and a spirit which seems to me more pernicious and more important to oppose than anything which is outside

---

[43] Newman to Acton, 7 June 1861, *ibid.*, pp. 32-3. There are two letters of this date, which together explain Newman's position.

[44] Newman to Acton, 7 June 1861, quoted by Ward, *Life of Newman*, I, 518-9.

the Church. . . . I really cannot discover a bridge by which
I can hope to get over the very wide chasm that seems to me
to separate me from you on this point."[45]

The chasm was soon widened. On 19 June, Acton informed Newman of the Antonelli letter, of which Manning
had just notified him. Acton was determined to carry on the
Rambler and suggested that the magazine might evade
censure by changing itself into a quarterly review. Newman
replied that this would be a difficult task. He was as indignant
as Acton at Antonelli's message: "If I were you, nothing
would bully me into giving up the Government, if I felt I
ought to go with them."[46] But Newman confessed that he
would not be sorry if Acton put an end to the *Rambler*; and
he suggested to Acton that he should retire to Aldenham to
produce a great historical work. In a later letter Newman
explained:

> It seems to me that a man who opposes legitimate authority is
> in a false position. . . . If they do not allow the *Rambler* to speak
> against the temporal power, they seem to me tyrannical—but
> they have the right to disallow it—and a Magazine, with a
> censure upon it from authority, continues at an enormous
> disadvantage.[47]

Acton was surprised by Newman's attitude. "There is
something in your view of the importance belonging to the
decrees of authority for which I was not at all prepared. . . .
In political life we should not be deterred, I suppose, by the
threat or fear even of excommunication from doing what we
should have deemed our duty if no such consideration had
presented itself." Acton maintained that having excluded
theology from the *Rambler*, there was nothing left in it over
which the ecclesiastical power possessed jurisdiction. He
thought the *Rambler* had a good effect, especially among
Protestants, by the spectacle of its independence. This effect
would be ruined "if it should appear that the only organ
among English Catholics of opinions with which it is possible

[45] Acton to Newman, 9 June 1861, *Selected Correspondence of Lord Acton*, pp.
33-4. Thirty years later, Acton was still troubled by Newman's approval of the
Dominican: there are three references to it in CUL Add. MS. 4988.
[46] Newman to Acton, 20 June 1861, *Selected Correspondence of Lord Acton*, p. 36.
[47] Newman to Acton, 30 June 1861, quoted by Ward, *Life of Newman*, I, 524.

for reasonable Protestants to sympathize was silenced by authority."[48]

Newman replied that the *Rambler* was in fact in the habit of touching on theological questions; it therefore came under the jurisdiction of the ecclesiastical power, which ought to be deferred to. He spoke out most sharply against Simpson. His comments on St. Pius V had been unnecessary and unjustified: "a Saint surely is not to be approached as a common man." It was hopeless to expect Simpson to reform. "He will always be flicking his whip at Bishops, cutting them in tender places, throwing stones at sacred Congregations, and, as he rides along the road, discharging pea-shooters at Cardinals who happen by bad luck to look out of the window. I fear I must say I despair of any periodical in which he has a part." If the *Rambler* were silenced, it would not be for its independence, but because it had gone out of its way to assail what was authoritative and venerable.

> The *Rambler* now is in a false position, if authority speaks against it. It has been sufficiently theological and ecclesiastical, to impress the world with the idea that it comes under an ecclesiastical censor, and if it caught it for tilting against Inquisition, Ecumenical Councils, and Saints, the world would be apt to say "Serve him right." This is how it appears to me.[49]

This letter indicated a cleavage between Newman and the *Rambler*: "I am very much afraid," Acton wrote to Simpson, "that he will not stand by us if we are censured."[50] Acton insisted to Newman that their difference was a matter of principle: "Has the Church a right to censure me because I say of a canonized Saint that on some occasion he committed an error in judgment, or even a mortal sin?" According to Newman's reasoning, "the fact might be as stated in the article, and yet the statement of the fact would give Rome a right to condemn us. If that were so it would justify the very attacks against which we are most anxious to defend the Church." Acton did not believe that a censure on

---

[48] Acton to Newman, 2 July 1861, cited in Woodruff, "Introduction," p. 24.
[49] Newman to Acton, 5 July 1861, cited in Ward, *Life of Newman*, I, 528-9.
[50] Acton to Simpson, 19 July 1861, Gasquet, *Lord Acton and his Circle*, p. 191.

these grounds would require his submission. He conceded that the public might support the authorities who condemned the *Rambler*, for the public did not admit "the authority of science, or the sanctity of truth for its own sake." But it was the mission of the *Rambler* to educate this public, to correct its errors by walking in the face of them.

> I cannot bear that Protestants should say that the Church cannot be reconciled with the truths or precepts of science, or that Catholics should fear the legitimate and natural progress of the scientific spirit. These two errors seem to me almost identical, and if one is more dangerous than the other, I think it is the last. So that it comes more naturally to me to be zealous against the Catholic mistake than against the Protestant. But the best weapon against both is the same, the encouragement of the true scientific spirit, and the disinterested love of truth.[51]

These principles, and not Simpson's pugnacity, explained the *Rambler*'s conflicts with authority. "I always feel," Acton said, "that I am deliberately and systematically farther away from the prevailing sentiments of good and serious Catholics than Simpson with all his imprudence."[52]

After this letter, the correspondence between Acton and Newman tapered off. Newman had shown the limitations of his Liberal Catholicism. He differed from Acton and Simpson on two fundamental points: the theoretical independence of history and the practical duty of submission to authority. Newman's theory of development had opened up for historical exploration the entire field of theology; but Newman himself was inclined to be cautious in applying his theory. He was fearful of the consequences to religion of an entirely disinterested history, of the search for "truth for its own sake" without reference to the effect it might have on the weak and ignorant. He had a distrust of mere scholarship, of unmixed intellectualism; he felt that a certain narrowness was necessary to avoid being overwhelmed by facts which the human mind was unprepared to digest. It was better, he thought, to defer even to uneducated public opinion:

[51] Acton to Newman, 8 July 1861, quoted by Ward, *Life of Newman*, I, 530-1.
[52] *Ibid.*, p. 532.

securus judicat orbis terrarum. It was necessary, in any case, to
submit to authority. "Authority, the certain legitimacy and
rectitude of its acts, became his centrepiece and refuge.
This was what development pointed to."[53] Newman stated
his view in the *Apologia*: "In reading ecclesiastical history . . .
it used to be forcibly brought home to me, how the initial
error of what afterwards became heresy was the urging
forward some truth against the prohibition of authority at
an unseasonable time."[54] Ecclesiastical authority possessed a
legitimate power of restraint over the intellect; even when its
action appeared to be founded on ignorance and prejudice,
there was a presumption that it was right, that its restrictions
were ultimately salutary for the progress both of religion and
of learning. At the worst, Newman thought, the decisions of
authority were entitled to be received with respectful
silence.

This revelation of Newman's attitude came as a shock to
Acton. Newman's profound submissiveness to authority
eventually led Acton to conclude that he was an Ultramontane at heart, whose apparent liberalism was due to mere
personal animosity towards the representatives of Ultramontanism in England, an incompatibility of temperament
rather than of principles: "he was heart and soul, far more
than he ever suffered to appear, an advocate of Rome."[55]
His apparent approval of the Dominican who wished to
burn Simpson, and his readiness to justify the intolerant
St. Pius V, identified Newman in Acton's mind with the
persecutors and Inquisitors. Newman's willingness to
subordinate historical truth to ecclesiastical expediency and
popular prejudice led Acton to believe that he had no
principle of truth independent of religion. Acton spoke in

[53] Acton, CUL Add. MS. 5644, cited in Stephen J. Tonsor, "Lord Acton on
Döllinger's Historical Theory," *Journal of the History of Ideas*, XX (June-Sept.
1959), 329 n.4. See also Thomas S. Bokenkotter, *Cardinal Newman as an Historian*
(Louvain, 1959), p. 70.

[54] Newman, *Apologia pro vita sua*, ed. Wilfrid Ward (London, 1931), pp.
349-50. It should be noted that Newman wrote the *Apologia* to defend the
Catholic clergy against a charge of indifference to "truth for its own sake."

[55] CUL Add. MS. 4989. These were Acton's notes for a projected article on
Newman in 1892, intended for the *English Historical Review*. See Maisie Ward,
The Wilfrid Wards and the Transition (London, 1934), p. 249.

later years of his "deep aversion" for Newman, "the most cautious and artful of apologists."[56]

This intellectual divergence from Newman was, however, slow in maturing. For some years, Acton held hopes of reconciling Newman to the Liberal Catholics; his youthful sanguineness delayed his realization of the extent of their disagreement. Nonetheless, 1861 marks a stage in Acton's mental development. He had learned that his views were too advanced for the English Catholics and were opposed by the hierarchy not only in England but in Rome. His youthful dreams of a revived Catholicism, liberal, scientific and ethical, were reduced to the level of a factional programme. Even the one eminent Catholic on whom he had relied for understanding and support—Newman—had failed him. Acton had a glimpse of the isolation of his position, foreshadowing the more complete isolation he was to face in later decades. From this time there may be found a certain bitterness in his attitude.

---

[56] Cited in Gertrude Himmelfarb, *Lord Acton: A Study in Conscience and Politics* (Chicago, 1952), pp. 156-7. See also my review of Bokenkotter in *Victorian Studies*, IV (March 1961), 278-9.

CHAPTER X

QUARTERING THE *RAMBLER*, 1861-1862

THE warfare of parties among the English Catholics became more intense in the latter months of 1861. Former friends of the *Rambler* were turning against it. Northcote, once its editor, aligned himself with its opponents. Dr. Todd, who had assisted Simpson in 1856, was now opposed to his views. Other contributors were critical: Canon Macmullen remonstrated with Acton, and Ryley concluded that he was "treading in the footsteps of Lamennais."[1] Meanwhile the official antagonism to the *Rambler* increased. A rescript censuring the magazine was sent to the English bishops by Propaganda; Acton's bishop, Dr. Brown of Shrewsbury, described it to him as "a very solemn thing."[2] Brown vaguely suspected some unorthodoxy in Acton but was overawed by his erudition. He sent a cautious old priest, Green, to replace the too liberal J. B. Morris as Acton's chaplain at Aldenham; Green was warned "to be well up in all his points" to combat Acton's infidelity.[3]

The hostility towards the *Rambler* affected its publisher, James Burns, whose business was largely dependent upon ecclesiastical patronage. Early in September 1861, Burns wrote to Simpson (who was acting as editor again, due to Acton's absence and Wetherell's illness) urging that the *Rambler* be surrendered to a committee to be named by Manning, Ward and Northcote. Only thus, Burns said, could a Catholic periodical be carried on to the satisfaction of the public. If Simpson rejected this proposal, Burns suggested that he would have to find another publisher.[4]

Simpson forwarded this letter to Acton, who recognized

---

[1] Acton to Simpson, 5 Dec. 1861, Downside MSS.
[2] Acton to Newman, 10 Nov. 1861, Newman MSS.
[3] Acton to Döllinger, 27 Dec. 1861, Woodruff MSS. Green, however, was won over by Acton's charm.
[4] Simpson to Newman, 30 Sept. 1861, Newman MSS.

in it "the complement of Manning's insinuations"[5] of two
months earlier. Acton suggested, as an "ingenious dodge,"
that "I would agree to any arrangement by which Newman
should be made editor, but that none of the other names give
me a guarantee for Catholic principles in the conduct of the
Review."[6] Acton was fairly certain that Newman would not
accept the editorship, but he thought that the proposal of his
name would either break the force of the opposition or bring
it out into the open. Burns refused to have anything to do
with Newman; he said that Newman's connection with any
periodical would injure its chances of success, by reason of his
unpopularity.

On 27 September, Simpson received a letter from Burns,
saying that he was leaving on a journey to Rome. Burns had
authorized Northcote to act on his behalf; he would be
willing to publish the *Rambler* under any management of
which Northcote and Manning might approve. "Of course
you will not bring out another number with our name until
this matter is settled."[7] This meant, in effect, that Burns
refused to publish the next number of the *Rambler* unless the
magazine were surrendered to Manning's control. It
appeared that Burns wanted nothing less than the destruction
of the *Rambler*.

If the proprietors wished to carry on the magazine, they
had to find another publisher; and since Catholic publishers
were vulnerable to the pressure of the hierarchy, it was
necessary to secure a Protestant publisher. Acton welcomed
the independence which the *Rambler* might obtain by this
means. It was not intended, however, that the *Rambler*
should give up its character as a Catholic magazine. When
one of the publishers to whom Simpson applied said that its
Catholicity was the one objection he had to publishing it,

---

[5] Acton to Simpson, 10 Sept. 1861, Abbot Gasquet, *Lord Acton and his Circle*
(London, 1906), p. 195. Acton later spoke of "Manning's Mephistophelean
treachery and craft" and described his proposals in June as "insulting and
dishonourable": Acton to Simpson, 11 Oct. 1861, quoted by [Dom] A[elred]
Watkin and Herbert Butterfield, "Gasquet and the Acton-Simpson Correspondence," *Cambridge Historical Journal*, X (1950), 81.

[6] Acton to Simpson, 10 Sept. 1861, Gasquet, *Lord Acton and his Circle*, p. 196.

[7] Cited by Simpson to Newman, 30 Sept. 1861, Newman MSS.

Simpson replied that "this objection was insuperable."[8]

While these negotiations were proceeding, Simpson, who was not aware of Acton's quarrel with Newman, applied to Newman for advice and support. Newman now informed Simpson of the "deliberate opinion" he had formed about the *Rambler*:

> I thought it was in a false position—which it never would get out of—and I thought it was sure to be stopped, or to come to an end, in one way or another. Accordingly I said that it would be best for the proprietors to stop it themselves;—and at once, because if they did not, others would do it for them. . . . I have had no reason up to this day to change this view of the matter.[9]

In Newman's opinion, no move which Simpson might make could retrieve the *Rambler* from its "false position." He expressed the same opinion, a few days later, in refusing a similar appeal for assistance made by Wetherell.[10] He said that he had not been able for several months to approve of the line taken by the *Rambler*, and he was thereby precluded from co-operating with its proprietors.

Simpson and Wetherell were not deterred. A Protestant publishing house was soon found which was willing to accept the *Rambler* on its own terms. In November 1861, the name of "Williams and Norgate" replaced that of "Burns and Lambert" on the title page of the *Rambler*. It was clear now that the Liberal Catholics were determined to maintain their organ regardless of official opposition. "The result of all this," Acton prophesied, "is that we shall soon have a regular opposition and open war declared by the other side."[11]

It was necessary for the *Rambler* to publish some statement announcing the change. Simpson, extremely bitter about the treatment the *Rambler* had received, wished to make this an occasion for a virtual declaration of war. He proposed to write a slashing article on "Catholic Liberty of the Press,"

---

[8] Simpson to Newman, 3 Oct. 1861, Newman MSS. The publisher was Chapman and Hall.
[9] Newman to Simpson, 2 Oct. 1861, quoted by Wilfrid Ward, *Life of John Henry Cardinal Newman* (London, 1912), I, 535.
[10] Newman to Wetherell, 5 Oct. 1861, Newman MSS.
[11] Acton to Simpson, 1 Oct. 1861, Gasquet, *Lord Acton and his Circle*, p. 202.

giving a full history of the conflicts of the *Rambler* from 1856 to the present and exposing all the attempts to destroy it. Wetherell, who shared Newman's views on Simpson's "imprudence," resisted this proposal. Wetherell was still suffering from an illness which had prevented him from working on the *Rambler* for eight months, but he resumed the sub-editorship in order to restrain Simpson. Acton, writing from Munich, also urged moderation. He was alarmed by Simpson's "disposition to take advantage of the change for more vigorous and bitter polemics" and sought to check his "just indignation" and "highly cultivated pugnacity." A "manifesto" against the authorities would weaken the moral position of the *Rambler*, which must rely upon the slow process of influencing habits of thought. Acton proposed that the *Rambler* should simply announce the fact of its change of publishers and indicate that the magazine would go on "as before, regarding as open to free discussion all questions not decided by the authority of the Church."[12] A statement to this effect, based largely on Newman's prospectus of 1859, was published.[13] It was a declaration of independence, but not of war.

Simpson soon found a way to ventilate his indignation and pugnacity. Manning had been lecturing on the Temporal Power with more zeal than discretion, treating it as if it were a dogma of the Church and drawing his arguments from scriptural prophecies; he was in an apocalyptic mood and saw signs of Anti-Christ in the revolutions of Italy. Even in Rome Manning's sermons were regarded as inopportune. It was an excellent opportunity for Simpson to attack him. He did so with Acton's approval: some of his sentences were taken *verbatim* from Acton's letters. Simpson criticized Manning for raising the external possessions of the Church to the same level as its internal truths. The Temporal Power was not an article of faith but a matter of ecclesiastical politics. Under existing political circumstances it was necessary to preserve it, but it was at best an imperfect means

---

[12] Acton to Simpson, 6 Oct. 1861, *ibid.*, pp. 207-8.
[13] "To Readers and Correspondents," *Rambler*, n.s., VI (Nov. 1861), 147-8.

of securing the freedom of the Papacy. "What the Pope wants is, not a positive right of governing, but a negative right of not being governed; not a centre of political power, but a basis of independence."[14]

Acton thought that Simpson's article was "not too severe" on Manning: "It is impossible to exaggerate the danger of such doctrines as his."[15] Manning, however, was offended by the article: he saw in it both personal hostility and infidelity to the Holy See. He erroneously attributed the article to Newman, whom he regarded as the head of the English opposition to Roman influence. This error was largely responsible for Manning's hostility to Newman in subsequent years.

Acton was also writing on the Temporal Power. In July he had published an obituary article on Cavour, critical of his policies but respectful of his ability as a statesman. So exacerbated were the tempers of Catholics on the subject of the Temporal Power that a statement in Acton's article, to the effect that Cavour was not "consciously an enemy of religion,"[16] was criticized as too eulogistic. In the November *Rambler*, Acton found another occasion to state his views on the Temporal Power, in a review of Döllinger's book on that subject.

The storm of criticism which had greeted Döllinger's Odeon lectures had come as a surprise to the lecturer. It was necessary for him to give a more complete statement of his views, which appeared in a book, *Kirche und Kirchen, Papstthum und Kirchenstaat*. Döllinger sought to explain the motive of his lectures: to reconcile Catholics to the impending fall of the Temporal Power, and to show how this apparent disaster was part of the historical development of the Church. Döllinger saw the crisis of the Catholic Church in terms of its relation to German Protestantism. Protestantism had

---

[14] Simpson, "Dr. Manning on the Papal Sovereignty," *Rambler*, n.s., VI (Nov. 1861), 111-2. This sentence was supplied by Acton. See Simpson to Acton, 22 Jan. 1862, Woodruff MSS.

[15] Acton to Simpson, 9 Oct. 1861, Gasquet, *Lord Acton and his Circle*, pp. 211-2.

[16] Acton, "Cavour," *Historical Essays and Studies*, ed. J. N. Figgis and R. V. Laurence (London, 1907), pp. 200-1; reprinted from the *Rambler*, n.s., V (July 1861), 141-65. See Gertrude Himmelfarb, *Lord Acton: A Study in Conscience and Politics* (Chicago, 1952), pp. 83-4.

proved incapable of resisting the dissolving forces of modern
infidelity; a reconciliation with the Catholic Church, on
terms of mutual respect, was now possible. The great obstacle
to reunion was the conviction that the Catholic religion was
ineradicably bound up with abuses in the political sphere,
connected with Temporal Power. Döllinger freely admitted
the faults of the ecclesiastical government of Rome, though
he explained them as innovations, not proceeding from
Catholic principles, which Pius IX had tried to reform.
He held that the Temporal Power was legitimate and
necessary and prophesied that if it were overthrown it
would eventually be restored. But the overthrow of the
Temporal Power would not be an unmixed evil. It would
remove from the Papacy the reproach of misgovernment and
begin a process of purification of the Church. Döllinger urged
the Pope to flee from Rome and take up his exile in Catholic
Germany. His presence there would lead to the reunion of
the Churches; it would also serve to teach the Italians who
held the high offices of the Church the value of a Catholicism
based not on compulsion but on freedom:

> If the Court of Rome should reside for a time in Germany,
> the Roman prelates will doubtless be agreeably surprised to
> discover that our people is able to remain Catholic and
> religious without the leading-strings of a police, and that
> its religious sentiments are a better protection to the Church.
> ... Throughout Germany we have been taught by experience
> the truth of Fénelon's saying, that the spiritual power must
> carefully be kept separate from the civil, because their union
> is pernicious.[17]

The Papal sovereignty, originally designed to safeguard the
spiritual independence of the Church, had resulted in a
political dependence on a temporal institution. The remedy
which Döllinger proposed was to distinguish the Temporal
Power from the essence of the Catholic faith and to give
renewed emphasis to the spiritual mission of the Church.

The coldly objective analysis of the defects of the Papal

---

[17] J. J. I. von Döllinger, *Kirche und Kirchen, Papstthum und Kirchenstaat* (München,
1861), quoted in Acton, "Döllinger on the Temporal Power," *The History of
Freedom and other Essays*, ed. J. N. Figgis and R. V. Laurence (London, 1907),
pp. 370-1; reprinted from the *Rambler*, n.s., VI (Nov. 1861), 1-62.

government was perhaps the "first, unconscious, unpre-
meditated step" in Döllinger's process of detachment from
Rome: "The historian here began to prevail over the divine,
and to judge Church matters by a law which was not given
from the altar."[18] His defence of the Temporal Power was
in reality an exposure of its weaknesses. Nonetheless,
Döllinger's exaltation of the Pope's spiritual authority and
his critique of Protestantism disarmed resentment; much to
Acton's surprise, the book was well received. The Pope said
that it would do good, though he did not agree with all of it.[19]
The *Dublin Review* virtually apologized for the harsh tone of
Purcell's review of the Odeon lectures.[20] Montalembert, a
staunch defender of the Temporal Power, said that he
would willingly subscribe to every word of Döllinger's book;
and Lacordaire and Gratry were of the same opinion.[21]

Acton reviewed *Kirche und Kirchen* in the leading article in
the November *Rambler*, giving an extensive summary of the
book. Acton interpreted Döllinger's thought in a Whig
sense, stressing the suspicion of the State which was shared
by both Ultramontanes and Whigs. The State most deserving
of suspicion was the France of Napoleon III, which sought to
dominate the Papacy under the guise of protecting it; it was
better, Acton implied, for the Pope to lose the Temporal
Power than to maintain it by the aid of French bayonets.
He lamented that those who shared Döllinger's views on the
Temporal Power did not speak out: this was an allusion to
Newman's conduct. Acton, differing slightly from Döllinger,
held that the Temporal Power could not exist unless it was
guaranteed by the Catholic Powers. The Powers, in turn,
were entitled to a guarantee that the Pope's Government
would be reformed so that the Roman people would not be
faced with the dilemma of choosing "between the right of
insurrection against an arbitrary government and the duty of

---

[18] Acton, "Döllinger's Historical Work," *The History of Freedom*, pp. 415-6.
[19] Acton to Döllinger, 26 Aug. 1862, cited in J. Friedrich, *Ignaz von Döllinger*,
3 vols. (München, 1901), III, 269.
[20] See Charles Russell, "Dr. Döllinger's Protestantism and the Papacy,"
Dublin Review, III (April 1863), 467-503.
[21] Acton to Simpson, 6 Dec. 1861 and 13 Jan. 1862, Gasquet, *Lord Acton and
his Circle*, pp. 239, 257. See also Acton to Döllinger, 6 Dec. 1861 and 28 Jan.
1862, Woodruff MSS.

obedience to the Pope."[22] Acton shared Döllinger's hope that the Pope would take up his exile in Bavaria. Privately he regarded this as the solution to the *Rambler*'s conflicts with authority:

> The time cannot be distant when the great source of hostility to us, the Roman question, will be solved for a time in a way which will be a confirmation of our views. Then the quarrel between us and the Roman party will have no interest, for we shall be as zealous as any in support of the dispossessed and fugitive Pope. . . . Of course, with the Pope in Bavaria our antagonism on the ground of freedom of inquiry will remain, though a German exile will soon effect a change even in this respect.[23]

The Pope, however, obstinately remained in Rome, and the Temporal Power survived almost another decade, during which the Liberal Catholics had to face an increasingly militant Ultramontanism. Acton, recognizing the isolation of his party, saw the need for allies. New writers, of the most diverse character, were recruited for the *Rambler*. Acton won over his chaplain, Green, a respectable old Catholic. On the other hand, there was John Moore Capes, the *Rambler*'s former editor, who had left the Church and taken a position outside all religious communions. Acton willingly accepted Capes' offer to review books; perhaps he still hoped, by kindness, to draw Capes back into the Church. He felt considerable sympathy for those who found themselves in the limbo between Catholicism and Anglicanism. This was the position of the "corporate reunion" movement, which recognized the supremacy of Rome but discouraged conversions. Simpson and Wetherell had written against the "union" movement; but Acton, without subscribing to its doctrines, valued it as a bridge between the Churches and wanted the *Rambler* to engage in friendly "Irenics with the Union party."[24] Their organ, the *Union Review*, showed marked friendliness towards the *Rambler*; and Acton obtained articles from a leading "unionist," E. S. Ffoulkes, an

---

[22] Acton, "Döllinger on the Temporal Power," p. 373.
[23] Acton to Simpson, 11 Oct. 1861, Gasquet, *Lord Acton and his Circle*, p. 217.
[24] Acton to Simpson, 3 Oct. 1861, *ibid.*, p. 204.

eccentric convert. Another person of unionist views was the troublesome H. N. Oxenham, whom Acton hoped to make a leading member of the Liberal Catholic circle.

Acton had obtained for Oxenham a post at Newman's Oratory School at Edgbaston. At the end of 1861 there arose a difference between Newman and the headmaster, Father Darnell, over the special position accorded by Newman to the school's matron. The masters, including Oxenham, resigned in protest; Newman immediately recruited a new staff. Acton was inclined to favour Darnell and Oxenham, but he could not intervene in Newman's affairs. He was unhappy that Newman did not consult him, "although initially I contributed more than anyone to the founding of the school," and he felt that "Newman has obviously changed his views on education since the Dublin Lectures."[25] Darnell, a friend of Acton and one of Döllinger's translators, was replaced by Newman's friend Ambrose St. John. This tended to diminish the Liberal Catholic influence on Newman; but one of the new masters at the school was a contributor to the *Rambler*, Thomas Arnold, Jr.

Meanwhile the Ultramontanes were not idle. Wiseman was sending private reports on the *Rambler* to Rome;[26] he warned his clergy against the magazine and denounced it in a pastoral letter.[27] W. G. Ward was also active. On 21 January 1862, he delivered in the Catholic Academy a lecture on the intellect, which asserted the subordination of intelligence to the non-intelligent will guided by the Church; "his peroration was clearly directed against the *Rambler*."[28] Simpson, seeking an opportunity to reply to Ward's lecture, moved that it be printed, and Ward agreed. The review appeared in the May *Rambler*. It accused Ward of a want of charity to his opponents and a perverse tendency to press Catholic dogmas beyond their necessary consequences.

[25] Acton to Döllinger, 28 Jan. and 9 Feb. 1862, Woodruff MSS. See also Acton to Simpson, 1 and 5 Jan. 1862, Downside MSS.

[26] Wiseman to Manning, 23 Nov. and 26 Dec. 1861, and 25 March 1862, Manning MSS.

[27] Acton to Döllinger, 27 Dec. 1861, Woodruff MSS, and to Simpson, 23 Dec. 1861, Gasquet, *Lord Acton and his Circle*, p. 251. Acton refused to notice Wiseman's denunciation in the *Rambler*.

[28] Simpson to Acton, 22 Jan. 1862, Woodruff MSS.

Ward's disparagement of the intellect was "unsound and un-Catholic," for "theologians consider that the ideal of man's perfection requires intellectual excellence in its highest degree."[29]

The May *Rambler* also contained a letter by Acton on "The Danger of Physical Science," replying to a correspondent who had argued that physical science was the great enemy of religion. Acton asserted that a conflict between the facts of physical science and the dogmas of the Church was impossible, for the facts alone could not contradict religion. The danger came from the importation into the physical sciences of theories drawn from the moral sciences; the solution was to confine each science to its own sphere, operating according to its own principles. Similarly, theology must keep itself free from obsolete opinions on the physical universe. "It is a religious duty as well as an intellectual necessity to strive continually to bring existing faith into agreement with increasing knowledge, to reconsider old solutions in obedience to new problems. . . . Thanks to this constant alternation of difficulties and answers, religious ideas expand and science advances."[30]

The May 1862 issue of the *Rambler* was its last. Henceforth it was to be published as a quarterly review, under a new name. This change had long been mooted. There seemed to be a course of "natural development" for the *Rambler*, leading it to assume "a less ephemeral character,"[31] appearing less frequently but increasing in size and scope. Its tendency was to approximate the gravity of a quarterly review, to favour literature over journalism. Acton, in particular, had no liking for journalism, and wished to devote himself to more serious writing. As early as 1858, he had explored the possibility of transforming the *Rambler* into a quarterly. The idea had arisen again in 1861, when Acton had suggested changing the *Rambler* into a quarterly as a means of escaping the censure that was expected from Rome.

[29] "Dr. Ward on Intellect," *Rambler*, n.s., VI (May 1862), 487.
[30] "N.N." [Acton], "The Danger of Physical Science," *ibid.*, 529.
[31] "Enlargement of the 'Rambler'," *ibid.*, 430.

That possibility was kept in mind, but when, in 1862, Acton, Simpson and Wetherell decided to transform the *Rambler*, their primary motive was to improve the magazine.[32]

The great obstacle to "quartering" the *Rambler* was the fact that this would bring it into competition with the *Dublin Review* and might appear to be an outright defiance of Cardinal Wiseman. By 1861, however, the *Dublin* was evidently in decline. Bagshawe, the editor, was ineffective, and the publisher, Richardson, unco-operative; Wiseman had ceased to contribute; issues were published at irregular intervals. In June 1861, Acton heard that "Ward and his friends talk of starting a new review, and that the Cardinal abandons the *Dublin* to its decline."[33] In November, Bagshawe received an appointment as a Welsh judge and had to resign the editorship of the *Dublin*. The sub-editor, Dr. Russell, assisted Bagshawe in carrying on the review until some new arrangement could be made; but he was not sanguine about its prospects. The *Dublin* was generally regarded as a dying publication. Under these circumstances, it appeared to the conductors of the *Rambler* that they could safely transform their magazine into a quarterly without seeming to set themselves up as rivals of the *Dublin*. In March 1862, Acton, Simpson and Wetherell began to make arrangements for the change.

Acton was concerned to disarm opposition to this move. Accordingly, he wrote to Dr. Russell, announcing his intention of making the *Rambler* quarterly, and assuring him that there was no intention of striking at the *Dublin* in making this "change, the great object of which is conciliation."[34] The change was designed to enable the *Rambler* to pursue its natural development and to allow of more adequate treatment of great questions and a wider comprehension of views. The "communicated" section of the new *Rambler* would be open to contributions from all sections of Catholic opinion, and the correspondence, which had caused so many conflicts, could be omitted. Acton expressed his desire to

---

[32] Acton to Döllinger, 28 Jan., 9 Feb. and 19 March 1862, Woodruff MSS.
[33] Acton to Newman, 19 June 1861, cited in Ward, *Life of Newman*, I, 523.
[34] Acton to Russell, 26 March 1862, Westminster Archives.

come to an understanding with the managers of the *Dublin*. Russell accepted Acton's professions of good faith and proposed that the *Dublin* should be merged with the quarterly *Rambler*. Neither Wiseman nor Bagshawe, however, was willing to join with Acton and his friends. The news that the *Rambler* was to be made quarterly caused them to increase their efforts to save the *Dublin*, in order to prevent the Liberal Catholics from having the field entirely to themselves. Wiseman entered into negotiations with Burns to take over the publication of the *Dublin* and sought to find a new editor. These negotiations were not immediately fruitful, but they put an end to Russell's project of merging with the *Rambler*.[35]

Acton regarded this development as a manifestation of opposition to the *Rambler* on the part of Wiseman. "Here is the end of the *Dublin* negotiations and the beginning of the fight; a stand-up fight it will be."[36] It was necessary now to be the first in the field. An announcement was placed in *The Times*, stating that the *Rambler* would be enlarged to double its present size and become a quarterly on 1 July.

The notion of merging the two reviews was suddenly revived, however, by Burns, who was anxious to resume the publication of a magazine. He proposed that both the *Dublin* and the *Rambler* should give way to a new quarterly, which would be jointly edited by Acton and some member of Ward's party, such as T. W. Allies; the "communicated" section could be opened to all parties.[37] Wetherell was strongly opposed to dealing with Burns, and Acton regarded Wiseman's rejection of the merger as final. Nonetheless, Acton did not wish the Liberal Catholics to assume the responsibility for perpetuating Catholic factionalism. He therefore took a conciliatory line, writing to Canon Morris, Wiseman's secretary, offering to accept Burns' proposal and to merge the *Rambler* in a new quarterly open to all parties, provided that the *Dublin* should cease to exist.[38] Acton

[35] Russell to Wiseman, 4 April 1862, Westminster Archives. The idea of merging was Russell's, not Acton's.
[36] Acton to Simpson, 5 April 1862, Gasquet, *Lord Acton and his Circle*, p. 267.
[37] Burns to Simpson, 12 April 1862, Downside MSS.
[38] Acton to Simpson, 16, 26 and 28 April 1862, Gasquet, *Lord Acton and his*

N

insisted only that the review should preserve its independence and freedom of discussion: he "loved peace much, knowledge and honesty more."[39] Morris was willing to negotiate; but he was acting without Wiseman's approval, and Wiseman had no intention of sanctioning a Catholic quarterly independent of his supervision. Furthermore, Wiseman had learned that proceedings were pending in Rome which would lead to the censure of the *Rambler*.[40] He therefore put an end to all negotiations and resumed his attempts to revive the *Dublin*.

Meanwhile an attempt had been made to detach Simpson from his party. His bishop, Dr. Grant, wrote to him, complaining that his articles in the *Rambler* did not tend to "save souls" or "draw wanderers to the sacrament of Penance," and urging him "to take henceforth the part of silence, or, if you write and publish, the choice of subjects that do not affect the Church and the Holy See."[41] Simpson's reply, drafted after consultation with Acton, was a justification of the Liberal Catholic point of view:

Being a Catholic, I cannot help writing as a Catholic—in matters defined, taking the one side defined; in doubtful matters, choosing my side according to my convictions. . . .

I have written in a journal which deals necessarily with public topics, and cannot handle the private spiritual concerns of individuals, and so cannot lead men to contrition and penance—a journal which is not theological, and so cannot deal directly with matters of faith. It is only left to me to try and take the side of faith by defending the truth, and by proving that a man may be sincerely Catholic and may defend his religion without *suppressio veri* and *suggestio falsi*. . . .

I am certain that the cessation of the *Rambler*, or its change,

Circle, pp. 268-9, 273-6. This Canon John Morris is to be distinguished from the Liberal Catholic John Brande Morris, sometime canon of Plymouth and Acton's former chaplain at Aldenham.

[39] Acton to Simpson, 26 April 1862, *ibid.*, p. 274. Acton told Döllinger that the main point was the management of the Review, which "I can not give up now, because I alone afford security for freedom, scientific method and independence." Acton to Döllinger, 1 May 1862, Woodruff MSS.

[40] Russell to Wiseman, 29 April 1862, Westminster Archives.

[41] Grant to Simpson, Good Friday 1862, Downside MSS. Partially printed in Gasquet, *Lord Acton and his Circle*, p. 270n. According to Acton, Simpson's Redemptorist priests at Clapham had refused him absolution on account of his work on the *Rambler*: Acton to Döllinger, 1862, Woodruff MSS.

would do great harm to the Catholic cause in England. I know, for I have experienced the thing, that the great prejudice against the Church among educated Englishmen is not a religious one against her dogmas, but an ethical and political one; they think that no Catholic can be truthful, honest or free, and that if he tries to be so publicly he is at once subject to persecution. The existence of the *Rambler* is more or less a reply to this prejudice.[42]

Simpson complained that his studies necessarily bore some relation to theology, and therefore he was accused of writing theologically; but when he tried to avoid theology, he was accused of ignoring the supernatural. The main objection to him, however, was his politics, his history, and above all his independence. Simpson explained his position:

I desire to see the Catholic doctrine professed by all the world. I know by experience that the great objection to it in the minds of educated Englishmen is the political objection. I know by history that it was very much by political measures and in the pursuit of political ends that the Holy See lost England. And I see that there still exists a widespread opinion among English Catholics that the same infallibility attaches to the dicta of the Holy See about political matters as attaches to its definitions in matters of faith. Hence there is a disposition to overlook the lessons of history, and the dictates of reason in politics, and to commit oneself blindly to the political guidance of an authority which has no promise of political wisdom. . . . I submit *ex animo* to the Church in all questions of faith, and interpretation of the divine law—But I assert a right to follow my reason in matters of science and experience of the senses and of practical reason and secular prudence.[43]

This was the spirit in which the Liberal Catholics transformed the *Rambler* into its quarterly successor, the *Home and Foreign Review*.

---

[42] Simpson to Grant, 23 April 1862, Downside MSS. Portions of this letter are reprinted in Gasquet, *Lord Acton and his Circle*, pp. lvii-lviii, 270-271n. See also Simpson to Acton, Easter Monday 1862 (Woodruff MSS.), and Acton to Simpson, 22 April 1862 (Gasquet, pp. 270-1), containing some passages which Simpson employed in his reply to Grant.

[43] Draft letter by Simpson, 1862, Downside MSS. It is not certain whether this draft was incorporated into the letter sent to Grant.

CHAPTER XI

CHALLENGE AND RESPONSE, 1862

THE new name of the transformed *Rambler* signified no change in policy: the personnel, the motto and the spirit of the *Rambler* were retained. The title of the *Home and Foreign Review* was adopted in order to allow a fresh start, free of the unfavourable associations which the name of the *Rambler* bore in the public mind, and incidentally in order to escape the censures which were expected from Rome.[1] The change to a quarterly was announced in the last issue of the *Rambler*:

> Its aim will still be to combine devotion to the Church with discrimination and candour in the treatment of her opponents; to reconcile freedom of inquiry with implicit faith; and to discountenance what is untenable and unreal, without forgetting the tenderness due to the weak and the reverence rightly claimed for what is sacred. Submitting without reserve to infallible authority, it will encourage a habit of manly investigation on subjects of scientific interest.[2]

The new title and format did not save the Liberal Catholic organ from the wrath of the hierarchy. A censure was being prepared in Rome, the news of which had led Wiseman to terminate the negotiations with the *Rambler*. Acton had had some intimation of this; in April 1862 he told Newman that "the violence of the feeling in the Curia seems to have reached its height. . . . They have lately attempted to do me a private injury, for the purpose of serving their public ends."[3] This appears to refer to an attempt by a Roman

---

[1] Acton to Döllinger, 26 May 1862, Woodruff MSS. Newman had advised this course: Newman to Wetherell, 21 March 1862, Newman MSS. Acton proposed the name *Home and Foreign*, which had appeared in the subtitle of the original *Rambler*.

[2] "Enlargement of the 'Rambler'," *Rambler*, n.s., VI (May 1862), 431. Much of this was taken from Newman's prospectus for the bi-monthly *Rambler* in 1859.

[3] Acton to Newman, 5 April 1862, cited in Douglas Woodruff, "Introduction" to Acton, *Essays on Church and State* (London, 1952), p. 27.

monsignor to turn Acton's fiancée against him.[4] In May, Cardinal Barnabò, Prefect of Propaganda, sent a circular letter to the English bishops, listing the offences of which the *Rambler* was guilty: "abstruse questions closely connected with the Faith are raised, and one of the principal writers often puts forward temerarious and scandalous propositions; the temporal authority of the Holy See is openly attacked, and the administration of the Pontifical States; it is said that Paul III, Paul IV, Pius V, preferred temporal emolument to the good of souls, and were the cause of England's loss to the Catholic Faith."[5] Particular passages which had given offence were specified. The bishops were required, within three months, to publish pastoral letters warning the faithful against the *Rambler*. Some of the bishops were unwilling to deliver the required censure. Their resistance obtained a reprieve for the *Home and Foreign*.[6] In August, however, the storm broke.

Wiseman had visited Rome in the spring of 1862, on the occasion of the canonization of the Japanese martyrs. The bishops assembled for this event decided to present an address to the Pope supporting the Temporal Power, and Wiseman was president of the commission to draft it. A rumour became current that there had been some disagreement over the terms of the address; and Acton mentioned the story, without confirming it, in the first issue of the *Home and Foreign Review*: "This address is said to be a compromise between one which took the violent course of recommending that major excommunication should be at once pronounced against the chief enemies of the temporal power by name, and one still more moderate than the present. The opening

[4] "The Curia has used a most dishonourable weapon against me. Nardi has written to Marie every possible derogatory thing against me." Acton to Döllinger, 1 Nov. 1862, Woodruff MSS. Countess Marie von Arco-Valley was betrothed to Acton in 1860; they were not married until 1865. The delay was primarily due, however, to the instability of the lady's affections.

[5] Digest of the Propaganda circular, from the Oscott archives, by Dom Cuthbert Butler, *The Life and Times of Bishop Ullathorne*, 2 vols. (New York, 1926), I, 322.

[6] J. Friedrich, *Ignaz von Döllinger* (München, 1901), III, 299. See also Newman to Acton, 19 July 1862, in Wilfrid Ward, *The Life of John Henry Cardinal Newman* (London, 1912), I, 639.

paragraphs are certainly unfortunate."[7] The *Home and Foreign* appeared on the first day of July; on the fourth and fifth, a more violent account of the address, harshly (and erroneously) criticizing Wiseman's conduct, was published in a French paper, *La Patrie*. Wiseman mistakenly saw a connection between these two reports, and he made this the occasion for censuring the *Home and Foreign*.

Addressing the clergy of Westminster on his return from Rome, Wiseman denied the account which had been published in *La Patrie*. Then he adverted to "a covert insinuation of the same charges, in a publication avowedly Catholic, and edited in my own diocese, consequently canonically subject to my correction." The conduct of the *Home and Foreign*, Wiseman said, was not surprising in view of

> the antecedents of that journal under another name, the absence for years of all reserve or reverence in its treatment of persons or things deemed sacred, its grazing over the very edges of the most perilous abysses of error, and its habitual preference of uncatholic to catholic instincts, tendencies, and motives. In uttering these sad thoughts, and entreating to warn your people, and especially the young, against such dangerous leadership, believe me I am only obeying a higher direction than my own impulses, and acting under much more solemn sanctions. Nor shall I stand alone in this unhappily necessary correction.[8]

Wiseman's prediction that the other bishops would join in his condemnation of the *Rambler* and its successor was soon fulfilled. In September and October, all but one of the bishops censured the *Rambler* in their pastorals. Bishop Cornthwaite, in Yorkshire, was the most severe, and he and Ullathorne required their clergy to read the condemnation from their pulpits. On the other hand, Acton's bishop, Brown of Shrewsbury, consulted with him before issuing his pastoral, which condemned only the *Rambler*, ignoring the *Home and Foreign*.[9] Most of the bishops employed a common

---

[7] *Home and Foreign Review*, I (July 1862), 269.

[8] *Rome and the Catholic Episcopate: Reply of His Eminence Cardinal Wiseman to an Address presented to him by the Clergy Secular and Regular of the Archdiocese of Westminster* (London, 1862), pp. 26-7.

[9] Acton to Simpson, 9 Oct. 1862, Downside MSS.

formula in their pastorals, quoting Wiseman's remarks and adding a brief endorsement. The circular of Bishop Clifford of Clifton may be cited as an example:

> We feel it our duty to call your attention to a periodical hitherto known as the *Rambler*, and now published under the title of *The Home and Foreign Review*. This journal professes to be a Catholic publication, and therefore, its readers are naturally led to suppose, that the opinions advanced by it, and the tone which pervades it, may safely be regarded as expressions of Catholic thought and feeling. We regret to say that such has not been the case for some time past, and it is our duty to call your attention to this fact, and, through you, to warn the faithful committed to your care, lest they be led to conclude, from our silence, that they may safely follow the guidance of this professedly Catholic paper in the discussion of sacred and doctrinal subjects. . . . We fully concur in the remarks made by his Eminence, and we trust that you will prudently exert your best endeavours, to prevent any of those committed to your care, allowing themselves to be led astray by dangerous teachers.[10]

It was a curiously limited censure: the *Rambler* was condemned for general faults, and the faithful were warned against dangerous tendencies in the *Home and Foreign*, which was deprived of its character as a recognized Catholic organ. This was neither a prohibition nor a formal theological condemnation; it was simply a strong expression of disapproval.

More than this was needed to counteract the influence of the *Home and Foreign*. A new attempt was made to revive the *Dublin Review*. Wiseman made over his rights in the *Dublin* to Manning, to whom he gave a complete freedom which he allowed to nobody else.[11] Burns replaced Richardson as publisher of the *Dublin* and placed its finances on a sound footing. The editorship was given to W. G. Ward, the ablest and most extreme of Ultramontanes. "You will find me," he told his sub-editor, "narrow and strong—*very* narrow and

---

[10] Circular of Bishop Clifford, 24 Sept. 1862, quoted in Simpson to Acton, Sept. 1862, Woodruff MSS.
[11] Wiseman to Manning, 9 Sept. 1862, Manning MSS.

very strong."[12] Manning required that all theological articles be submitted to censors and exercised a strict control himself; but the spirit of the new *Dublin* was that of Ward, brilliant, logical, predominantly theological and devotional, always aggressively Ultramontane. Unlike the *Rambler*, the *Home and Foreign Review* had to contend with an effective rival.

When Wiseman's censure appeared, Simpson proposed to publish a "confession," apologizing for the faults of the late *Rambler*, in order to enable the *Home and Foreign* to make a fresh start. Acton, however, was opposed to taking any notice of the Cardinal's denunciation. He spoke of Wiseman's statement as "a tissue of lies" but preferred to "submit to an unjust accusation of error [rather] than subject him to a true accusation of falsehood."[13] The *Home and Foreign*, Acton said, could not apologize for the tone of the *Rambler*, because it was not the tone but the principles that were at issue, and its principles remained unchanged. Any apology for the *Rambler* must involve Newman's article on "Consulting the Faithful," which was, "theologically, the most offending thing of all." Higher interests, "Newman's school, the future university (whether our own or at Oxford), and the whole interest of thought and science, are mixed up in our cause. In order to save them, I am persuaded that patience and a duck's back are the only safeguards."[14]

Nonetheless, it was decided to publish a reply to Wiseman in the October *Home and Foreign*. Newman advised Acton to write "a counter-statement to the Cardinal" which would be "a manly, simple, eloquent avowal of what you aim at"[15] and would reassure Catholics as to the future conduct of the review. Acton was less sanguine:

I remember how important I thought it to state in the reply to the Cardinal that Rome had virtually spoken, and that we

[12] Quoted by Wilfrid Ward, *William George Ward and the Catholic Revival* (London, 1912), p. 223.

[13] Acton to Simpson, 27 Aug. 1862, Downside MSS. This letter is published by Abbot Gasquet, *Lord Acton and his Circle* (London, 1906), p. 292; but Gasquet altered the word "lies" to read "mistakes" and omitted the words "of falsehood."

[14] *Ibid.*

[15] Newman to Acton, 17 Sept. 1862, cited in Woodruff, "Introduction," p. 27.

were going on in despite of her. We are in a position which obliges us to defy the thunders of the Vatican. Rome defends the political and temporal rights and possessions of the Church by spiritual censures. We say that if there is politically a sound reason against them we must incur excommunication.[16]

Acton's sharpness, however, was moderated by Wetherell; and the result was a cautious and respectful statement of the position of the *Home and Foreign Review*.[17]

The reply to Wiseman began by describing his censure of the review as the result of a misapprehension. No criticism of his conduct had been intended in the report on the bishops' address to the Pope; it was stated only that "a rumour was current, not that its purport was true."[18] The real difficulty lay, not in the erroneously censured report in the *Home and Foreign*, but in the prejudice against its conductors, founded upon the conduct and character of the *Rambler*. It was acknowledged that Wiseman's censure represented the views of Rome and was supported by a majority of the English bishops and clergy. The only response which could be made to this ecclesiastical hostility was a statement of the purposes and principles of the review.

The review existed for the service of the Church; if anything published in it was contrary to her doctrine or incompatible with devotion or respect to her authority, "we sincerely retract and lament it."[19] But a literary periodical could only serve religion indirectly, by following the laws of the intellect which are independent of the authority of the Church. Independent politics and science support religion by discovering truth and upholding right; and whatever diverts them from their own spheres, even for religious interests, is ultimately subversive of faith and morals and

[16] Acton to Simpson, 9 Dec. 1862, Downside MSS. Acton insisted that the Temporal Power was the essential issue. Acton to Döllinger, 26 Aug. 1862, Woodruff MSS.

[17] Newman found it lacking in "warmth." Wetherell's reply (Wetherell to Newman, 6 Nov. 1862, Newman MSS.) suggests, by its use of the first person, that Wetherell had written part of the article, which is usually assigned to Acton alone. Acton, however, wrote the major portion.

[18] Acton, "Cardinal Wiseman and the Home and Foreign Review," *The History of Freedom*, p. 443; reprinted from the *Home and Foreign Review*, I (Oct. 1862), 501-20.

[19] *Ibid.*, p. 447.

"argues either a timid faith which fears the light, or a false morality which would do evil that good might come."[20] This was the weakness of Ultramontane thinkers; but with the advance of learning and the development of impartial scholarship, the principles of politics and science

> have become, not tools to be used by religion for her own interests, but conditions which she must observe in her actions and arguments. Within their respective spheres, politics can determine what rights are just, science what truths are certain. . . . Political science can place the liberty of the Church on principles so certain and unfailing, that intelligent and disinterested Protestants will accept them; and in every branch of learning with which religion is in any way connected, the progressive discovery of truth will strengthen faith by promoting knowledge and correcting opinion, while it destroys prejudices and superstitions by dissipating the errors on which they are founded. . . . The moment has come when the best service that can be done to religion is to be faithful to principle, to uphold the right in politics though it should require an apparent sacrifice, and to seek truth in science though it should involve a possible risk. Modern society has developed no security for freedom, no instrument of progress, no means of arriving at truth, which we look upon with indifference or suspicion.[21]

In intellectual matters, there was no necessary gulf between Catholics and Protestants; and a Catholic review could best accomplish its purpose by pursuing studies with which Protestants as well as Catholics could sympathize, following principles and methods which were common to both. Such was the programme of the *Home and Foreign Review*.

This justification of the principles of the *Home and Foreign* did not mollify the bishops. In particular, Ullathorne felt that something more was needed to counteract its influence: the reasons for the censure of the *Rambler* and its successor

---

[20] *Ibid.*, p. 454.

[21] *Ibid.*, pp. 453, 456. Acton said that this was "the first time that the ideas of scientific method and political justice have been established from the Catholic standpoint in England . . . it is a standard, whereby parties will have to be defined from now on." Acton to Döllinger, 10 Oct. 1862, Woodruff MSS.

must be clearly stated.[22] He therefore published a letter to his clergy, giving the reasons for his opposition to the *Rambler* and the *Home and Foreign Review*.

Ullathorne criticized the *Home and Foreign* for its unsound principles regarding the separation of science and politics from religion. He concentrated his criticism on two writings in the *Rambler*, both by Simpson: the letters on Original Sin in 1855 and 1856 and "Reason and Faith" in 1861. The passages he noticed in the former had been specified in Barnabò's letter to the bishops: Simpson was charged with denying that original sin comes by propagation and with making God the author of sin. Simpson's remarks on Adam's animal nature and on the possibility of descent from the apes had taken on a new interest in the light of Darwin's work and were included in Ullathorne's censure. The articles on "Reason and Faith" were criticized as erroneous in theology and rationalistic in philosophy. Ullathorne concluded by asserting that "in the *Rambler*, of which the *Home and Foreign Review* is a continuation, there are contained propositions which are respectively subversive of the faith, heretical, approaching to heresy, erroneous, derogatory to the teaching Church, and offensive to pious ears."[23]

Ullathorne's pamphlet is most significant for its effect on Newman's attitude. Newman had read the early issues of the *Home and Foreign Review* with interest and admiration; he wrote friendly letters to its editors and deplored its condemnation by Wiseman. "I am very sorry," he said, "that the Bishops have set themselves against the ablest publication we have, though I can't quite trust its conductors."[24] Nonetheless he advised Acton to continue the review despite Wiseman's censures, and he praised the reply to the Cardinal.[25] Acton thought that he had finally won Newman

---

[22] See Newman's memorandum, 26 Dec. 1862, in Ward, *Life of Newman*, I, 550-1. Manning had suggested that the *Rambler* be put on the Index; Ullathorne preferred to leave its condemnation to the English Bishops.

[23] *A Letter on the Rambler and the Home and Foreign Review. Addressed to the Clergy of the Diocese of Birmingham, by the Right Rev. Bishop Ullathorne* (London, 1862), p. 42.

[24] Newman to Mrs. W. Froude, cited in Ward, *Life of Newman*, I, 538-9.

[25] Newman to Acton, 17 Sept. 1862, and to Wetherell, 6 Oct. 1862, *ibid.*, 539-541.

over to Liberal Catholicism, that Newman had "identified our cause with his own": "for the first time Newman declared himself completely on my side."[26]

Then, in October, Newman read an article in the *Home and Foreign* which seemed to "renew the worst faults of the *Rambler*."[27] Simpson, reviewing Döllinger's book on *Heathenism and Judaism*, found occasion to indulge in some Biblical criticism of his own. The first chapters of Genesis, he said, represented the creed of primitive religion and expressed primitive notions of the physical universe; "when the seed suddenly grew up into Christianity, . . . religion became entirely moral and metaphysical, without retaining a single fibre of physical speculation among its essential constituents."[28] Therefore Genesis should be read simply as a religious document, not as a treatise on astronomy or geology. Simpson was attempting to develop a Catholic answer to the problems posed by recent scientific discoveries; but Döllinger's narrative did not really justify the metaphysical structure which Simpson built upon it. Newman was extremely "put out" by the way in which "a theological discussion is lugged in without any occasion."[29] He objected to the article as off-hand theological speculation which insinuated its conclusions without giving a reasoned argument. "If this article is to be a sample of the *Home and Foreign*, I hope the Review and I may henceforth be 'better strangers'."[30]

At this juncture appeared Ullathorne's condemnation of the *Home and Foreign*. Newman regarded Ullathorne's judgment as decisive in a manner in which Wiseman's was not. Ullathorne was Newman's own bishop; he had condemned specific faults, giving reasons for his censures; and he was acting with the sanction of the Holy See, inasmuch as the

[26] Acton to Döllinger, 26 Aug. and 10 Oct. 1862, Woodruff MSS.

[27] Newman to Wetherell, 8 Nov. 1862, cited in Gasquet, "Introduction," p. lxxiii.

[28] Simpson, "Döllinger on Heathenism and Judaism," *Home and Foreign Review*, I (Oct. 1862), 452.

[29] Newman to Thomas Arnold, Jr., 12 Oct. 1862, quoted by Ward, *Life of Newman*, I, 543.

[30] Newman to Wetherell, 8 Nov. 1862, cited in Gasquet, "Introduction," p. lxxiii. Wetherell agreed that the article was bad: Wetherell to Newman, 15 Nov. 1862, Newman MSS.

passages he censured had been specified by Propaganda. Newman promptly wrote to Ullathorne to assure him of his submission. It was the duty of the writers and editors, he said, to repudiate the doctrines which were condemned and to withdraw the articles in which they were found. Newman also wrote to Acton, saying that Ullathorne's letter was "the voice of the Church."[31] He regarded it as irrelevant whether or not the censured articles actually contained the propositions which Ullathorne found in them: they had been condemned by a competent authority, and the Liberal Catholics were bound to submit.

Acton regarded Newman's letter as "singularly absurd."[32] Acton's own bishop had shown him the letter of Propaganda; Acton had found nothing in it which required him to adopt a different course than that which he was following. The Propaganda letter possessed greater force than that of the Bishop of Birmingham, who had no jurisdiction over the editors of the *Home and Foreign*. Acton would only follow Newman's advice to the extent of making no protest or reply.[33] Wetherell, however, was more seriously affected. Always cautious and inclined to follow Newman's views, he proposed to resign from the *Home and Foreign*. Acton "had all manner of difficulty in inducing the reluctant Wetherell to withdraw his resignation."[34]

Ward and Manning rejoiced at the apparent change in Newman's attitude; and Acton feared that "we may lose him altogether this time."[35] But meanwhile Newman once again modified his views. He came to the conclusion, after reading the reply to Ullathorne which Simpson wrote in December, that the Bishop had misinterpreted Simpson's articles in the *Rambler*. His own letter of submission, Newman found, had also been misinterpreted. Ullathorne had sent a copy to Monsignor Talbot in Rome, to show to the authorities

[31] Newman to Acton, 29 Oct. 1862, Woodruff MSS.
[32] Acton to Simpson, 31 Oct. 1862, Gasquet, *Lord Acton and his Circle*, p. 289.
[33] Acton to Newman, 31 Oct. 1862, Newman MSS.
[34] Acton to Simpson, 4 Nov. 1862, Downside MSS. Wetherell told Newman that there were things in the *Rambler*, notably Simpson's remarks on Pius V, of which he had disapproved. Wetherell to Newman, 6 Nov. 1862, Newman MSS.
[35] Acton to Simpson, 4 Nov. 1862, Downside MSS.

there as proof of Newman's loyalty. Newman feared that his submission to the Bishop's judgment had been taken to mean intellectual agreement with his arguments. He wrote to Ullathorne to make it clear that he had given only his submission and not his judgment on Simpson. While he disliked the tone of Simpson's articles, many of Simpson's views were also his own: "a certain sympathy with him has been at the root of my pain with his performances."[36]

Acton and Simpson managed to convince Newman that he was not bound to regard Ullathorne's condemnation as decisive. Conscious of the importance of the work which the *Home and Foreign Review* was attempting to do, Newman shrank from accentuating his differences with its conductors. Newman's position was a complex one. "A man who has been mixed up with two such different people as Ward and Simpson," he said, "cannot explain himself without writing a volume."[37]

It was Simpson, however, who wrote the volume. Simpson was conscious that much of the hostility to the *Home and Foreign Review* was based on his articles in the *Rambler*. He proposed to disembarrass the review by publicly assuming responsibility for those articles, at the same time replying to Ullathorne's criticisms of them. His reply was to be a personal one, and it was arranged that Acton and Wetherell should have no part in it, so that the *Home and Foreign* would not be responsible for Simpson's remarks, and Simpson could assert that he was "writing without the sanction or knowledge of its conductors."[38]

Simpson explained that his articles on "Reason and Faith" were not an exposition of the Catholic faith, but a reply to *Essays and Reviews*, a justification of the Catholic position in terms which might be understood by non-Catholics. This was the cause of Ullathorne's misinterpretations. Simpson had not asserted that faith is opposed to reason, but the contrary. He had distinguished the "inward

---

[36] Draft of Newman's letter to Ullathorne, Dec. 1862, quoted by Ward, *Life of Newman*, I, 553.

[37] Cited in Wilfrid Ward, *William George Ward and the Catholic Revival* (London, 1912), p. 205.

[38] Simpson, *Bishop Ullathorne and the Rambler* (London, 1862), p. 3.

core" of faith from its external appurtenances in order to demonstrate that faith was immune to scientific attacks and that Catholics were not committed to oppose the advance of science. The "inward core" of faith meant the entirety of the articles of the creed and revealed dogma; Simpson acknowledged the infallibility of the Church in defining faith and morals, although it was fallible in other respects. Simpson also defended his letters on Original Sin, which, he said, had been based on the Jesuit Perrone's lectures in Rome and were approved by priests before being published. Ullathorne had also criticized Simpson's remarks on Pius V; Simpson replied that "episcopal censures cannot change the truth of history." Insofar as Ullathorne had censured him in his capacity as a bishop, Simpson protested against his judgment, appealing "from the Bishop ill informed to the Bishop better informed"[39] and to the public at large.

Newman regarded Simpson's pamphlet as a satisfactory reply to Ullathorne. Ullathorne, however, was not satisfied. He told Newman that Simpson's system "was one of Pantheism mixed up with the Catechism, etc., that Science was exalted against Religion; that an Hegelian transcendentalism was professed or implied; that political conscience is made at variance with moral; that Simpson was not the worst of the party; that he had wished to knock under and take Manning for his director, but there was a more subtle mind at the bottom; that various young men had left Sir John Acton and given out loose, half-infidel opinions."[40] Simpson's reply irritated Ullathorne and indicated to him that a more complete treatment of the subject was required. He therefore published a second letter to his clergy at the beginning of 1863.

Ullathorne took no notice of Simpson's reply other than to observe that there was nothing in it which required him to modify what he had written. He concentrated his criticism

---

[39] *Ibid.*, p. 42.
[40] Memorandum by Newman, 26 Dec. 1862, quoted by Ward, *Life of Newman*, I, 551. Ullathorne described Simpson's mind as "at one time Kantian, at another pantheistic." Ullathorne to Newman, 1 Jan. 1863, in Butler, *Life of Ullathorne*, pp. 327-8.

on the "rationalistic system"[41] of the *Home and Foreign Review*, which sowed the seeds of doubt and irreverence in Catholic minds. The methods and tone of the *Home and Foreign* were not Catholic; it seemed more like an enemy than a friend of the Church. Ullathorne mocked its scientific pretensions:

> The position from which the reviewers prefer looking on their English Catholic brethren seems situated as it were in a misty dawn, through which the stars of German science are about to rise, and to search the obscure places of our faith. What we have faintly heard of, they have seen; and advancing through the twilight, they use the privileges of travellers to tell what they have seen to a simple hearted people.[42]

Ullathorne found the *Home and Foreign* guilty of a "tendency to pull down faith, diminish truth and dissolve authority."[43]

The controversy between Ullathorne and the *Home and Foreign Review* ended inconclusively. Simpson had succeeded in answering the gravest charges; Ullathorne's biographer acknowledges that he "had missed the point of Simpson's argument and had misrepresented his meaning."[44] But, as Newman observed, if Ullathorne had misunderstood Simpson, the average layman was more likely to do so. Ordinary Catholics knew only that the *Home and Foreign* was a source of irritation and that it had been condemned by the bishops. Against such a prejudice, no effective reply was possible.

The controversy, indeed, had skirted the main issue. The principle which the Liberal Catholics upheld was the right of the individual Catholic to freedom of intellectual inquiry within the limits set by the defined dogmas of the Church. It was thus irrelevant whether their particular speculations were right or wrong; the issue was their right to speculate. On this issue "there was a consensus of Bishops to the point, that questions not yet decided ought not to be popularly

---

[41] Ullathorne, *On Certain Methods of the Rambler and the Home and Foreign Review: A Second Letter to the Clergy of the Diocese of Birmingham* (London, 1863), p. 30.

[42] *Ibid.*, pp. 31-2.

[43] *Ibid.*, p. 95.

[44] Butler, *Life of Ullathorne*, p. 325. Butler considers, however, that many of Simpson's views were reckless and unsound and that he was affected by the philosophy of Ontologism.

discussed."[45] The bishops had failed to prevent the transformation of the *Rambler* into the *Home and Foreign Review*, nor had they succeeded in forcing the review to submit; but, by the mere fact of their hostility, they had isolated it from the sympathies of a majority of the English Catholics.

Acton was fully aware of the extent of his isolation. The years 1861 and 1862 had seen the first great crisis in his life. He was marked by the experience: "something in him had been bruised by the spectacles that he had had to witness."[46] In 1861 he had experienced the shock of learning that he was separated on basic issues from all respectable Catholics, even Newman. By the end of 1862 he had come to the conclusion that the real ground of his isolation was a moral one—and that his own Church had placed itself on the side opposed to morality:

> The antitheses lie very deep, and I regard any reconciliation as impossible, since my article in October, in which I worked out my theory of science. All accusations against Simpson or myself are actually mere pretexts by which they want to conceal, so that it will not be recognized, the fundamental principle that the Church must be defended only by moral methods. . . . Judge by this Ullathorne's principle, that souls must be won *at all hazards*. This is now the wide chasm between the Review and the Episcopate.[47]

Acton's principle that the Church may not fight with immoral weapons leads straight to the ethical rigorism of his later years; it is the characteristic sign of the mature Acton. In the crises of 1861 and 1862, Acton had reached maturity.[48]

---

[45] Newman to Acton, 19 July 1862, Woodruff MSS.
[46] Herbert Butterfield, *Lord Acton* (London, 1948), p. 9.
[47] Acton to Döllinger, 7 Jan. 1863, Woodruff MSS.
[48] The distinction between the "early" and the "mature" Acton is the subject of debate among biographers. See Lionel Kochan, *Acton on History* (London, 1954), p. 45, who, however, dates maturity around 1870.

O

Chapter XII

THE *HOME AND FOREIGN REVIEW*,
1862-1864

AGAINST the background of episcopal hostility and popular suspicion, the *Home and Foreign Review* had to make its way. In its principles and policies, the *Home and Foreign* was substantially a continuation of the *Rambler*; but there were certain significant differences between the two periodicals. Even before the censure of the bishops had deprived the *Home and Foreign* of its character as a representative organ of English Catholicism, its conductors had proposed to "diminish the religious speciality" which had characterized the *Rambler*. "It is no longer a Catholic review," wrote Simpson, "but a review whose conductors happen to be Catholics; it challenges notice no longer as representing Bishops and Priests, but as a literary rival of the old reviews."[1] Simpson did not deny the essentially Catholic character of the *Home and Foreign*; but it had passed from the narrow field of Catholic journalism, represented by *The Tablet*, the *Weekly Register* and the *Dublin*, to the wider ranges of the great English reviews, the *Quarterly*, the *Edinburgh* and the *Westminster*. It sought an audience which was not exclusively Catholic. One of its foremost objects, Acton said, was "by instructing English readers generally concerning Catholic ideas, and by familiarizing Catholics with the facts and thoughts of the world around them, gradually to break down some of those obstacles to an understanding at least which are not founded on purely religious grounds."[2]

The contributors to the *Home and Foreign* were of a more

---

[1] Simpson to Orestes Brownson, 4 July 1862, Downside MSS. Portions of this letter are printed in Abbot Gasquet, "Introduction" to *Lord Acton and his Circle* (London, 1906), pp. lxiv-lxv. Simpson had invited Brownson to write for the *Home and Foreign*.

[2] Acton to Gladstone, 30 June 1862, BM Add. MS. 44093 ff. 8-9.

diverse character than those of the *Rambler*. Acton obtained the services of several writers from the Continent. The contributors were not exclusively Catholic. One of the regular writers was an Anglican, D. C. Lathbury. Another frequent contributor was a French Jew, Maurice Block: "I do not see," Acton wrote, "why Judaism is an objection to a man writing current events."[3]

The management of the *Home and Foreign Review* was not identical with that of the *Rambler*. Frederick Capes, who had been a part-proprietor of the *Rambler*, had no share in the *Home and Foreign*.[4] Acton and Simpson remained as proprietors, and Acton as editor. Wetherell continued as subeditor, though he insisted that he was actually joint editor with Acton. Wetherell was under Newman's influence and came to share Newman's belief that Simpson's imprudence and reputation for unsoundness were largely responsible for the hostility towards the *Home and Foreign*. The review, Wetherell said, could not bear, "in the present state of opinion and feeling about it, the existence of any suspicion that a terrible infant has anything to do with its management."[5] He thought that the fact that Simpson was a proprietor, and was therefore known as one of the "conductors" of the review, created a prejudice against it. In December 1862, Wetherell proposed that Simpson surrender his proprietorship and assume the status of an ordinary contributor. Simpson was willing to placate Wetherell by giving up his nominal proprietorship, which produced no financial benefit. He placed the matter in Acton's hands, stipulating only for the maintenance of "some point of moral, or if you like it, sentimental interest"[6] in the *Home and Foreign*. Acton insisted that the change should be merely nominal: he would be no party, he told Simpson, "to any scheme really to diminish your influence, or to make the Review less your organ than it is. . . . All that I ever contemplated . . . would

[3] Acton to Simpson, 10 Jan. 1864, Gasquet, *Lord Acton and his Circle*, p. 309. Acton expected Simpson to revise Block's articles and "give them an H. & F.-ical aspect."

[4] Simpson to Acton, n.d. [Dec. 1862], Woodruff MSS.

[5] Wetherell to Simpson, 27 Oct. 1862, Downside MSS.

[6] Simpson to Acton, n.d., Woodruff MSS. Simpson asked to retain the privilege of refusing payment for articles.

be an understanding preserving your present position really intact, sacrificing only the name of proprietor."[7] It was agreed that Simpson would resign his proprietorship, with the right of resuming it if he should later be dissatisfied with the new arrangement; but, except for the title of proprietor, he was to retain his share in the management.

The arrangement was not a satisfactory one. The prejudice against the *Home and Foreign* arising from Simpson's association with it was not removed, because no announcement of the change was made to the public. Wetherell, who had been told only that Simpson was no longer a proprietor, did not always consult him as much as Simpson thought he ought to be consulted. Simpson came to feel that in many ways he was superfluous: "I got off the coach to lighten the load, and it has driven on without me."[8] Acton relied increasingly on the assistance of Wetherell, whom he described as his "*alter ego* in the *Home and Foreign Review*, and to all better intents and purposes practically its Editor."[9] On several occasions Simpson expressed his dissatisfaction with the new arrangement. Acton strove to mediate between Simpson and Wetherell, but he found the task a difficult one.

In 1863 a new member was added to the staff of the *Home and Foreign*, a convert, Peter le Page Renouf. Acton described Renouf, who was professor of ancient history at Dublin, as "the most learned Catholic in the country,"[10] and credited him with having suggested the theory of development to Newman. Renouf had been one of the leading writers of the *Atlantis*. That journal had declined since Newman left Dublin and was virtually suspended. Most of its literary staff transferred their support to the *Home and Foreign*. Renouf was one of the first to offer his services. In the summer of 1862, he proposed to write an article in favour of

[7] Acton to Simpson, 21 Dec. 1862, Downside MSS.

[8] Simpson to Acton, 13 Dec. 1863, Downside MSS. Gasquet misquotes this: *Lord Acton and his Circle*, p. liv.

[9] Acton to Gladstone, 1 Jan. 1867, BM Add. MS. 44093 ff. 55-8. Acton had a high opinion of Wetherell's talent and judgment and regarded him as "a very good restraint against Simpson's lack of discretion." Acton to Döllinger, 29 March 1862, Woodruff MSS.

[10] Acton to Simpson, 2 Sept. 1862, Downside MSS. See also CUL Add. MS. 4988.

founding a Catholic college at Oxford. Acton, however, although convinced of the necessity of higher education for English Catholics, was never enthusiastic for the Oxford scheme: he preferred to found an entirely new Catholic University. He had discussed the matter with Newman and had offered him land for the university at Bridgnorth, with access to his large library at Aldenham. Acton therefore declined Renouf's article, fearing that it might injure the prospects of the Catholic University; at the same time, he urged Renouf himself to undertake the founding of the university.[11]

Acton proposed to make Renouf an additional sub-editor of the *Home and Foreign*. He hoped that "the purely objective, scientific nature of Renouf's mind"[12] would tend to moderate the quarrels of Wetherell and Simpson. Renouf accepted the sub-editorship in the autumn of 1863[13] and contributed a large number of reviews. Shortly afterwards, however, he was appointed an inspector of schools; this prevented him from assisting in the editorial work.

The many new contributors to the *Home and Foreign* enabled it to deal with a broader range of subjects than the *Rambler*. The political and religious departments occupied proportionately less space, while economics, philology, law, archaeology and science received greater emphasis. The *Home and Foreign* had in its service a staff of experts, such as the historical economist Roscher, the classicist Paley, Renouf on archaeology, W. K. Sullivan on science and Celtic lore, Acton and Döllinger on history and, on foreign politics, correspondents in the various countries. The distinctive feature of the *Home and Foreign Review*, which gave it a distinguished place in the history of English periodical literature, was the section on "Contemporary Literature."

[11] Acton to Renouf, 14 Nov. 1862, and Renouf to Acton, 22 Nov. 1862, *Selections from the Correspondence of the First Lord Acton*, ed. J. N. Figgis and R. V. Laurence (London, 1917), pp. 162-5, 125-6. Renouf, however, felt himself unequal to the task of founding a university.

[12] Acton to Simpson, 2 Sept. 1863, Downside MSS.

[13] His rôle was kept secret. At the same time, Lathbury joined the staff as a reviser of articles. Wetherell remained as sub-editor and Simpson as "*amicus curiae*." Acton to Döllinger, 14 Aug. 1863, Woodruff MSS.

Each issue contained a large number of brief reviews of books, both English and foreign, covering all areas of serious literature, written by specialists. The erudition of these reviews, and the knowledge which they displayed of foreign literature, was unrivalled among English quarterlies. There were on the average fifty reviews an issue; one issue contained as many as ninety-seven. Acton did the largest share of the reviewing.

The most important reviews were those dealing with Biblical criticism. The Colenso controversy had shown that, in the case of some Protestants, the reaction against Biblical literalism could imperil all dogmatic belief. Simpson, who reviewed the controversy, maintained that this danger was one to which only Protestants, who had no standard of orthodoxy other than the text of the Bible, were liable, while Catholics, secure in the dogmatic infallibility of the Church, could safely allow the free scientific investigation of the Bible.[14]

> The great practical difference between biblical science as cultivated by Protestants and as cultivated by Catholics is that, with the former, the very foundations of Christian faith are put in question; and the results which Catholics might adopt with impunity lead, in the case of Protestants, legitimately, if not always in fact, to simple unbelief. . . . The inspiration of Scripture is a traditional belief of the Catholic Church, which has, however, cautiously abstained from defining the nature and limits of inspiration. A considerable amount of liberty is therefore left to scientific speculation, especially if we remember . . . that the substance of the Catholic faith, as positively defined by the Church, lies in a region to which real scientific speculation does not even tend to approach.[15]

Simpson combined his justification of the Catholic position with a plea for the freedom of the Catholic scholar. "Those

---

[14] This idea had been suggested to Acton by Jowett: "He said to me strikingly, it is easier for Catholics than Protestants to let biblical criticism and its results pass without opposition. If it should ever happen that this scientific freedom, which is so dangerous to Protestants, is allowed to Catholics, we would immediately stand on an entirely different footing with this entire school, and progress would not always lead to unbelief." Acton to Döllinger, 26 May 1862, Woodruff MSS.

[15] *Home and Foreign Review*, III (July 1863), 222.

who believe the Catholic Church to be divinely protected from dogmatic error in its decisions must of course accept its canon of Scripture as the true one; but there is nothing to prevent their discussing all the historical facts of which the history of the canon is composed."[16] In the realm of facts, Catholic theologians should be free to accept the conclusions of scientific history, or of any other science.[17]

The standard of the *Home and Foreign Review* was so high that it criticized some Biblical critics, such as Renan, for being insufficiently scientific, for lack of objectivity and reliance on unproved hypotheses. The most striking illustration of its attitude was an article by Renouf on Smith's *Dictionary of the Bible*. Renouf asserted that Catholics could, without sacrificing orthodoxy, come to the same conclusions on such questions as the authorship of Isaiah as the most advanced German critics. During the preceding century the external evidences of Christianity had undergone profound modification, not however to the disadvantage of Catholicism, for the only security that remained for the inspiration of the Bible was the tradition of the Church. Renouf admitted that recent Biblical criticism was the product of unbelief or indifference, but he held that Catholics must nonetheless accept the scientific truths that had been demonstrated: "facts and arguments are not disposed of by calling men 'rationalists' and unbelievers." "The interests of the most conservative theology are here in fact identical with those of critical science. It is not for the benefit of religion that all the positions taken up by its defenders should be evidently such as may be undermined, turned, or carried by assault."[18] Dean Stanley, in the *Edinburgh Review*, compared the boldness of this article with that of *Essays and Reviews*: "The writer, from the most orthodox point of view, decides fearlessly on all questions, and decides on what (for want of a

[16] *Ibid.* (Oct. 1863), 651.

[17] For an example of this freedom in science, see W. K. Sullivan, "Lyell on the Antiquity of Man," *ibid.*, II (April 1863), 456-503, which accepts Lyell's evolutionary theories of geology.

[18] P. le P. Renouf, "Dr. Smith's Dictionary of the Bible," *ibid.*, IV (April 1864), 626, 655. Acton remarked in jest that "we shall incur excommunication for the review of Smith, where we reject the greater part of Isaiah." Acton to Simpson, 28 March 1864, Downside MSS.

better word) we must call the liberal side—on the side of the Essayists."[19]

The scholarly integrity and ability of the *Home and Foreign Review* won for it the admiration of the English world of thought. Matthew Arnold remarked that "perhaps in no organ of criticism in this country was there so much knowledge, so much play of mind."[20] Max Müller described it as "one of the best edited of our quarterlies."[21] The *Home and Foreign* was judged to have surpassed, "alike in knowledge, range, and certainty, any of the other quarterlies, political, or ecclesiastical, or specialist, which the nineteenth century produced."[22]

In politics, the *Home and Foreign* was more closely associated with the Liberal party than the *Rambler* had been. At first, indeed, it had professed indifference to parties. "Our purpose," Acton said, "is to maintain that old Whig system of which Burke is the greatest exponent, and which it seems necessary at the present day to have been a Tory to understand. It is obvious therefore that we cannot undertake to support any party."[23] In practice, however, the principles of the *Home and Foreign* drew it into the camp of the Liberals. The Tories, Acton believed, were indifferent to principles and represented merely the interests of the Established Church and the landlords. It was Gladstone, who had passed from the Tories to the Liberals, who represented Acton's political ideal, the practical doctrinaire who could reconcile constitutionalism and reform. Acton's friendship

[19] [A. P. Stanley], "The Three Pastorals," *Edinburgh Review*, CXX (July 1864), 304.

[20] Matthew Arnold, "The Function of Criticism at the Present Time," *Essays in Criticism* (London, 1928), p. 20; first published 1865. Arnold's next words are striking: "but these could not save it. The *Dublin Review* subordinates play of mind to the practical business of English and Irish Catholicism, and lives." Matthew Arnold's brother Thomas was a contributor to the *Home and Foreign*.

[21] Cited in Wilfrid Ward, *The Life of John Henry Cardinal Newman* (London, 1912), I, 538-9. Praise could also be cited from the *National* and the *Union Review*. The "phenomenal" *Home and Foreign* was an influence leading to the conversion of the liturgical historian Edmund Bishop. See Nigel Abercrombie, *The Life and Work of Edmund Bishop* (London, 1959), pp. 19, 292.

[22] J. N. Figgis and R. V. Laurence, "Introduction" to Lord Acton, *The History of Freedom and other Essays* (London, 1907), pp. xii-xiii.

[23] Acton to Gladstone, 30 June 1862, BM Add. MS. 44093 ff. 8-9. See also Simpson, "The Conservative Reaction," *Home and Foreign Review*, I (July 1862), 26-51.

for Gladstone was steadily growing; in 1863 it was transformed into enthusiasm. He welcomed Gladstone's speech on qualification for offices, in March, as "a great event. He has jumped with both feet into Home and Foreigndom."[24] In July the *Home and Foreign* hailed Gladstone as the destined leader of the Liberals. "Henceforward the future of the party is bound up with him. . . . if it will have more defeats, it will have greater triumphs."[25]

The *Home and Foreign* endorsed, not the Liberal party as a whole, but only its Gladstonian element, the political heirs of Peel. Acton cared less for the existing government of Palmerston than for the former government of Lord Aberdeen, in which the Peelites had played a leading role. The conduct of Aberdeen's government had been criticized in Kinglake's book on the Crimean War. Acton arranged for Lathbury, who was reviewing Kinglake, to receive confidential information from Gladstone and other survivors of the Aberdeen government which would enable him to vindicate its policy.[26] Acton repeatedly urged Gladstone to write for the *Home and Foreign*: "the objects and principles of the Review fit it to be your organ on many important matters, more perhaps than any other journal."[27] Gladstone was willing to write for the review, but he would not do so while in office. However, he assisted the editors by giving them political information and suggesting new contributors.

In January 1864, the *Home and Foreign* reviewed Gladstone's latest budget in an article by Robert Lowe, a junior minister. The article was highly favourable to Gladstone, with just enough criticism to make its praise persuasive. Gladstone, filled with admiration at the ability of the article, thought that Acton was its author; Acton disclaimed authorship but declined to give the writer's name.[28] Gladstone appears to have learned that Lowe was the author: this

[24] Acton to Simpson, 5 March 1863, Downside MSS.

[25] *Home and Foreign Review*, III (July 1863), 368.

[26] Acton to Gladstone, 26 and 28 Feb. 1863, BM Add. MS. 44093 ff. 18-21. See Lathbury, "Kinglake on the Causes of the Crimean War," *Home and Foreign Review*, II (April 1863), 398-432.

[27] Acton to Gladstone, 28 Feb. 1863, BM Add. MS. 44093 ff. 20-1. See also Acton to Gladstone, 1 July and 29 Oct. 1863, *ibid.*, ff. 28-31.

[28] Gladstone to Acton, 6 Jan. 1864, and Acton to Gladstone, 8 Jan. 1864, *ibid.*, ff. 32-42.

article is credited with making Lowe Chancellor of the Exchequer in Gladstone's first ministry.[29]

The foreign politics of the *Home and Foreign* were peculiarly Acton's. Its treatment of the American Civil War was somewhat less than objective. Acton was a partisan of the Confederacy, holding that the principle of states' rights was necessary for constitutional liberty. He refused to condemn the institution of slavery. In European affairs, the *Home and Foreign* continued the *Rambler*'s opposition to the policies of Napoleon III. It paid great attention to German politics. Acton, who had never shaken off the effects of his Bavarian education, placed his hope in the small constitutional monarchies of south Germany and rejected the doctrinaire nationalism which turned to Prussia. He was opposed to Bismarck from the start and therefore was favourable to Austria. He was not unaware of the defects of the Austrian government; he lamented that it had failed to adopt the principles of constitutionalism and federalism. What attracted him in the Austrian system was the very thing which made it abhorrent to nationalists: the union of diverse nationalities under a common state. Acton rejected the doctrine that the nation and the state should be co-extensive. His critique of nationalism is perhaps his most lasting contribution to political thought.[30]

Acton regarded the Italian question as connected with the German: Austria and the Temporal Power were menaced by the same revolutionary nationalism. In opposing Italian nationalism, however, the *Home and Foreign* showed no enthusiasm for the Temporal Power. "We neither identify the cause of freedom with the kingdom of Italy, nor the independence of the Church with the government of the Papal States."[31] It proposed that the Pope should flee from

[29] Herbert Paul, "Introductory Memoir," *Letters of Lord Acton to Mary Gladstone* (New York, 1904), p. 25. See Robert Lowe, "Mr. Gladstone's Financial Statements," *Home and Foreign Review*, IV (Jan. 1864), 1-18.

[30] Acton, "Nationality," *Home and Foreign Review*, I (July 1862), 1-25; reprinted in *The History of Freedom*, pp. 270-300. It has become "perhaps the most widely studied of all his writings" in connection with the recent revival of conservatism; see Richard M. Weaver, "Lord Acton: The Historian as Thinker," *Modern Age*, V (Winter 1960-1), 16.

[31] *Home and Foreign Review*, II (Jan. 1863), 319.

Rome and invited him to take refuge in England or Ireland. Such an event would put an end to "the old attitude of estrangement founded on superstition and suspicion," for the rulers of the Church "would become familiar with the spectacle of a free and tolerant community, in the light of whose example they would perceive the benefits which liberty confers on religion."[32] The Church would find that the principles of constitutional liberty were more appropriate and serviceable to her than those of reaction: "Cavour, by his formula of a free Church in a free state, opposed to the policy of the Church a principle which is essentially her own, and which she cannot resist without being unfaithful to herself."[33] Acton criticized Manning's "Sermons on Ecclesiastical Subjects" for treating the Temporal Power as a matter of dogma. This "atempt to protect the weak and earthly element [in the Church] by lifting it into the sphere of the spiritual and eternal" demonstrated, Acton said, an "inability to distinguish between the things of Caesar and the things of God."[34]

The distinction between the things of God and the things of Caesar, between that which pertained to the Church and that which had nothing to do with it, was fundamental to Liberal Catholicism. The attempt of the Liberal Catholics to limit the sphere of faith proceeded from a desire to maintain the "inward core of irreversible dogma"[35] in its divine purity, unmixed with human elements, and to prevent the Church from being identified with the sins and weaknesses of its adherents. This was the basis of their opposition to the Ultramontanes, who did not recognize such distinctions and appeared willing to sacrifice political right and intellectual honesty to the immediate temporal interests of the Church. "The great scandal of the present day," Simpson said, "is the attempt of pious sentiment to advance what it considers to be God's glory by untruth and injustice."[36]

[32] *Ibid.* (April 1863), 698-9.
[33] *Ibid.* (Jan. 1863), 313.
[34] *Ibid.*, IV (Jan. 1864), 311.
[35] Acton, "Ultramontanism," *Essays on Church and State*, ed. Douglas Woodruff (London, 1952), p. 82; reprinted from the *Home and Foreign Review*, III (July 1863), 162-206.
[36] Simpson to T. W. Marshall, n.d., Woodruff MSS.

The name of "Ultramontane," Acton asserted, had been wrongly assumed by the opponents of Liberal Catholicism.

> Ultramontanism stands in the same relation to Catholicism in matters of opinion as Catholicism to Christianity in matters of faith. It signifies a habit of intellect carrying forward the inquiries and supplementing the work of authority. It implies the legitimate union of religion with science, and the conscious intelligible harmony of Catholicism with the system of secular truth. Its basis is authority, but its domain is liberty, and it reconciles the one with the other.[37]

Knowledge is one of the ends of the Church, and progress a necessity of her existence; and Catholics who feared knowledge and resisted progress were not entitled to be called Ultramontanes. In a significant article on "Ultramontanism," Acton claimed that designation for the historical school which was represented in England by the *Home and Foreign Review*. Catholics, he said, must solve the problems of the day scientifically as well as religiously, satisfying both conscience and reason.

> The Ultramontane is therefore one who makes no parade of his religion; who meets his adversaries on grounds which they understand and acknowledge . . . who discusses each topic on its intrinsic merits—answering the critic by a severer criticism, the metaphysician by closer reasoning, the historian by deeper learning, the politician by sounder politics and indifference itself by a purer impartiality. In all these subjects the Ultramontane discovers a point pre-eminently Catholic, but also pre-eminently intellectual and true. He finds that there is a system of metaphysics, and of ethics, singularly agreeable to Catholicism, but entirely independent of it.[38]

As Acton saw it, Ultramontanism should be a liberating force, giving freedom to intellectual inquiry in the confidence that it would lead to the discovery of a truth which could not fail to be compatible with Catholic faith. Acton's sketch of his "grandiose and paradoxical conception of a liberal Ultramontanism"[39] was perhaps the purest expression of the

[37] Acton, "Ultramontanism," p. 40.

[38] *Ibid.*, p. 84. Gasquet ("Introduction," p. lxv) suggests that this article was written "conjointly" by Simpson and Acton.

[39] Ulrich Noack, *Katholizität und Geistesfreiheit, nach den Schriften von John Dalberg-Acton* (Frankfurt a.M., 1936), p. 96.

Liberal Catholic doctrine. In asserting the pre-eminent necessity of pursuing justice and truth, it placed the cause of Liberal Catholicism on a foundation which was essentially ethical.

To Acton, scientific history was synonymous with intellectual honesty. His opposition to the actual Ultramontanism of the nineteenth century was due to an ethical revulsion from a system which taught false history in the name of religion and bound up the cause of the Church with a system of lies. He discerned in the Ultramontanes' reliance upon authority "a sort of latent scepticism covered by a habit of flinching from difficulties, or of assuming that there is nothing which cannot be converted into a support of religion by a very superficial examination and manipulation." Suppression of facts or glossing over difficulties amounted, in Acton's opinion, to a "wilful lie."[40]

Acton was less than just to the ablest of his opponents, W. G. Ward. Ward's anti-intellectualism was the product of a rigorous logic which led him to conclude that the intellect was an insufficient and a dangerous guide; certainty could only be attained by absolute submission to infallible authority. To be Catholic, Ward said, "is to live as it were in an atmosphere of authority; to look for direction at every moment towards the Church and the Vicar of Christ."[41] Catholics were bound to give an interior assent "not only to the definitions but to the doctrinal intimations of the Holy See"; and a Catholic thinker or writer ought "so to think and write, as he judges that the Holy See . . . would wish him to think and write."[42]

To combat the unbridled intellectualism of the *Home and Foreign* was the purpose of Ward's editorship of the *Dublin Review*. A direct clash between the two reviews did not occur during the lifetime of the *Home and Foreign*; but every issue of

[40] Acton to Newman, n.d. [1862], Newman MSS. Acton was referring to a Jesuit work which pretended that Pope Paul III was not the father of an illegitimate son and spoke of his grandson as his "nephew." See Acton's review of Prat's *Histoire du Père Ribadeneyra, Home and Foreign Review*, I (July 1862), 242-3.

[41] Ward, "Catholic Controversies," *Dublin Review*, n.s., XII (April 1869), 377.

[42] Ward to Newman, 20 Jan. 1875, cited in Wilfrid Ward, *Life of Newman*, II, 565-6.

the *Dublin* under Ward's editorship was a manifesto of those principles which were diametrically opposed to Liberal Catholicism. In Ward's first issue, Manning set forth the goals which he proposed for the Catholics of England. He urged them to separate themselves from the main stream of English society, which was heading towards "worldliness" and rationalism, and to show themselves "more Roman than Rome, and more ultramontane than the Pope himself."[43] Ward went so far as to describe Liberal Catholicism as material heresy and mortal sin and its adherents as unsound and disloyal Catholics. Ward's conduct of the *Dublin Review* thus contributed towards raising the temper of those internal disputes among English Catholics which were already notorious for their virulence. It was clear, said the *Saturday Review*, "that an amount of pugnacity exists among Roman Catholics, which by no means finds a sufficient vent in onslaughts on Protestantism."[44]

The Liberal Catholics were also infected by the spirit of party. In 1862, Acton proposed that Simpson should bring the case of Liberal Catholicism before the Protestant public by secretly writing an article for the *Edinburgh Review* on the state of Catholic parties in England and the history of their conflicts. This, he thought, would effect "a diversion in our fight"[45] and develop sympathy among Protestants for the Liberal Catholic cause. In this instance Simpson was less pugnacious than Acton; not wishing to emphasize the quarrel between the Liberal Catholics and the hierarchy, he eventually produced a relatively tame article on English Catholic history which was useless for Acton's purpose. It was published in the *Home and Foreign* in April 1863, under the title of "Milner and his Times." Its most remarkable feature was a reference to the variety of opinions among Catholics, which might be construed as a plea for a more tolerant attitude towards Liberal Catholicism:

[43] Henry E. Manning, "The Work and the Wants of the Catholic Church in England," *Dublin Review*, n.s., I (July 1863), 162.

[44] Cited in Gasquet, "Introduction" to *Lord Acton and his Circle*, p. xliii.

[45] Acton to Simpson, 3 Oct. 1862, in [Dom] A[elred] Watkin and Herbert Butterfield, "Gasquet and the Acton-Simpson Correspondence," *Cambridge Historical Journal*, X (1950), 94. See also *ibid.*, pp. 79, 93; and Acton to Simpson, 14 and 16 Oct. 1862, Downside MSS.

Catholicism is a fact, and not a theory. Whatever schools of thought have their existence within the Church, and are not cast out from her communion, are, *ipso facto*, shown to be consistent . . . with the generous spirit of historical Catholicism, which is tolerant of differences in doubtful matters, provided that unity is not broken in the necessary points of faith and morals.[46]

The *Home and Foreign* succeeded to the *Rambler*'s complex and unsatisfactory relationship with Newman. The intellectual cleavage between Newman and Acton could not be bridged, but their association was not terminated. Newman remained the symbol of the hopes of Liberal Catholicism, though he was not part of the movement; and the *Home and Foreign* was the only English Catholic review devoted to those intellectual interests which Newman had so much at heart. At the same time, Newman insisted that in matters of principle he was in agreement with Ward, although he disliked Ward's uncompromising tactics. Newman sought to assume the role of mediator between the two parties and declined to write for either the *Dublin* or the *Home and Foreign*.

Newman's attitude is most clearly expressed in his correspondence with William Monsell. Monsell, a close friend of both Newman and Montalembert and a Liberal in politics, had contributed several articles on Irish subjects to the early issues of the *Home and Foreign*. Alarmed by the censures of the bishops, he wrote to Acton urging him to place the management of the *Home and Foreign* in the hands of a council, with a theological censor. Acton declined to make any change. Monsell, who regarded the success of a review conducted on Acton's principles as "a matter of the deepest interest to us all," feared that "if Acton does not change, not his principles but his tone, he will be set aside by Catholics, and the resuscitated *Dublin*, which under Ward will be, I presume, a sort of echo of the *Univers*, will be the only acknowledged Catholic organ."[47] Newman sympathized with Monsell's complaints but held out hopes that the *Home*

[46] Simpson, "Milner and his Times," *Home and Foreign Review*, II (April 1863), 557.

[47] Monsell to Newman, 7 Nov. 1862, quoted by Douglas Woodruff, "Introduction" to Acton, *Essays on Church and State*, p. 28.

and Foreign would mend its ways. At the beginning of 1863 he thought that the review was in an improved position. Monsell, however, found one article in the January issue which shocked him by implying that there was a contrast between "Catholic" and "Christian" morality. He asked Newman whether he ought to continue his contributions to the *Home and Foreign*.

Newman was also shocked by the article; and he had recently seen a letter by Acton which clearly indicated that there would be no change in the spirit of the *Home and Foreign*. He therefore told Monsell:

> I think you ought, and have a right, to bargain that there should not be the smack of Protestantism in the Review, which is unmistakable in the article you remark upon. It was a smack of something or other, which I should call a tone, which ruined the *Rambler*; not its doctrines, but a tone in stating or alluding to them; and a Protestant smack will be fatal to the *H. and F.* If, then, you continue to write for it, you really must insist on this ambiguous, uncomfortable style of writing coming to an end.

Newman acknowledged that Simpson had been "hardly treated" by Ullathorne, but thought that he had no right to complain. "Why did he begin? Why did he fling about ill-sounding words on sacred and delicate subjects?"[48] On the other hand, Newman said, there was one substantial ground of complaint in regard to the proceedings against the *Rambler* and the *Home and Foreign*: the interference by Propaganda in English affairs, leaving no independence to the Bishops. This direct control by Rome left no room for the relative freedom of debate and provisional toleration of opinions which had prevailed in the Middle Ages and which was Newman's ideal of Catholicism. Monsell summed up Newman's attitude to the *Home and Foreign* in two words: "interest and disappointment."[49] Deeply as Newman sympathized with its principles, he felt that its tone deprived it of the sympathies of good Catholics.

Later in 1863, however, Newman showed himself more

---

[48] Newman to Monsell, 13 Jan. 1863, in *Selected Correspondence of Lord Acton*, p. 39.

[49] Quoted in Ward, *William George Ward*, p. 205.

favourably disposed towards the *Home and Foreign*. The April issue led him to express to Wetherell his amazement at the "resources, vigour, and industry" displayed by the review, and to wish it "*every* success; *among* these successes, for which I wish and pray, and for which I have before now said Mass, of course the foremost is, that, by its soundness and prudence in treating matters quasi-religious and cognate to religion, it may obtain the approbation and confidence of our Bishops."[50] In August, Renouf reported that Newman "spoke without any qualification of his admiration"[51] for the *Home and Foreign*. The report was exaggerated: Newman's admiration was never unqualified. "The *Home and Foreign*," Newman wrote early in 1864, "has to amend its ways most considerably before it can be spoken well of by Catholics—so I think; but it realizes the fact that there *are* difficulties that have to be met, and it tries to meet them. Not successfully or always prudently, but still it has done something."[52] The review appeared to him to be "improving, number after number, both in religious character and in literary excellence"; and there seemed "no inconsistency between my submitting to my own Bishop's judgment, when the Review began, and hoping for a reversal of the judgment, as it proceeded."[53]

Acton, however, did not attach much value to these sentiments of Newman. "Now Newman has great sympathy with our cause, inasmuch as he is enlightened and liberal and highly cultivated; but I do not believe he really understands our theory."[54] In 1864 an event occurred which tended to confirm Acton's opinion. Thomas Arnold, Jr., a master at the Oratory School, offered as a prize to one of his students a copy of the English translation of Döllinger's *Kirche und Kirchen*. Newman and Ambrose St. John interfered and refused to allow the boy to receive the book. The "note of Liberalism was the chief objection."[55] The revelation of

[50] Newman to Wetherell, 22 April 1863, Newman MSS.
[51] Acton to Simpson, Sept. 1863, Downside MSS. Acton emphasized that this was to be kept secret. See also Acton to Döllinger, 14 Aug. 1863, Woodruff MSS.
[52] Newman to Robert Ornsby, 1864, cited in Ward, *Life of Newman*, II, 49.
[53] Newman to Acton, 18 March 1864, *ibid.*, I, 565-6.
[54] Acton to Simpson, 7 Feb. 1864, Gasquet, *Lord Acton and his Circle*, p. 315.
[55] Thomas Arnold, Jr., *Passages in a Wandering Life* (London, 1900), p. 179.

Newman's illiberalism proved too great a shock for Arnold's faith to bear: he resigned from the school, moved to Oxford, and in 1865 returned to the Church of England.[56]

Meanwhile the reversal of the bishops' judgment against the *Home and Foreign*, for which Newman prayed, seemed likely to become a reality. In August 1863, Acton learned that Bishop Brown of Newport had been "overcome by our last number" and had declared openly "that there has never been anything so good in England."[57] In September, Acton's own bishop came to make his visitation at Aldenham and incidentally to persuade Acton to give up the *Home and Foreign*. Acton, however, "converted the Bishop, who came to curse, and went away yesterday after giving his blessing to the Review and expressing himself gratified at my explanations." The bishop assured Acton that "in spite of the strong feelings of some bishops, a reaction has been setting in among them, and that he would try and promote it."[58] A similar reaction had been setting in among some lower clergy and laymen. E. S. Ffoulkes, in the *Union Review*, urged that "our laity will be sadly wanting if they do not step forward in behalf of this, by far the ablest and best conducted of any Roman Catholic publication of the kind in the English language that our age has yet witnessed, and claim its recognition as their own special organ by the clergy."[59]

Early in 1864, Acton was invited to make a political speech to the Catholics at Dudley. He used the opportunity to inculcate the doctrines of Liberal Catholicism while ostensibly refuting Protestant prejudices against the Catholic Church:

> What we want is the broad light of day. The faults of in-
> dividuals will continue to be attributed to the system as long

[56] In 1875 Arnold returned to Roman Catholicism. See *ibid.*, pp. 180-6; and the autobiography of his daughter, Mrs. Humphry Ward, *A Writer's Recollections* (New York, 1918), pp. 134-5.
[57] Acton to Simpson, Aug. 1863, Gasquet, *Lord Acton and his Circle*, p. 305.
[58] Acton to Simpson, 9 Sept. 1863, *ibid.*, pp. 305-6. Acton was assisted in "converting" the bishop by Wetherell, Arnold, and Roger Vaughan, a Benedictine monk, brother of the future Cardinal Vaughan.
[59] E. S. Ffoulkes, *Experiences of a 'Vert* (London, 1865), p. 22; reprinted from the *Union Review* (May 1864), p. 295.

as the system is not clearly understood. There must be no pretext for misunderstanding us, for we are engaged, not in a trial of strength with our fellow countrymen, but in a race of enlightenment.

He appealed for the removal of Catholic grievances, particularly "the iniquity of the Protestant Establishment in Ireland," but held that "these are not Irish, or Catholic, but imperial questions," on which Catholics claimed the common liberties of Englishmen. He disclaimed the doctrine of persecution, asserting that the only persecution by which the Church benefited was that which it had suffered rather than inflicted.

> The Catholic Church and the English nation have both traversed a period when they were exposed to the influence of the spirit of intolerance. That period has gone by for both. We have suffered too long from the effects of evil examples and fatal traditions, and the time has come when all men ought to understand that the liberty of the Church is part of the liberty of the subject, and that the reforms which Catholics still demand are the most important part of what remains to be done in order to bring to its perfection the fabric of the British Constitution.[60]

This speech, Acton found, was "well received by several of the Staffordshire clergy, who, I was told, do not take their bishop's part against us."[61]

Acton welcomed these signs of growing favour for the *Home and Foreign*, but he had no hopes for any substantial alteration in its relations with the ecclesiastical authorities. He warned Wetherell, who dreamed of "a conversion in high places," that "there was no triumph in store for our doctrines, and the authorities could never adopt them or sincerely admit us to be other than rogues."[62] Wetherell, however, believed that the *Home and Foreign* might eventually be restored to favour if it followed a cautious policy.

In the spring of 1864, the *Home and Foreign Review* was in the

---

[60] *The Times* (London), 4 Feb. 1864, p. 12.
[61] Acton to Simpson, 28 Jan. 1864, Downside MSS. "Their bishop" was Ullathorne.
[62] Acton to Simpson, 7 Feb. 1864, Gasquet, *Lord Acton and his Circle*, p. 315. This letter has been altered by Gasquet, who omitted Wetherell's name.

best position it had ever known. Although it could not overcome the hostility of the Ultramontanes, it had established
itself as a journal and had gained an honourable place among
English quarterlies. Events outside England, however, were
casting their shadows on these bright prospects; and "in
affairs of the mind," as Simpson remarked, "shadows are
more penetrating than substance."[63]

[63] Simpson to Acton, 2 March 1864, Woodruff MSS.

CHAPTER XIII

CONFLICTS WITH ROME, 1863-1864

THE Liberal Catholic movement in England was essentially a native product; its course had run parallel to the Liberal Catholicism of the Continent, but there had been relatively little direct interaction between the two movements. In the 1860s, however, the several branches of Liberal Catholicism began to draw together, to develop common answers to common problems, and eventually to share a common fate.

The emergence of the issue of the Temporal Power had forced the English Liberal Catholics to deal with a question with which their Continental brethren were equally concerned. On this question, however, the counsels of Liberal Catholicism were divided. Lacordaire thought the Temporal Power undesirable; Döllinger thought it desirable but untenable; Montalembert and Dupanloup regarded it as absolutely necessary. Acton, who suspected that French Liberal Catholicism contained more of policy than of principle, had "no confidence in Montalembert's Italian politics."[1] After 1862, however, Montalembert was increasingly preoccupied with the question of toleration and religious freedom, and on this question the principles of Liberal Catholicism led him into opposition to Rome.

At a Congress of Belgian Catholics at Malines in 1863, Montalembert delivered two speeches. The first, on "A Free Church in a Free State," urged the independence of Church and State. The second, on "Liberty of Conscience," rejected the principles of religious intolerance and condemned persecution in all its forms. These speeches, Montalembert's boldest expression of Liberal Catholic principles, were enthusiastically cheered by his Belgian audience.

---

[1] Acton to Simpson, 1 Nov. 1859, Downside MSS. Acton, however, wished "not to dispute publicly among ourselves" on the issue.

Montalembert's speeches aroused the opposition of the Ultramontanes. He had, however, guarded against theological criticism by making it clear that he was dealing, not with the "thesis" of Catholic doctrine, but with the "hypothesis" of its adjustment to actual circumstances. Because of this, and also out of respect for his defence of the Temporal Power, the authorities were unwilling to censure him. Cardinal Wiseman, who was present at Malines, took pains to avoid the appearance of criticizing Montalembert and prevented Ward from publishing an article attacking him in the *Dublin Review*. The *Civiltà Cattolica*, published by the Jesuits in Rome, explicitly approved the distinction between thesis and hypothesis.[2] The Pope refused to censure Montalembert publicly, although he sent him a private letter of rebuke.

Acton, in the *Home and Foreign*, found Montalembert's speeches cause for rejoicing, describing them as "the most perfect production that we yet possess of the matured genius of the great French orator."[3] Monsell, a close friend of Montalembert, evidently influenced by his views, made a speech in the House of Commons in which he criticized Catholic intolerance in Spain and urged the Church to rely on liberty instead of privilege.[4]

Shortly after Montalembert spoke at Malines, Döllinger delivered a speech of even greater significance. As President of a Congress of Catholic scholars at Munich in 1863, Döllinger gave an address on "The Past and Present of Catholic Theology." It was the clearest exposition he had given of the spirit of his historical theology. He maintained that the scholastic theologians were limited by their Aristotelian method: "without the elements of biblical criticism and dogmatic history they possessed only one of the eyes of theology." To meet the new challenges which had developed

---

[2] The article in the *Civiltà Cattolica*, "The Congress of Malines and Modern Liberties," was reprinted in the *Dublin Review*, n.s., II (Jan. 1864), 242-7. The article is said to have cost the editor, Fr. Curci, his position. See E. E. Y. Hales, *Pio Nono* (London, 1954), p. 284.

[3] *Home and Foreign Review*, III (Oct. 1863), 729.

[4] *Hansard's Parliamentary Debates*, CLXXII (1863), 1006-8. Newman refused to sanction the principle of absolute toleration and told Monsell that it was simply a question of expediency. See Wilfrid Ward, *William George Ward and the Catholic Revival* (London, 1912), p. 268.

since the Middle Ages, Döllinger argued, Catholic theology must be transformed by "the idea that Christianity is history, and that in order to be understood it must be studied in its development." Failure to recognize this had led to the decline of theology in Italy and France. Germany was the home of the new theology, and German scholarship was destined to revitalize Catholic thought and prepare the way for the reunion of the Churches. German theology, employing the weapons of modern science, does not shrink from the results of scholarship and is unafraid of error. Indeed, error is essential as a part of the process of development of doctrine. Because scientific theology contains within itself the elements necessary for correcting its faults, Döllinger said, it should be allowed complete freedom, except in the rare cases of real dogmatic error. Above all, the opinions of a school must not be exalted into dogmas, nor should the weapons of authority be used to correct the errors of scholarship. "The faults of science must be met with the arms of science; for the Church cannot exist without a progressive theology."[5]

Acton hailed Döllinger's address as "the dawn of a new era"[6] in Catholic theology. His report on the Congress in the *Home and Foreign* was an enthusiastic endorsement of Döllinger's speech, whose importance, he said, "extends beyond national boundaries."[7] Acton thought that Döllinger, by proclaiming his complete submission to the defined dogmas of the Church, had given adequate security for his orthodoxy and had satisfied the lawful claims of authority.

The suspicions of the Ultramontanes were aroused by the very features which evoked Acton's enthusiasm. Döllinger's distinction between revealed dogma and theological elaborations upon it, between the infallible Church and particular ecclesiastical authorities which were not infallible, was the

---

[5] Acton's summary of Döllinger's address: Acton, "The Munich Congress," *Essays on Church and State*, ed. Douglas Woodruff (London, 1952), pp. 181, 182, 188; reprinted from the *Home and Foreign Review*, IV (Jan. 1864), 209-244.

[6] *Ibid.*, p. 199. Acton had been present at the Congress.

[7] *Ibid.*, p. 159. It should be noted that, in justifying Döllinger, Acton criticized (p. 192) the "errors" of those who, going beyond him, asserted "that not only is the expression of dogma modified by the initiative of science, but that even its substance is altered in the progress of religious knowledge." This is a clear repudiation of the Modernist doctrine.

root of his offence. His doctrines were capable of an orthodox interpretation, but they seemed to strike a blow at the apparatus for the control of thought, centred around the Roman Congregations of the Index and Inquisition, which had been built up since the Reformation. For this reason, Ward regarded Döllinger's philosophical doctrines as more alarming than Montalembert's merely political views. Döllinger's rejection of scholasticism and his criticism of Italian theologians were bound to be distasteful to the authorities at Rome. At the Munich Congress itself, the neo-scholastics had taken alarm and had drawn up a protest against his speech; but Döllinger had circumvented the protest by complaining that it impeached the orthodoxy of his theology. The whole assembly, Ultramontanes as well as Liberals, thereupon rose to bear testimony to his orthodoxy, and the protest was withdrawn. It was the high-water mark of Döllinger's career as a Catholic theologian; but the triumph was an illusion. Döllinger had repeated, in 1863, the tactical error of the conductors of the *Avenir* in 1831. Propounding views which were novel and distasteful to authority, he had claimed that those views should be not merely tolerated but accepted by the Church. Rome regarded this as a challenge to which it was bound to reply.

Rome's reply came in the form of a Papal Brief to the Archbishop of Munich, dated 21 December 1863 but not published until 5 March 1864. The Brief did not specifically censure Döllinger, but it implicitly condemned his doctrine of the freedom of scholarship by insisting that the researches of scholars must be conducted with full deference to the ecclesiastical authorities. Catholic thought was bound, not only by dogmatic definitions, but by the opinions of the theological schools and the decisions of the Roman Congregations; and it was wrong, though not heretical, to reject those opinions and decisions.

> Even though the question concerned that subjection which is to be yielded in an act of divine faith, yet that would have not to be confined to those things which have been hitherto defined by the express decrees of Œcumenical Councils or of Roman Pontiffs and this Apostolic See, but to be extended to

those things which are delivered as divinely revealed by the ordinary authority (*magisterium*) of the whole Church dispersed throughout the world, and are therefore accounted by Catholic theologians, with universal and consistent consent, to appertain to the faith. . . It is not sufficient for learned Catholics to receive and revere the before-mentioned dogmas of the Church; but that it is also necessary(*opus esse*) for them to subject themselves, as well to the doctrinal decisions which are issued by the Pontifical Congregations, as also to those heads of doctrine which are retained by the common and consistent consent of Catholics as theological truths, and as conclusions so certain that opinions adverse to the same, though they cannot be called heretical, yet deserve some other theological censure.[8]

The language of the Brief was vague, and its censures were couched in general propositions, but there could be no doubt of its intentions. A basic principle of Liberal Catholicism, the independence of scholarly research from ecclesiastical authority, was condemned by Rome. The Brief did not possess the character of an *ex cathedra* dogmatic definition, but it was a clear intimation of the will of the Holy See. Its censures were capable of being extended to the *Home and Foreign Review*, which had, by its endorsement of Döllinger's speech, made itself a party to his condemned doctrines.

The Munich Brief was published in March 1864, when Acton, Simpson and Wetherell were preparing the April issue of the *Home and Foreign*. It came as a stunning and decisive blow to Acton. He recognized that what the Pope condemned was the fundamental principle which justified the existence of the *Home and Foreign*. Several years earlier Acton had indicated his position: "we submit where the authority is infallible, but hold ourselves free where it is not, and when it is not, for instance, the Index or the bishops."[9] This distinction between fallible and infallible authorities was disregarded by the Brief, which required submission to all authorities. The Brief was

an elaborate statement of opinions and intentions on a point practically fundamental which are incompatible with our own.

[8] Ward's translation of the Munich Brief; W. G. Ward, "Rome and the Munich Congress," *Dublin Review*, n.s., III (July 1864), 86.

[9] Acton to Simpson, 11 Oct. 1861, in Abbot Gasquet, *Lord Acton and his Circle* (London, 1906), p. 216.

I, at least, entirely reject the view here stated. If it is accepted by the *Home and Foreign*, the Review loses its identity and the very breath of its nostrils. If it is rejected, and the proclamation of the Holy See defied, the Review cannot long escape condemnation, and cannot any longer efficiently profess to represent the true, authoritative Catholic opinion. In either case I think the Review forfeits the reason of its existence. It cannot sacrifice its traditions or surrender its representative character.

There is nothing new in the sentiments of the rescript; but the open aggressive declaration and the will to enforce obedience are in reality new. This is what places us in flagrant contradiction with the government of the Church.

Acton told Simpson that the Brief made it "impossible for me to carry on the Review as hitherto with a good conscience."[10]

Acton therefore proposed to terminate the career of the review with its next issue, doing so with Simpson's approval, but on his own responsibility as proprietor, and making a public declaration of his reasons for the act. Simpson gave his "full consent and approbation" to the course which Acton proposed. "It is clearly as impossible to carry on a professedly Catholic Review on our principles," he said, "as it is for us to change our principles." He hoped that Acton would "let it be clearly understood that we in no sense accept the views of Pio IX."[11] Wetherell and the other conductors of the *Home and Foreign Review* were also in full agreement with Acton's proposal.

Acton spoke of the "calm composure" with which he had reached his decision.[12] "Submission is as little to be thought of as resistance," he wrote: intellectual integrity forbade the one and respect for ecclesiastical authority the other. What influenced him most was the practical consideration that in a conflict with Rome, which the Munich Brief seemed to foreshadow, the *Home and Foreign Review* could win only

---

[10] Acton to Simpson, 8 March 1864, *ibid.*, pp. 317-8.
[11] Simpson to Acton, 9 March 1864, Woodruff MSS.
[12] Acton to Döllinger, 12 March 1864, Woodruff MSS. It should be noted that in this crisis, as in others, Acton sought Döllinger's approval of his course, but only after he had reached his own decision.

barren triumphs, while the cause of Liberal Catholicism would be permanently ruined by the very fact of its reiterated opposition to authority: "The scandal which would be given here by a struggle with Rome . . . is so great that I do not dare to provoke it—to say nothing of the gloating among Protestants, whereby all the good which has been effected by our theories will be nullified."[13] A reasoned book, which Acton and Simpson hoped to write, might survive the wreck of the *Home and Foreign*; but the continuance of the review in conflict with Rome would only lead to more drastic measures being taken against the Liberal Catholics. These prudential considerations, with which Acton justified his decision to Döllinger, were repeated in his correspondence with Newman. The intention expressed in the Munich Brief, Acton said,

> seems to promise further measures if opportunity be given by resistance or contradiction. A conflict with the authorities would not only be a grievous scandal, but would destroy the efficiency and use of the Review, and I have determined not to risk a censure, but to take the significant warning of this document, and to put an end to the Review after the appearance of the next number. . . . I shall find means of giving a full and intelligible explanation of my motives, which will be as satisfactory as it can be made without in any way renouncing any of our principles.[14]

"Conflicts with Rome," the article in which the cessation of the *Home and Foreign Review* was announced and explained, was written by Acton and signed with his name.[15] It was based upon an article on Lamennais and Frohschammer which had been prepared before the appearance of the Munich Brief. Lamennais and Frohschammer had both been

---

[13] Acton to Döllinger, 9 March 1864, Woodruff MSS.

[14] Acton to Newman, 15 March 1864, Newman MSS. Partially quoted by Douglas Woodruff, "Introduction" to Acton, *Essays on Church and State*, p. 30. For another statement of motives, see Wetherell's letter to the *Pilot*, 19 July 1902, quoted by Gasquet, "Introduction" to *Lord Acton and his Circle*, pp. lxxv-lxxvi.

[15] Acton, "Conflicts with Rome," *The History of Freedom and other Essays*, ed. J. N. Figgis and R. V. Laurence (London, 1907), pp. 461-91; reprinted from the *Home and Foreign Review*, IV (April 1864), 667-96. It was the only article Acton had ever signed. It was extensively revised by Simpson.

condemned by the Church, the latter in 1862, the former
thirty years earlier; their doctrines had been imputed to the
Home and Foreign, and it was important to dissociate the
review from them.[16] At the root of their errors Acton found
a false conception of the relationship between science and
religion and an inability to distinguish between the infallible
truths of religion and the fallible authorities of the Church.[17]
Failure to recognize the harmony of religion and science on
the basis of their independence was responsible for the errors
both of the Ultramontane opponents of liberty and of its
unworthy defenders. Lamennais and Frohschammer identified the Church with its rulers and therefore fell into error,
the one by exaggerating the claims of authority, the other by
exaggerating the right of resistance. Frohschammer had been
censured by the Index, unjustly, as he believed, for a philosophical work. Acton maintained that he ought first to have
inquired whether the authority which censured him was
actually the voice of the Church. "It should have been
enough for him to believe in his conscience that he was in
agreement with the true faith of the Church."[18] Frohschammer went further: reacting against the "monstrous error of
attributing to the congregation of the Index a share in the
infallibility of the Church."[19] he asserted that philosophical
systems might be constructed without reference to the dogmas
of the Church and even in contradiction to them. Acton
condemned this doctrine. He would not allow to philosophy
the independence which he claimed for history. "The
philosopher cannot claim the same exemption as the historian. God's handwriting exists in history independently of
the Church, and no ecclesiastical exigence can alter a fact."[20]
By exaggerating the independence of philosophy, Frohschammer had provoked a reaction against the rightful independ-

[16] Acton had already criticized Frohschammer, in July 1863, for "an
unconscious surrender of dogmatic truths." Acton, "Ultramontanism," *Essays
on Church and State*, pp. 65-6. See also Acton to Döllinger, 21 May 1863, Woodruff MSS.
[17] In this article, for the first time, Acton explicitly denied Papal Infallibility.
"The Holy See is not separately infallible," he said; it has "repeatedly erred."
Acton, "Conflicts with Rome," p. 477.
[18] *Ibid.*, p. 481.
[19] *Ibid.*, p. 478.
[20] *Ibid.*, p. 473.

ence of science and history, of which the first symptom was
the Munich Brief.

It was possible to interpret the words of the Brief in a sense
not inconsistent with the habitual language of the *Home and
Foreign Review*. Acton rejected such a "plausible accommoda-
tion"; he preferred "to interpret the words of the Pope as
they were really meant." One of the first principles of the
review was to exemplify the distinction between dogma and
opinion, between acts of infallible authority and those
possessing an inferior sanction. The practical purpose of the
Brief was to obliterate this distinction; and the will of the
Holy See was manifested with unusual forcefulness and
distinctness. The relative tolerance which had been conceded
to the principles of the *Home and Foreign* was now withdrawn.
This posed a problem to the conductors of the review, who
were "unable to yield their assent to the opinions put
forward in the Brief." They would not give up their principles; but to continue the review in opposition to Rome
would be both derogatory to the Holy See and fruitless for
the cause of truth. "It would be wrong to abandon principles
which have been well considered and are sincerely held, and
it would be wrong to assail the authority which contradicts
them. The principles have not ceased to be true, nor the
authority to be legitimate, because the two are in contradiction."[21] Acton would not repeat the error of Lamennais and
Frohschammer or challenge their fate by provoking Rome
to a more explicit repudiation of Liberal Catholic doctrines
which would place religion in apparent opposition to science.
He chose instead to "sacrifice the existence of the *Review* to
the defence of its principles, in order that I may combine
the obedience which is due to legitimate ecclesiastical
authority, with an equally conscientious maintenance of the
rightful and necessary liberty of thought."[22] He placed his
hope in the future, in the development of an educated public
opinion which would eventually sway the ecclesiastical
government. The *Home and Foreign Review* "was but a partial
and temporary embodiment of an imperishable idea—the

[21] *Ibid.*, p. 487.
[22] *Ibid.*, p. 489.

faint reflection of a light which still lives and burns in the hearts of the silent thinkers of the Church."[23]

In "Conflicts with Rome," the swan song of English Liberal Catholicism, Acton found occasion once more to define the principles and defend the Catholicity of the movement. Thus the cessation of the *Home and Foreign* was not a surrender or a submission; the principles of Liberal Catholicism were upheld in the very act of renouncing the struggle. The *Home and Foreign Review*, Ward declared, "has died like a wasp, leaving its sting in the wound it inflicted."[24]

The cessation of the *Home and Foreign*, nonetheless, meant, in effect, the end of the Liberal Catholic movement in England. Acton had long maintained that Liberal Catholicism could expect no triumph, but would be fortunate if it could obtain toleration from the authorities of the Church. The Munich Brief was a sign that toleration would be denied. By ending the career of the *Home and Foreign*, Acton hoped to avoid a direct and fatal conflict with authority. "We must give up our notion of Catholic literature as a bad job,"[25] said Simpson. The struggle for Liberal Catholic principles was not, indeed, abandoned, but it was changed in character. Liberal Catholics must henceforth advocate their principles either, in particular situations, as isolated individuals within the Church, or as participants in endeavours which were not confined exclusively to Catholics. Liberal Catholicism had no future as an organized movement; and its adherents could only hope that its principles might, through the progress of Catholic thought, secure a quiet acceptance in future generations. For the present, they must resign themselves to silence.[26]

[23] *Ibid.*, p. 491. At the conclusion of this article was printed the Latin text of the Munich Brief: *Home and Foreign Review*, IV (April 1864), 691-6.

[24] Ward, "Rome and the Munich Congress," p. 67. Ward criticized Acton's article at great length and maintained that the Munich Brief had the force of infallible teaching.

[25] He added that "literature for Catholics must clearly come out in a non-Catholic form." Simpson to Acton, 9 March 1864, Woodruff MSS. The idea, which Acton entertained, of publishing a book of *Essays by Catholic Laymen* was soon abandoned. See Acton to Döllinger, 12 March 1864, Woodruff MSS.

[26] "For the present it seems to me better to be silent—although not quite in the sense of 'respectful silence'." Acton to Döllinger, 12 March 1864, Woodruff MSS. The term "respectful silence" (*silence respectueux*) was coined by the Jansenists, who wished to evade submission to Rome's condemnation of

This was an attitude which Newman could approve. He was grieved by the news of the cessation of the *Home and Foreign*. He had read the Munich Brief, observing in it the points which Acton mentioned, "nor had I any difficulty in acquiescing in them, in their letter and in their principle; but I dread their application."[27] Newman supposed that the Brief meant more than it said; "and thus there are serious grounds for apprehension, lest there be some ultimate intention of proceeding against you, and that the more easily, because we in England are under the military regime of Propaganda."[28] While he congratulated Acton on being released from an occupation which was unworthy of him, he regretted that the English Catholics must henceforth be subjected to "the dull tyranny of Manning and Ward."[29]

Newman's attitude toward the Munich Brief reveals both his sympathy with the intellectual principles of Liberal Catholicism and his fundamental reliance on authority. Examining the Brief in detail, he found in it an insistence that Catholic men of science must keep the conclusions of theology before them even in their scientific researches. This, he felt, denied them "freedom of logic in their own science" and made it impossible for Catholic scholars to deal successfully with current scientific controversies. "So that, if I understand this brief, it is simply a providential intimation to every religious man, that, at this moment, we are simply to be silent, while scientific investigation proceeds . . . and I am not sure that it will not prove to be the best way."[30]

Newman was engaged, at this time, in preparing his *Apologia pro vita sua*. In the last chapter of the *Apologia*, he discussed at length the problem posed by the Munich Brief,

Jansen's work. Hence Acton remarks: "Pius called us Jansenists. He meant not in point of grace, but of authority. He alluded to the silence respectueux, and meant to indicate the ceremonious practice by which men veiled their displeasure and disrespect." CUL Add. MS. 4992, cited in Gertrude Himmelfarb, *Lord Acton: A Study in Conscience and Politics* (Chicago, 1952), p. 108.

[27] Newman to Acton, 18 March 1864, Woodruff MSS; partially quoted by Wilfrid Ward, *Life of John Henry Cardinal Newman*, 2 vols. (London, 1912), I, 565-6.

[28] *Ibid.* This sentence is not quoted by Ward.

[29] *Ibid.*, quoted by Ward, *Life of Newman*, I, 565-6.

[30] Quoted in *ibid.*, 567. The full text of Newman's analysis of the Brief is given in *ibid.*, 641-2.

the action of authority in going beyond the province of faith and arresting the course of scientific thought. Newman found occasion to criticize the Ultramontanism of Veuillot and Ward by referring to "a violent ultra party, which exalts opinions into dogmas, and has it principally at heart to destroy every school of thought but its own."[31] But Newman was mainly concerned with providing a rationale for submission to authority. He described the authority of the Church in terms which gave it the full extent claimed by the Munich Brief, and he professed his own absolute submission to that claim. He acknowledged that there was a great trial to the reason in this claim of authority, in that it extended beyond the province of faith and, without the gift of infallibility, interfered in matters of secular science. These prohibitions, Newman said, were binding on actions and writings, but not on thought. "We are called upon, not to profess anything, but to be silent." Newman believed that authority was generally likely to be right in its actions. It was sometimes necessary to arrest the course of intellect out of tenderness for souls. The duty of the Catholic thinker was to submit in silence, waiting for a more propitious moment to bring forward his ideas. Newman interpreted "recent acts of authority" (the Munich Brief) as "tying the hands of a controversialist";[32] and he professed to be thankful for so clear a direction.

Newman's profound submissiveness to authority led him to the same practical conclusion as Acton: to be silent, without surrendering principles, and to trust in the future. The language of the *Apologia* implied a greater sympathy with the doctrines of the Munich Brief than Newman actually felt. He believed that the terms of the Brief made it impossible to write an original work on a serious subject without risking a charge of heresy. "I think it is very hard," he said, "that I may not write under the antecedent condition that I am a

---

[31] Newman, *Apologia pro vita sua*, ed. Wilfrid Ward (London, 1931), p. 351. Acton supplied some materials to Newman for the *Apologia*. Newman wrote: "Your letter is very valuable to me. . . . As to the points you mention, you may be sure I shall go as far as ever I can." Newman to Acton, 15 April 1864, Newman MSS.

[32] Newman, *Apologia pro vita sua*, pp.349-50 , 354.

fallible mortal, but that every turn of expression is to be turned into a dogmatic enunciation."[33] Newman's trust in authority was mingled with disappointment at the course which authority was pursuing. "It is so ordered on high that in our day Holy Church should present just that aspect to my countrymen which is most consonant with their ingrained prejudices against her, most unpromising for their conversion."[34]

As if to confirm this statement, the Pope published, on 8 December 1864, the Encyclical *Quanta cura*, which was accompanied by the *Syllabus of Errors*. These documents completed the work which had been begun by the Munich Brief. The Encyclical condemned "naturalism," the doctrine that society should be governed without regard to religion, from which proceeded the erroneous principles of freedom of speech and of conscience. It also censured the Liberal Catholic doctrine that assent may be withheld from those decisions of the Holy See which did not deal with the dogmas of faith and morals. By itself, the Encyclical would probably have attracted little attention; but it was accompanied by the *Syllabus*, a list of propositions which had been condemned by Pius IX in previous encyclicals and allocutions. Most of the eighty censured propositions were doctrines which were reprobated by all Catholics; but many of the special doctrines of Liberal Catholicism were condemned, including some of the opinions which Döllinger had expressed at the Munich Congress.[35] The last proposition condemned in the *Syllabus* is an almost perfect statement of the Liberal Catholic creed: "The Roman Pontiff can and ought to reconcile himself to, and come to terms with progress, liberalism, and modern civilization."[36]

[33] Newman to Aubrey de Vere, 6 July 1864, quoted by Wilfrid Ward, *Aubrey de Vere: A Memoir* (London, 1904), p. 307.

[34] Cited in Ward, *Life of Newman*, I, 14.

[35] Paul M. Baumgarten, "Döllinger," *Catholic Encyclopedia* (New York, 1913), V, 98. See proposition 13 of the *Syllabus*, under the heading "Moderate Rationalism": "The method and principles by which the old scholastic doctors cultivated theology are no longer suitable to the demands of our times and to the progress of the sciences." Anne Fremantle, *The Papal Encyclicals in their Historical Context* (New York, 1956), p. 145.

[36] This is the conventional translation; perhaps the last clause ought to read "recent civilization". It is taken from the allocution *Jamdudum cernimus*

The *Syllabus* was drawn up in the technical language of
theology and was intended simply for the guidance of the
bishops; but it was published to the world, and the summary
terms of its condemnations created the impression that they
had a universal application—"a gesture of defiance hurled
by an outraged Pope against the nineteenth century."[37]
This impression that the Papacy had committed itself to a
policy of blind reaction seemed to be confirmed by the
conduct of the Ultramontanes, who claimed the Encyclical
and *Syllabus* as a triumph for their party. Ward, maintaining
that the Encyclical confirmed his views on the necessity of
assent and submission to all the decisions of the Pope,
proclaimed that "its doctrinal declarations possess absolute
infallibility."[38]

The *Syllabus* threw consternation into the ranks of the
Liberal Catholics. It was that further condemnation of their
doctrines which Acton had hoped to avoid by putting an end
to the *Home and Foreign Review*. Dupanloup, Bishop of
Orléans, attempted to calm the storm. In a hastily-written
pamphlet, he minimized the effect of the *Syllabus*. Dupanloup
made use of the distinction between thesis and hypothesis:
the Pope, he argued, was speaking in terms of absolute
principles and an ideal society; in the realm of hypothesis,
the Liberal Catholic doctrines might still be maintained.
The condemnation of the *Syllabus* possessed no more force
than the encyclicals and allocutions in which they were
originally propounded, and in their original form they were
of merely specific and limited application.[39] By such argu-

---

(1861), which, criticizing political liberalism as it was manifested in Italy,
denied that "the Roman Pontiff should reconcile himself and come to terms
with *what they call* progress, with Liberalism, and with recent civilization."
See Dom Cuthbert Butler, *The Life and Times of Bishop Ullathorne*, 2 vols.
(New York, 1926), II, 96-7.

[37] E. E. Y. Hales, *Pio Nono* (London, 1954), p. 274.

[38] W. G. Ward, "The Encyclical and Syllabus," *Dublin Review*, n.s., IV
(April 1865), 443. Ward also found occasion to animadvert against "that
extreme form of Catholic misbelief which animated the late 'Home and Foreign
Review'." It should be noted that Ward later moderated his theory of Infallibility after being criticized by Roman theologians.

[39] This point was elaborated for English readers, ten years later, by Newman,
*A Letter to his Grace the Duke of Norfolk, on occasion of Mr. Gladstone's recent
Expostulation* (London, 1875). Newman also took occasion to criticize the "wild
words and overbearing deeds" of Ultramontanes who used their own private

ments Dupanloup virtually reduced the *Syllabus* to a nullity. His pamphlet purported to be a defence of the *Syllabus*, correcting the mis-statements of the enemies of the Church; because of this, and because he had combined his explanation of the *Syllabus* with a defence of the Temporal Power, he received the thanks of over six hundred bishops and the qualified approval of the Pope. But Dupanloup was less sanguine than he appeared, saying privately: "If we can tide over the next ten years we are safe."[40]

Acton was not satisfied with Dupanloup's subtleties and equivocations.[41] He insisted, as he had done in the case of the Munich Brief, on reading the words of the Pope as they were meant: "The *Syllabus* entirely rejected the moderate State and the position obtained by liberalism."[42] Acton did not regard the *Syllabus* or the Encyclical as documents of infallible authority or as having any claim to his assent; but he recognized them as expressions of the will of the Pope which were utterly incompatible with the doctrines of Liberal Catholicism.

Because of the cessation of the *Home and Foreign Review*, Acton possessed no organ in which he could state his views on the *Syllabus*. He could only indicate his attitude by his silence. When the Encyclical and *Syllabus* were published, Acton was in Rome, and he was asked to join with the other English residents in Rome in a congratulatory address to the Pope. Acton drafted an address which deliberately avoided all mention of the two documents; but the committee responsible for the matter rejected his draft as an insult to the Pope. Acton withdrew from the committee and did not sign the address which it prepared.[43]

Acton's dream of a Liberal Church was at an end. Hence-

judgment "for the purpose of anathematizing the private judgments of others" (pp. 4, 131).

[40] Quoted by Newman to E. B. Pusey, 17 May 1865, cited in Ward, *Life of Newman*, II, 101.

[41] Acton was "appalled" at Dupanloup's "ignorance" and said that to a man accustomed to rigorous thinking Dupanloup "appears a mere windbag." Acton to Lady Blennerhasset, 1879, *Selections from the Correspondence of the First Lord Acton*, ed. J. N. Figgis and R. V. Laurence (London, 1917), pp. 50-1. One of the reasons for Acton's eventual break with Döllinger after 1879 was Döllinger's refusal to condemn Dupanloup, who had defended the *Syllabus*.

[42] Acton, CUL Add. MS. 4903.

[43] See Himmelfarb, *Lord Acton*, p. 62.

forth Liberal Catholicism was capable of little more than a
rear-guard action, attempting to limit the extent of the
Ultramontane triumph. In the next years, a certain bitterness and even desperation marked the conduct of the leading
Liberal Catholics, Montalembert, Döllinger and Acton.
In 1865, standing for election at Bridgnorth, Acton informed
his constituents that he belonged "rather to the soul than the
body of the Catholic Church."[44] A man who could speak
thus had passed beyond Liberal Catholicism into a more
advanced form of opposition to the rulers of his Church.

---

[44] John Neville Figgis, "Acton," *Dictionary of National Biography*, 2 suppl.
(London, 1912), p. 9. Acton did not wish to stand for re-election at Carlow,
where he had dissatisfied his constituents. He stood for Bridgnorth, near
Aldenham, and was elected but unseated on a petition in 1866. See James J.
Auchmuty, "Acton as a Member of the House of Commons," *Bulletin of the
Faculty of Arts*, Farouk I University [Alexandria, Egypt], V (1949), 31-46.

ROMAN TRIUMPH

THE Munich Brief and the *Syllabus* had sounded the death-knell of Liberal Catholicism. Its agonies were prolonged until 1870, however, as the Liberal Catholics struggled to salvage some fragments of accomplishment from the wreckage of their movement.

Their earliest hopes were centred on Newman. As he had done during his brief editorship of the *Rambler* in 1859, Newman served as the clerical spokesman of the educated laity. In lieu of the project of founding a Catholic University, which had been abandoned, he proposed to found an Oratory at Oxford, which would serve the spiritual needs of the Catholic students who were beginning to frequent that University. This project was eagerly supported by many of the laity; Wetherell was particularly active in organizing a subscription to finance it. Manning and Ward, however, were alarmed by Newman's project: they saw that it would attract Catholic students to Oxford and feared that it would lead to "mixed education" and the breakdown of Catholic exclusiveness. They appealed to Wiseman and to Propaganda; and the result was a meeting of the bishops at the end of 1864, which unanimously agreed to discourage Catholics from attending the Protestant Universities. This meant the defeat of Newman's project. A number of laymen drew up a petition urging that Catholics be allowed to attend the Universities; Wetherell took the petition to Rome, but he obtained no hearing.

The frustration of Newman's Oxford project was Wiseman's last significant act; he died in February 1865. Enfeebled by illness in his last years, Wiseman had come to rely on Manning in the management of English Catholic affairs, and Manning was appointed to succeed him as Archbishop of Westminster. This appointment completed the triumph of

Ultramontanism in England; it "seemed to force the action of the Catholics of England into one only channel."[1]

In 1867, however, Newman revived his Oxford project, with the support of his bishop, Ullathorne. Propaganda did not forbid the project, but Ullathorne was instructed that Newman himself was not to be allowed to settle in Oxford, lest his presence attract Catholic students there. When this instruction became known, the project was abandoned.[2] Manning and Talbot had effectively intrigued to thwart Newman's plans; but the incident ultimately proved beneficial to Newman. Monsell arranged for an address to be presented to Newman, signed by nearly all the prominent lay Catholics of England, testifying that "every blow that touches you inflicts a wound upon the Catholic Church in this country."[3] Fathers St. John and Bittleston of the Oratory went to Rome to obtain an explanation of the restriction imposed on Newman. They learned that Newman's unexplained article on "Consulting the Faithful" was responsible for the prejudice at Rome against him. The article was satisfactorily explained, and Newman's reputation for obedience and orthodoxy was cleared.

Manning's distrust of Newman remained unabated. He described Newman as "the centre of those who hold low views about the Holy See, are anti-Roman, cold and silent, to say no more, about the Temporal Power, critical of Catholic devotions, and always on the lower side."[4] There

[1] Newman to Acton, 21 July 1865, Newman MSS. Manning was at first conciliatory, and Acton was surprisingly calm about his appointment: "Peace reigns provisionally." Acton to Döllinger, 23 June 1865, Woodruff MSS.

[2] Manning maintained the policy of discouraging Catholic students from attending the Universities; nonetheless, Acton sent his son to Cambridge in the late 1880s.

[3] Quoted by Wilfrid Ward, *The Life of John Henry Cardinal Newman*, 2 vols. (London, 1912), II, 143. The names of Acton, Simpson and Wetherell do not appear on the address. The organizers declined to include Acton and Simpson because their presence on the list might deter others from signing; Wetherell refused to sign without them. Simpson asked to sign, and was informed that his name "stank in the nostrils of the orthodox, and . . . would be more useful in its absence than in its presence." Simpson to Newman, 20 April 1867, Newman MSS. Acton, Simpson and Wetherell had all contributed funds to Newman's project.

[4] Manning to Talbot, 25 Feb. 1866, quoted in Edmund Sheridan Purcell, *Life of Cardinal Manning, Archbishop of Westminster*, 2 vols. (New York, 1896), II, 322-3. Talbot's language was even stronger.

was some truth to these charges. Newman, in replying to
Pusey's *Eirenicon* in 1865, had criticized the Italian devotions
introduced by Faber. In 1866 he accepted the dedication of
Oxenham's translation of Döllinger's Church history, and
in 1867 he encouraged Father Ryder of the Oratory to write
against Ward's views on the Pope's Infallibility. In 1868
Newman approved a book by Renouf on the case of Pope
Honorius, which sought to show the difficulties of the
doctrine of Papal Infallibility. But these manifestations of
sympathy for Liberal Catholic views were limited in number.
After the failure of his second Oxford project, Newman
tended to withdraw from public activity.

Meanwhile the conductors of the *Home and Foreign* had,
after an interval of uncertainty, resumed their journalistic
activities, not, however, in a distinctively Catholic fashion.
In 1867 they commenced a weekly newspaper called the
Chronicle, which was edited by Wetherell. The funds for this
venture were supplied by Sir Roland Blennerhasset, who
had, like Acton, been a pupil of Döllinger. Wetherell made
the *Chronicle* an avowedly secular journal and took pains to
deny that it was a Catholic organ.[5] The sub-editor, Lathbury,
and most of the contributors were Protestants. Although the
Chronicle offered the Liberal Catholics an opportunity to
express their views, its main interest was political. It sought
to establish itself as the organ of Gladstonian Liberalism:
"Implicit confidence in you," Acton told Gladstone,
"personally and politically, is the bond by which Wetherell
holds his friends together."[6]

Acton served as Roman correspondent for the *Chronicle* and
contributed many articles and reviews. One of his articles
caused some embarrassment for the journal. In an attempt to
expose the attempts of Catholic historians to conceal the
crimes of the Inquisition, Acton erroneously charged St. Pius
V, instead of Pius IV, with procuring the murder of Italian
Protestant refugees.[7] Newman protested against these

[5] Wetherell to Simpson, 16 March 1867, cited in Abbot Gasquet, "Introduction" to *Lord Acton and his Circle* (London, 1906), p. lxxix.

[6] Acton to Gladstone, 5 Dec. 1867, BM Add. MS. 44093 ff. 66-7.

[7] Acton, "Fra Paolo Sarpi," *Essays on Church and State*, ed. Douglas Woodruff
(London, 1952), pp. 258-9; reprinted from the *Chronicle*, 30 March 1867, pp.

remarks in terms similar to his criticism of Simpson in 1861;[8] he also instructed Father St. John, who was then in Rome, to disavow on his behalf any connection with the *Chronicle*. When St. John had an audience with the Pope, Pius spoke of Acton as one of those who were not Catholics at heart and were bringing in a sort of semi-Catholicism.[9]

In general, the *Chronicle* was too liberal for the Catholics, while its Catholicism lost it support among Liberals. It failed to secure enough subscribers to pay its costs, and for this financial reason it went out of existence after one year of publication.[10]

In 1869 the Liberal Catholics made a last venture into journalism. They took control of the *North British Review*, the former organ of the Scottish Free Kirk; again Wetherell assumed the editorship, with Acton and Simpson among the contributors. Even more than the *Chronicle*, the *North British* was a secular and not a religious review; its prospectus, drafted by Acton, explicitly disavowed any religious affiliation, while proclaiming its devotion to the scientific study of religion, history and politics, and announcing its intention of supporting the policies of Gladstone.[11] Simpson told Newman that "we intend this time to steer quite clear of any religious declarations whatever, and to make it only political and literary."[12] Newman observed that "did not I know the quarter whence it came, I should think it written by liberal Scotchmen, religious in a way, who looked at the Church as a fiction of past times."[13] Despite its secular

---

14-17. Acton admitted that "there is no excuse for my blunder about Pius IV": Acton to Wetherell, 13 May 1867, in [Dom] A[elred] Watkin and Herbert Butterfield, "Gasquet and the Acton-Simpson Correspondence," *Cambridge Historical Journal*, X (1950), 103.

[8] Newman to Wetherell, 2, 3, 4 and 9 April 1867, Newman MSS. Newman liked the *Chronicle* in other respects but would have nothing to do with its management.

[9] Ambrose St. John to Newman, 4 May 1867, in Ward, *Life of Newman*, II, 167.

[10] Wetherell to Gladstone, 4 Feb. 1867, BM Add. MS. 44414 ff. 73-6. See also Acton to Gladstone, 11 Feb. 1867, BM Add. MS. 44093 f. 70.

[11] Draft by Acton, 1 July 1869, *Selections from the Correspondence of the First Lord Acton*, ed. J. N. Figgis and R. V. Laurence (London, 1917), pp. 312-6. See also Acton to Gladstone, 23 Jan. 1869, BM Add. MS. 44093 ff. 83-4.

[12] Simpson to Newman, 24 Dec. 1868, Newman MSS.

[13] Newman to Wetherell, 7 Nov. 1869, cited in Gasquet, "Introduction,"

character, the *North British* provided Acton and his friends
with an organ in which they could express their views during
the critical days of the Vatican Council in 1870. In 1871,
however, Wetherell's health, always precarious, broke down,
and he was unable to continue as editor. No one could be
found to replace him: the events of the last years had convinced Acton and Simpson that no useful work could be
accomplished by journalism. The *North British Review*, the
last of the periodicals conducted by the English Liberal
Catholics, came to an end in 1871.

A change had come over the character of Liberal Catholicism in the years after 1864. A sharper antagonism to Rome
marked the conduct of Montalembert, Döllinger and Acton.
The question of persecution was decisive for them. Montalembert's speech at Malines on "Liberty of Conscience" was the
first sign of a hatred of intolerance which eventually caused
him to break with his colleagues on the *Correspondant*. The
subject was brought home to Döllinger by the *Syllabus*, by
Montalembert, and by Oxenham, who had become Döllinger's close friend.[14] In 1867, the canonization of an
Inquisitor, Peter Arbues, signified to Döllinger that the
Church had sanctified the principle of persecution; from this
time he found himself in ethical opposition to Rome. Acton
had already been alienated from the rulers of the Church by
their rejection of scientific history, which he regarded as no
more than wilful dishonesty; their endorsement of persecution seemed to him to constitute an assertion that it is lawful
to commit murder for the good of the Church. He accused
the authorities of the Church of perverting morals and
promoting sin: "It is the fiend skulking behind the Cruci-
fix."[15] This is the characteristic note of the new phase in

p. lxxxii. Newman later expressed his appreciation of the *Review*'s ability,
though he did not support its policy.

[14] See CUL Add. MSS. 4906, 4909. Acton, who deplored Oxenham's
peculiarities but regarded him as "the ablest convert since Wilberforce," had
sent him to Munich in 1863 to study under Döllinger. See Acton to Döllinger,
7 Jan., 21 April and 13 May 1863, Woodruff MSS.

[15] Acton to Lady Blennerhasset, Feb. 1879, *Selected Correspondence of Lord
Acton*, p. 56,

Acton's life, marked by an extreme "ethical rigorism."[16]

Rome made no effort to heal the breach and seemed determined to complete the defeat of Liberal Catholicism. An Ecumenical Council was summoned to meet at the Vatican in 1869, and it soon became apparent that a purpose of the Council was to define as dogma the Infallibility of the Pope. This aroused the fears of the Liberal Catholics. Papal Infallibility, they believed, might lead to the dogmatizing of the Temporal Power and the *Syllabus*; furthermore, there seemed to be a conflict between the doctrine of Infallibility and the facts of history. Although the dangers that the Liberal Catholics anticipated were averted by the actual wording of the definition, this could not be foreseen in 1869, and the overbearing conduct of the Ultramontanes afforded some justification for these fears. Newman, who personally believed in Papal Infallibility but did not wish it to be defined as dogma, spoke of the impending definition as the work of "an aggressive and insolent faction."[17]

Acton was especially active in the efforts to prevent the definition of Papal Infallibility. Gladstone, who was now Prime Minister, had made Acton a peer just before the Council opened in December 1869. Acton employed his influence with Gladstone in an unsuccessful attempt to bring about diplomatic action by the great powers which would restrain the Council. His letters from Rome were among those published by Döllinger under the pseudonym of "Quirinus" in an effort to sway public opinion against the definition. Acton himself, although a layman, was active in organizing an opposition among the bishops at the Council.[18]

[16] Ulrich Noack, *Katholizität und Geistesfreiheit, nach den Schriften von John Dalberg-Acton* (Frankfurt a. M., 1936), p. 20. Professor Butterfield has described Acton's hatred of persecution as "frantic." Herbert Butterfield, "Reflections on Religion and Modern Individualism," *Journal of the History of Ideas*, XXII (Jan.-Mar. 1961), 36.

[17] Newman to Ullathorne, 28 Jan. 1870, quoted by Ward, *Life of Newman*, II, 280. Even after the Council, Newman said that its proceedings "constitute a grave scandal." Newman to Alfred Plummer, 15 Jan. 1871, quoted by Frank Leslie Cross, *John Henry Newman* (London, 1933), p. 167.

[18] This reliance upon the governments and the bishops has given rise to a charge of "Gallicanism" against the Liberal Catholics. It must be remembered that this was a tactical device, used in a moment of desperation. Acton's

The Liberal Catholics had turned to the episcopate in the hope that it would be able to resist the increasing power of the Papacy and restore a form of constitutional government to the Church. A strong minority of bishops, including many who had no sympathy with Liberal Catholicism, opposed the definition. Most of them, however, following the lead of Dupanloup, did so only on the grounds that the definition was "inopportune"; unlike Acton and Döllinger, they did not oppose the doctrine on its merits. Thus they possessed no basis for an effective resistance, and the disciplined Ultramontane majority was able to secure the definition of Papal Infallibility in July 1870.

The definition of Infallibility was the final triumph of the Ultramontanes and proved fatal to the Liberal Catholic movement. Although the wording of the Vatican decrees carefully restricted the number and character of Papal pronouncements which were declared to be infallible, the duty of obedience to the Pope, even where he was not infallible, was affirmed. The triumph of Papal autocracy was complete.

Döllinger, challenged to submit by his bishop, refused and was excommunicated. A relatively small number of Germans, mostly drawn from academic circles, withdrew from the communion of Rome and organized an "Old Catholic Church." Nothing of the sort happened in England, although a handful of individuals left the Church, and Capes, who had spent twelve years in isolation from religious bodies, returned to the Church of England in order to bear witness against the Vatican decrees. Newman had no difficulty in submitting and advising others to submit; he devised a "minimalistic" interpretation of the dogma which satisfied nearly all the Liberal Catholics.

Acton was less ready to submit. He wished to appeal from the Council to the consensus of the Church and, in September of 1870, published an open letter to a German bishop urging the minority bishops to continue their resistance. The bishops, however, submitted to the Vatican decrees; and the

---

"Gallicanism," like his earlier "Ultramontanism," were both aspects of his constant opposition to absolute power in any form.

sensus fidelium, as indicated by the attitude of the overwhelm-
ing majority of Catholics, evidently confirmed the decision
of the Council. Acton was fortunate in that he was not called
upon to declare himself until he had ceased to reject the
Vatican decrees. "No layman ever played such a part in
Church matters, and no Catholic more narrowly missed
excommunication."[19] What preserved his allegiance to the
Church was the distinction, which he had always made,
between the Church and its rulers, and his theory of development, which allowed him to hope that the dogma of Infallibility would eventually be assimilated with the traditions of
the Church and be rendered innocuous. At first he "yielded
obedience" to the decrees, without internal assent; later,
after Newman published his minimalistic interpretation in
1875, Acton found it possible to "accept"[20] the dogma of
Infallibility. But he never made a public act of submission,
and he risked excommunication in 1874 and 1875 by
deliberately evading a declaration of assent for which
Manning pressed him. He had "yielded obedience to Rome,
but on his own terms, so that it was less a submission than
an assertion of independence."[21]

After the Vatican Council and the cessation of the *North
British Review,* the English Liberal Catholics were silent,
except for a brief moment in 1874, on the occasion of
Gladstone's denunciation of the Vatican decrees. Gladstone,
partly influenced by the letters which Acton had written to
him during the Council, asserted that the dogma of Papal
Infallibility impaired the civil allegiance of Catholics. Acton
defended the loyalty of his fellow-Catholics, but at the same
time he managed to strike one last blow at Ultramontanism.
It was only by convicting the Papacy of sin—by pointing
out that for centuries the authorities of the Church had been

[19] Shane Leslie, *Henry Edward Manning: His Life and Labours* (London, 1921),
p. 220.
[20] Acton to Lady Blennerhasset, 13 April 1875, *Selected Correspondence of Lord
Acton,* p. 155. Acton's confessor and bishop were satisfied as to his orthodoxy.
[21] Gertrude Himmelfarb, *Lord Acton: A Study in Conscience and Politics* (Chicago,
1952), p. 126. Lionel Kochan has expressed an opposite point of view: "there
was a certain streak of pliability in Acton's nature. He lacked the courage of
his convictions. . . . He kept quiet in the full awareness that he was shirking
the struggle." *Acton on History* (London, 1954), pp. 31, 32.

guilty of political crimes without the aid of the dogma of Infallibility—that Acton could show that Gladstone was in error. His words gave much offence among Catholics; but to Acton the question was a purely historical one, and it provided a last opportunity for vindicating the independence of Catholic history:

It would be well if men had never fallen into the error of suppressing truth and encouraging error for the better security of religion. Our Church stands, and our faith should stand, not on the virtues of men, but on the surer ground of an institution and a guidance that are divine. Therefore I rest unshaken in the belief that nothing which the inmost depths of history shall disclose in time can ever bring to Catholics just cause of shame or fear. I should dishonour and betray the Church if I entertained a suspicion that the evidences of religion could be weakened or the authority of Councils sapped by a knowledge of the facts with which I have been dealing, or of others which are not less grievous nor less certain because they remain untold.[22]

Acton's words were the last cry of the Liberal Catholic movement. On the Continent, those Liberal Catholics who had accepted the Vatican decrees tended to be caught up in the new movement for Catholic unity which followed the war of 1870 in France and the *Kulturkampf* in Germany. In England, they confined their activities to matters which were not distinctively Catholic in nature. Wetherell had retired from journalistic activity in 1871;[23] Simpson, after turning to Shakespearian studies, died in 1876; and Acton embarked upon the pursuit of his "Madonna of the Future," the never-written *History of Liberty*, and developed a rigid moralism in ethics which led to his quarrel with Döllinger in 1879 and his virtual disablement from productive work for a decade.[24]

[22] Letter of Lord Acton, *The Times* (London), 24 Nov. 1874, p. 6. For Simpson's behaviour in this controversy, see the Appendix.

[23] Acton found him a post as private secretary to Lord Granville at the Foreign Office.

[24] See CUL Add. MS. 4863, quoted by Kochan, *Acton on History*, pp. 82-3. Acton said of his later and more extreme position: "It is no reminiscence of Liberal Catholicism. Rosmini and Lacordaire, Hefele and Falloux seem to me no better than De Maistre, Veuillot, or Perrone." Acton to Lady Blennerhasset, Feb. 1879, *Selected Correspondence of Lord Acton*, p. 56.

This was the end to which the Liberal Catholics had come: silence. It was less the novelty of their ideas than the circumstances of their times that had been fatal to their cause. Liberal Catholicism is basically an attitude of friendly receptivity to intellectual influences independent of the Roman Catholic Church—an attitude directly opposed to the mentality of the "state of siege" then dominant among Catholics. In order to bear its fruits, Liberal Catholicism required a measure of freedom and toleration from the authorities of the Church; and this had been denied. Under the pressure of events, the Liberal Catholics had been forced to become a party within the Church and to adopt a position of opposition to ecclesiastical authorities—an opposition in which they might win victories, but not victory. Once this opposition had become fully explicit, their cause was hopeless.

Too liberal to submit, too Catholic to secede, the Liberal Catholics rested their hopes in a posterity which has by and large ignored them. Under the pontificate of Leo XIII, the survivors of the movement saw some of their ideas adopted or allowed by the Church;[25] but that was in another era, when the old battle-cries were no longer shouted, and the terms "Ultramontane" and "Liberal Catholic" had become obsolete. Pius IX had outlived Liberal Catholicism; and the highest praise that Acton could find for his successor was that "he is the first Pope who has been wise enough to despair, and has felt that he must begin a new part, and steer by strange stars over an unknown sea."[26]

[25] Newman's nomination to the cardinalate in 1879 was regarded by many as a retrospective vindication of Liberal Catholic views; and Newman regretted that Simpson should not have lived to witness the event. Newman to Wetherell, 5 April 1879, Newman MSS.

[26] Acton to Mary Gladstone, 25 March 1881, *Letters of Lord Acton to Mary Gladstone*, ed. Herbert Paul (New York, 1904), p. 181.

SIMPSON, GLADSTONE, AND VATICANISM, 1874-1875

THE *Dictionary of National Biography* states: "When Mr. Gladstone was writing his treatise on 'Vaticanism', Simpson was constantly at his side, and the curious learning of that famous pamphlet is thus largely accounted for."[1] This assertion is taken almost *verbatim* from a gossipy and not especially trustworthy obituary notice of Simpson in the *Athenæum*.[2] This account has been followed by other biographical notices of Simpson.[3] In many cases it is associated with some questioning of Simpson's Catholicity. It is the gravest charge that has been made against him as a Catholic.

Cardinal Gasquet sought to disprove this charge by citing a letter from Acton to Simpson, dated 4 November 1874, as evidence that "Acton at least, and almost certainly Simpson, had no notion that Gladstone had any such pamphlet in preparation."[4] However, the letter of 4 November refers to Gladstone's first pamphlet in the Vatican Decrees controversy, whereas the *Vaticanism* pamphlet, to which Simpson's biographers refer, was not written until February of 1875. Gasquet failed to disprove the charge made against Simpson, and it would be profitable to examine the evidence anew.

After Gladstone's first pamphlet was published, Simpson wrote to Acton, criticizing Gladstone's remarks on the question of civil marriage. Acton forwarded this letter to

---

[1] T(hompson) C(ooper), "Richard Simpson," *DNB*, XVIII, 276. This article is largely culled from obituary notices.

[2] "Richard Simpson," *Athenaeum*, 22 April 1876, p. 567.

[3] Almost *verbatim* by Joseph Gillow, *A Literary and Biographical History, or Bibliographical Dictionary of the English Catholics*, 5 vols. (London, n.d.), V, 509; also by Edwin Burton in the *Catholic Encyclopedia* (New York, 1913), XIV, 4; in *British Authors of the Nineteenth Century*, ed. S. J. Kunitz and H. Haycraft (New York, 1936), p. 561; and by Bertram C. A. Windle, *Who's Who of the Oxford Movement* (New York, 1926), pp. 217-8.

[4] Gasquet, "Introduction" to *Lord Acton and his Circle* (London, 1906), p. lxxxvii.

Gladstone and later advised him to consult Simpson on the subject. Gladstone wrote to Simpson, 26 December 1874, on the marriage question, and a short correspondence followed,[5] in which Simpson sought to explain the Pope's condemnation of civil marriage in a favourable sense. Simpson did not criticize Gladstone for writing his pamphlet, but he thought that it had been adequately answered and that the papal utterances could be interpreted in two senses, one of which was inoffensive. The Vatican Council, he argued, "simply forbids us to contradict the proposition that the Pope speaking *ex cathedra* is infallible. It leaves us perfectly free to form our own ideas as to what is *ex cathedra*. . . . All the difference that I feel since 1870 is that I may no longer publicly contradict a proposition which I may still explain away."[6]

A month later, Simpson wrote again, pointing out that certain of Manning's criticisms of Gladstone's pamphlet, on the binding force of civil laws, were in contradiction with Catholic canon law.[7] This was the only letter which Simpson wrote unsolicited to Gladstone; it was prompted by the desire to catch Manning in an error. In this, the last letter in their correspondence, Simpson mentioned that his poor health did not permit him to go to the British Museum to document his arguments; it is therefore improbable that he would have travelled to Hawarden, where Gladstone was then writing his pamphlet on *Vaticanism*.

It is clear from this brief correspondence that Simpson was not "constantly at Gladstone's side" during the writing of *Vaticanism*. He commented and advised on certain limited questions, seeking to remove the offence given by Catholic doctrines. Though he minimized its significance, he did not

[5] BM Add. MSS. 44445, ff. 281, 289-292, and 44446, ff. 10-12, 170-173. Simpson had earlier declined to assist in translating Gladstone's pamphlet.

[6] Simpson to Gladstone, 28 Dec. 1874, BM Add. MS. 44445, f. 291. In another letter, Simpson described himself and Acton as "such liberal Catholics as submit to, and shelve, the decrees." They adopted a "conciliatory construction" taking the decrees "not as an isolated phenomenon, but as something to be incorporated and reconciled with the decrees of Trent and Constance. They do not stand alone, but have due order and subordination in the corpus of Ecclesiastical decisions. They do not supersede or change what was before." Simpson to Acton, 17 Nov. 1874, Woodruff MSS.

[7] Simpson to Gladstone, 8 Feb. 1875, BM Add. MS. 44446, ff. 170-173.

reject the dogma of Papal Infallibility, which Gladstone was denouncing.

There was, indeed, a Catholic at Gladstone's side during part of the time he was writing his pamphlet; but it was not Simpson. It was H. N. Oxenham. In February 1875, Acton wrote to Gladstone: "Oxenham, though not a discreet man, is a most pungent and persistent fault-finder, and therefore an excellent critic of unpublished proofs. I am glad he is to look through yours."[8] Oxenham's proof-reading activity is probably the basis for the story that was later told of Simpson.

---

[8] Acton to Gladstone, 19 Feb. 1875, in *Selections from the Correspondence of the First Lord Acton*, ed. J. N. Figgis and R. V. Laurence (London, 1917), p. 149.
R

INDEX

248